THE WINES OF FRANCE

Serena Sutcliffe is a Master of Wine and international wine broker and consultant. She travels the world's vineyards, and selects wines from some of the greatest estates as well as from country growers. Her job as a taster also involves her in numerous international jury panels and she is a member of the International Wine and Food Society's Wine Committee. She lectures on wine both in Great Britain and the United States, and is a regular contributor to many wine journals and publications. She is Wine correspondent for BBC Radio London, and frequently broadcasts and appears on television in Great Britain, America and France. Serena Sutcliffe has also edited and co-authored *Great Vineyards and Winemakers*, and written *The Wine Drinker's Handbook*. She is married to David Peppercorn M.W. – a vinous blend which they describe as 'beatific'.

THE WINES OF FRANCE is an extensively updated and revised version of Serena Sutcliffe's section on France in her 1981 edition of ANDRE SIMON'S WINES OF THE WORLD, which on publication was widely acclaimed on both sides of the Atlantic and hailed as wine book of the year.

no wine +
no white

for Alicia — only to know
how and what
exactly love usf?

orders 5/12/86

THE WINES OF FRANCE

Serena Sutcliffe

A Futura Book

First published as Chapter One of
ANDRE SIMON'S WINES OF THE WORLD
Second edition by Serena Sutcliffe
Copyright © The Rainbird Publishing Group Ltd 1967, 1972, 1982
First Edition 1967, revised 1972
Second Edition, fully revised 1981
First published in Great Britain in 1981 by
Macdonald & Co (Publishers) Ltd
London & Sydney

This edition, fully revised
Copyright © The Rainbird Publishing Group Limited 1985
First published in Great Britain in 1985 by
Futura Publications, a Division of
Macdonald & Co (Publishers) Ltd, London & Sydney

ISBN 0 7088 2706 3

Photoset in North Wales by
Derek Doyle & Associates, Mold, Clwyd
Printed in Great Britain by
William Collins, Glasgow

Futura Publications
A Division of
Macdonald & Co (Publishers) Ltd
Maxwell House
74 Worship Street
London EC2A 2EN

A BPCC plc Company

Contents

List of Maps

Introduction

When this study of the wines of France first appeared, it was as the first chapter in the Second Edition of André Simon's *Wines of the World*. Four years on, it has been thoroughly reviewed and updated, and is published as a book in its own right.

It would seem that although people will drink any wine from any country in the world, provided they like the taste and can swallow the price, they still prefer to read about French wines above all else. France is perceived to be the country where the 'finest' wines are produced, the setter of standards, the quality goal towards which the others are striving. It would be difficult for French wines always to live up to this exacting image, but nowadays the reality is probably closer to the myth. The very competition from other countries has forced France to assess her own wines in an unprecedented way, and the commercial facts of life have shown even the most arrogant exporter that there are other remarkable wines from around the world. The result has been even greater consistency of quality in French wines than ever before.

A vinous Tour de France means figures, facts and ampelography, or a brief round-up of the grape varieties in each region. But it also must be a celebration of how the wines actually taste, who makes them, how they do it, and whether it is all worthwhile once you have the liquid in the glass. Descriptions in this book are of the fine wines, rather than the failures, the memorable flavours and scents, rather than the disappointments.

Obviously, vintage up-dates are an important part of the book, as every year brings a set of wines which are miraculously different from each preceding vintage, in ways which are not altogether clear to even the most seasoned wine commentator. One of the most exciting aspects of overhauling a book on wine is the discovery of new wine-makers, sons taking over from fathers and bringing in a rush of enthusiasm and new talent. It compensates for the departure of certain wine producers, or the break-up of estates, always one of the saddest parts of wine history.

I love France, its wines and the people who make them. I suppose it is the country in which I feel most at home, although I can *make* myself at home almost anywhere, provided I have a good glass of wine in front of me! I hope the châteaux and the chais, the vineyards and the villages, will come alive for you while reading this book. Above all, may the evocation of tastes and smells tempt you to go out and find good French wine, to drink it and enjoy it, and to introduce its undoubted delights to all those as yet unconverted.

Serena Sutcliffe   London, 1985.

1 *Viticulture, Vinification and the Care of Wine*

Growing and making wine, from the vine to the bottle, is a judicious mixture of art and science, with the emphasis on science. It is true to say that pure technicians *can* make poor wine, and peasant growers with very little book-knowledge *can* make delicious wine, but on the whole, the best results are obtained with a blend of experience and training. The balance veers more towards science where conditions for making wine are not ideal, such as in very hot countries, or those with not enough sun. Man can juggle with Nature to a certain extent, blasting slopes so that they face the right way, spray irrigating to compensate for lack of rain, but he must always respect the basic terrain and climate.

At the basis of all wine-making lies the grape itself. It is amazing how often this can be overlooked, but miracles cannot be worked with poor raw material. Climate, soil and site all reflect on the grape, and the resulting health or otherwise of this most fascinating fruit is the answer to whether man has got the configuration right.

The ultimate taste and character of your wine will depend on a multitude of factors, embracing viticulture, vinification, right through to such mundane things as transport conditions and shelf-life. At the heart of it all lies the grape, and the way it *tastes*. The nobler the grape variety the more its basic quality will assert itself. Nothing will elevate a poor grape variety, not even the cleverest vinification, although poor vinification can ruin the noblest grape, with only glimpses of what the wine might have been peeping through. Quite apart from the inherent quality of the individual grape variety, no good wine can ever be made from unhealthy must. The grapes must be picked at optimum point (easier in a small vineyard than in a large one) and be free of rot and bacteria. It is here that the deadly sins of Sloth and Greed come in. If the vineyard owner has been lax in going through his vines with sprays against mildew, oidium and botrytis (the mould only becomes 'noble' when it attacks *ripe* grapes), if he has been less than energetic in watching leaf growth and encouraging good air circulation to avoid excess humidity, if he has neglected to spray insecticide against the dreaded red spider, particularly harmful to the Merlot in Bordeaux, and if he is too greedy to sort and throw out rotten or unripe grapes from the final harvest, the must will never make great wine.

Enormous progress has been made in judging the best moment to pick grapes in order to extract all the help that nature can give. The right balance between rising sugar content and falling acid content must be found for each region and grape variety, and the pH has to be watched. Inclement weather and contract labourers do not necessarily wait for grapes to reach perfect maturity, but increased scientific knowledge of the composition of the grape has enabled better harvesting decisions to be made. These run into high-risk areas with all late-harvested grapes, *Spätlese, Auslese*, and especially with *Eiswein*. The extensive use of the harvesting machine in certain parts of the world has dramatically shortened the picking time and reduced the risk element. Bordeaux is a prime example of this.

There exist more than 3,000 known grape varieties and nomenclature is an enormous problem. Local terminology is at its most fertile in viticulture, and one rather insignificant grape variety can sail under at least half a dozen names in different parts of the world. Some varieties are indigenous to their areas, and have been since time immemorial, others get transported across countries, and even oceans, and turn up newly baptized in some far-flung new vineyard. Others change somewhat in the move, become mutations of their original selves, but confusingly cling to family names that bear little resemblance to the original plant. Yet others are given endearing local nicknames which remain endearing only as long as one is drinking, not writing about, them. Some are named after the areas of their, supposed, birth (the

Traminer after the village of Tramin in Süd Tirol/Alto Adige), some after their inventors (to this family belong many new German varieties, such as Müller-Thurgau after Herr Müller from Thurgau in Switzerland, Morio-Muskat after Doktor Morio, and Scheurebe after the late Mr Scheu), and some names are what the French would term *fantaisie*. An idea of the multiplicity of names for the same grape variety can be given by a brief trip round Europe, hardly venturing to the other continents. You might not have come across the Abruzzo Bianco of Central Italy, but it is none other than the Trebbiano of Orvieto and one of the grapes making Soave – a small proportion can also be added to Chianti to give it lightness. But the Trebbiano is also none other than the Ugni Blanc of Southern France, which is known as the St Emilion in Cognac, where it makes the thin, acid wine so suitable for distillation. The one place it has never been near is St Emilion! The Sauvignon grape is known as the Blanc Fumé at Pouilly-sur-Loire (and sometimes in Napa, where it becomes the Fumé Blanc), but that name would not get you anywhere if you used it in Graves. The Chasselas of Pouilly-sur-Loire and Alsace is the Gutedel of Germany, which becomes the Fendant in Switzerland – and also becomes a better wine in the transition. The Elbling of the Upper Mosel and Luxembourg is almost unrecognizable as the sweet Pedro Ximénez of Jerez. But Germanic countries also call it the Räuschling or Kleinberger. The Muscadet of Muscadet is a refugee from Burgundy, where it is the Melon de Bourgogne and rather *ordinaire*. The Malbec of the Médoc becomes the Pressac in St Emilion, the Côt in the Loire and, quite inexplicably, the Auxerrois in Cahors. At St Emilion they also see fit to rechristen the Cabernet Franc the Bouchet. Pinots abound everywhere, some of doubtful parentage and of all colours. The Chardonnay is not strictly a Pinot, although some would claim a distant connection for it with Pinot Blanc. Then there is Pinot Gris (or Pinot Grigio, Pinot Beurot or Ruländer), Pinot Meunier (red, and one of the three grapes used for Champagne), and the ubiquitous Pinot Noir, which also masquerades under the

11

names of Spätburgunder or Blauer Burgunder in Germany, and Rotclevner in Switzerland: Clevner or Klevner being a sort of all-purpose name for Pinot. The Pineau de la Loire is not a Pinot at all, but another name for Chenin Blanc – in South Africa they call it Steen. The Rhein-riesling is the classic Riesling of Germany and the same as Johannisberg Riesling of California, but the Wälschriesling (or Olaszriesling or Laski Riesling or Italico Riesling) of Austria, Middle Europe and Northern Italy is probably not a Riesling at all in origin and came from France. The red Trollinger, chiefly grown in Austria, the Italian Tyrol and Germany, and useful for wine-making or eating, must take pride of place for the sheer diversity of its names. It also appears at the Gross-Vernatsch, the Blauer Malvasier, the Black Hamburg (of Hampton Court fame), the Frankenthaler, the Schiava-Grossa, to name but a few.

This is exhausting but, unfortunately necessary, as without the possibility of 'decoding' grape variety names, it is impossible to establish the relationship between grape varieties and the wines they produce, and to have some idea of what to expect when tasting. Tracking 'families' of vines across the world is difficult, especially before the grapes appear, as most grape varieties are extremely hard to identify from the leaf structure, even for the locals. All these grapes are varieties of *Vitis vinifera*, which originally came from the Middle East. The wild *Vitis vinifera sylvestris* of Europe cannot produce crops suitable for wine-making. *Vitis vinifera* is susceptible to that devastating aphid, phylloxera, and that is why nearly all European vines are grafted on to immune American root stocks. The three main American varieties are *Vitis riparia* (from river banks), *Vitis rupestris* (from rock and mountain) and *Vitis berlandieri* (a Texan vine) – all from the central, temperate zone of America. Many crossings of these original root stocks have been evolved and are now produced in Europe. The root stock must be chosen with great care with regard to the soil and to the marriage with the chosen European grape variety. The basic health and quality of the vine depends on the choice of both graft and root stock, and the failure rate can be high if due care and analyses are not employed. Only in a few places in Europe can the *Vitis vinifera* grow ungrafted and unaffected – in the Arenas area of Jerez, near Chipiona, where the sand prevents the aphid from harming the vine, and for the same reason at Colares near Lisbon, and near Montpellier and in some parts of the Mosel and the Douro (especially at Quinta do Noval) where the slate and schist are equally inhospitable.

There should not be any confusion (and not surprisingly, there often is) between a hybrid and a cross-bred grape. Hybrids, in viticultural terms, are crossings between American and European vines. Very few are permitted to be grown in European vineyards, and in fact their presence can now be detected by atomic absorption machines. These ungrafted vines are also known as *producteurs directs*. Some of these hybrids are very resistant to disease, but it is generally accepted that they do not produce the very best wines. Crossings of European varieties are not hybrids, and are grafted on to American stocks.

In the Vineyard
Grafting can take place in a nursery or directly in the vineyard, rather depending upon the clemency of the regional climate. Spacing of the vine plants is obviously of paramount importance, bearing in mind such things as mechanization and slope – in cool climates, slopes are preferred as they give better exposition to the sun. Drainage is vital everywhere, and apart from using slopes to this end, the natural make-up of the soil can sometimes be assisted, such as adding more pebbles. Use of stones in the vineyard helps heat reflection. As the viticultural year progresses, foliage must be watched, as too much leaf surface in humid conditions leads to rot. The age of the vines has a direct effect on the quality of red wine, increasing the concentration noticeably – young vines give lighter wine and usually more of it. To compensate for this thinness some wine-makers add *vin de presse* to the produce of young vines, but this is often unhappy, as the press wine does not 'marry' well with the soft, light yield from the young vines. The result is a hard wine, still hollow, but with a stalkiness in the

background. The best thing with young red vines is to delay picking as long as possible, to get maximum ripeness, and reduce yield as much as possible by reducing the amount of fertilizer used at the time of planting and pruning with severity. This age factor is not nearly so important for white wines. There are optimum points in the life of a vine, varying with the region and climate – but it could be said that vines of fifteen to twenty-five years old give generously and well, while thirty-five to forty-year old vines make greater wine. However, vines in hot countries, like the inhabitants, tend to mature faster.

Cleanliness of soil is all-important, and 'fatigued', overworked soil seldom gives of its best and is prey to disease. It remains to be seen what the long-term effects of heavy non-organic fertilization will bring. Fertilizer should go into the soil soon after the vintage, so that it has time to go down deep into the ground before the new growing season starts. Minerals in the soil are a boon to the wine-maker, when the roots can go down deep, and these 'trace elements' in a wine can greatly contribute to complexity in the final result. Mineral deficiencies or excesses can be corrected in the soil. After the aphid phylloxera – for a graphic description and diagrams of its life cycle, see Sherry, by Julian Jeffs, published by Faber, London (1982) – never beaten but outmanoeuvered, the fungoid diseases are always a danger. These include the dreaded oidium or powdery mildew, which affects all parts of the leaf, young shoots and grapes. A white, dusty covering is to be seen and the grapes subsequently split and rot, ultimately drying up. Spraying with sulphur, or sulphur dusting when applied regularly in warm and humid conditions will protect against oidium. There are other chemical, patent sprays, but some of these can produce side effects. Mildew (the downy variety) or Peronospora is another dangerous fungus. Once it has taken a hold, it can destroy the leaves, vital in the assimilation process of vines and, if not observed and treated, the grapes can be affected and shrivel, ruining the flavour of the resultant wine, if anyone is foolish enough to try to make wine from such sick material. The young leaves must be protected, and careful watch should be kept to see that oily patches are not appearing on them. Regular spraying with Bordeaux Mixture (basically copper sulphate) is a reliable preventive measure, and it has a good effect on other diseases such as black rot at the same time.

Pourriture grise, or grey rot, is the same fungus as *Botrytis cinerea*, the name also applied to *pourriture noble*. Botrytis is a danger to all grapes that are already not healthy due to bad weather or oidium. The stalks can also be affected, causing the berries to drop prematurely. When this rot attacks healthy ripe white grapes of certain varieties (such as Riesling, Sémillon, and sometimes Sauvignon), the desirable effect of noble rot occurs. The fungus punctures the skin of the grape, the water content evaporates, and the sugar and concentration of the grapes increase. There is also a specific flavour to grapes attacked by *pourriture noble*, without which, for instance, a top Sauternes is not really true. The fungus is not desirable on unripe grapes or on red grapes, and copper sulphate spraying can increase resistance. Good husbandry in the vineyard is another general precaution. *Court Noué* or fan leaf, is a virus, for which the only cure is uprooting. It is not something which is readily admitted by vine-growers who may have it, but it is a degeneration, often encouraged by overtired soil. Changes become visible on the leaves, and the vines' yield decreases. Until resistant root stocks are found, uprooting and thorough cleansing of the soil before replanting are the only remedies. Chlorosis of the vine is caused by incorrect soil balance, and when serious, can affect the shoots and the grapes. Correcting additions of sulphate of iron can restore the balance, as well as careful selection of root stocks. Moths, cochylis, eudemis and pyrpalis, can be devastating, but should not be so with strict observation for the first signs and good insecticide spraying. Red Spider is more common now in certain places of the world than it should be (prematurely browning leaves is often a sign), and requires early treatment. In some areas, birds are a problem, particularly where the grapes are the most enticing food in the radius.

Vines are also susceptible to conditions uniquely arising

15

from the weather. Bad weather at flowering can cause the blossoms to fall, or the embryonic berries immediately afterwards. *Coulure* such as this is responsible for small vintages. *Millerandage* is caused by unequal flowering and will result in a bunch of grapes having some berries that are normal, and others that remain small and green and never ripen. These unripe berries should not be made into wine and should remain unpicked (the best machines now do this) or be selected out by human hand. Frost is a danger in some areas of the world, and always looms over vineyards near woods and on plains. The most serious winter frosts freeze the sap in the vine, and can in extreme cases destroy the vine – this only happens with prolonged temperatures at well below freezing. Spring frosts are dangerous when there has been a mild winter and the vines are in advance. Hail is often very localized, but can be so fierce as to shred a whole area of vineyard. The whole plant is damaged, and can also impart a taste to the grapes. Rockets are sometimes used to disperse hail cloud formations, and aircraft can intercept the clouds to cause only rain to fall.

Pruning in a vineyard directly affects the yield, and therefore has to be slightly prophetic, since the ensuing climatic conditions of the year are not known. An experienced pruner is the most valuable member of the vineyard staff, as he will sense how strong a plant is and will adjust his pruning accordingly. Methods vary with the viticultural area and the training method employed, which will be discussed in individual areas. Generous pruning, to encourage high yield, will probably 'dilute' the final quality of the wine, but on the other hand, the grower has to prune for all eventualities. An old vine, which produces little quantity anyway, needs the help of an understanding pruning hand, but a vigorous, young vine probably needs restraining. When pruning, it is also necessary to know what is being done in the way of fertilization, for the general replacement of organic manures by chemical products has often pushed production too far. One hundred days is usually counted as the time necessary between flowering and harvesting (although Bordeaux is now averaging 110), but late-ripening varieties or top-sweet wines will obviously need up to a month more. After picking, automatically or by hand, the aim is to get the grapes to the winery or *cuvier* as quickly as possible. In hot countries this is particularly necessary, and in some areas of the world, night picking is practised in order to avoid the heat of the day. Most picking is done once only per vineyard, but in the case of top Sauternes/Barsac or *Beerenauslese* or *Trockenbeerenauslese* wines, pickers might go through the same vineyard three or four times, gathering each bunch, or sometimes berry, at its optimum point.

Vinification

The wine-maker's work begins in the vineyard; the picking must be organized with the aim of filling each vat with the most homogeneous material possible. This applies to grape variety, situation of the vine, size of the harvest, level of ripeness, and health of the grapes gathered. It is no use thinking that the deficiencies of one component can be made up by the qualities of another – all that happens is that the really good ingredients are lost in the whole. Later on, careful tasting of each vat can control those that do not quite make the grade, but if the first rule of homogeneity is followed, there are far fewer nasty surprises. Professeur Ribéreau-Gayon of the University of Bordeaux particularly stresses this point.

Red grapes usually go through a crusher-stemmer, unless the additional tannin from the stems is required and they are conserved. The crushing process is extremely light, with the aim of getting enough juice to run to start the fermentation. Fermentation either starts naturally, with natural yeasts, or selected, cultivated yeasts are used, if absolute control is desired. In a natural fermentation, the wild yeasts begin the process, and then the *Saccharomyces ellipsoideus* take over. A small amount of sulphur dioxide is used to cleanse the must and kill off bacteria. Fermentation can take place in wooden *cuves*, or barrels in lined or unlined concrete vats, or, more normally nowadays, in closed stainless-steel vats, where it is far easier to control the temperature – a vital necessity if real

17

quality is to be attained. Normal temperatures for the fermentation of red wine are between 28°C and 30°C maximum, but sometimes this is lower, thereby prolonging fermentation. As the sugar is transformed into alcohol and carbonic gas (but there are also many other side-products of fermentation, such as glycerine, succinic and acetic acid, lactic acid and acetaldehyde), the solid matter of grapes, skins and pips is forced to the top of the vat or other fermenting vessel to form a cap – or *chapeau*. This cap is dangerous if exposed undisturbed to the air (if the vats are open), as it attracts bacteria with great ease when dry. It is also necessary that the skins remain in permanent contact with the fermenting must in order to get good colour extraction. The cap can also cause the middle of the vat to rise alarmingly in temperature. The most successful way of keeping the cap in contact with the must, ensuring good colour extraction and an even working of the yeasts, is to practise the system of *remontage*. This is quite simply drawing off must from the bottom of the vat and pumping it over the top or spraying it over the top, or even pushing the pipe through the hat and pumping direct into the liquid. Open vats can also have a system of a permanently submerged cap, but *remontages* are still necessary.

Chaptalization (and deacidification if necessary) takes place during the process of *remontage*. More nonsense is probably written about chaptalization than anything else in the vinification process. Chaptalization is the addition of sugar to the must, therefore increasing the potential alcohol level. Ironically, Chaptal did not develop the process in 1801 for this reason, but to help in the conservation of wine. There are, of course, other ways of raising alcoholic level, such as the Italian method of adding concentrated must. For red wines, sugar from cane or from beetroots can be used, but the former must be used for white wines. Chaptalization cannot be envisaged unless the must in question already has the minimum alcoholic level required by the *appellation contrôlée* laws in France. It is totally erroneous to attribute sweetness in a wine to chaptalization – there are other methods of sweetening wine, such as the addition of

Süssreserve, called back-blending in some parts of the New World, or the process of stopping a wine's fermentation before all the sugar is converted – *mutage*. Sometimes when a dry wine appears to have sweetness to it it is because of the sheer ripeness of the grapes – unripe grapes can taste sour and green, just as grapes from a really ripe year give a really ripe, almost sweet, taste to the wine they make. But chaptalization does change the balance of a wine. It slightly lowers the fixed acidity (yet another reason why a chaptalized wine might appear softer than a non-chaptalized one), although the addition of concentrated must raises the fixed acidity level. The alcohol/extract ratio is also higher in chaptalized wines, and when tests are made for excessive chaptalization, this is taken into account. It is particularly important to control fermentation temperatures when wines have been chaptalized usually during the *remontage* process. Stainless-steel vats can have cold water which runs down the sides of the vats to cool them, or there is a system resembling a milk cooler through which the must passes.

It is essential that the alcoholic fermentation should pass steadily. It should not career forward, nor should it 'stick' as this attracts bacteria. If it is cold, it may be necessary to heat the surroundings of the *cuvier* in order to start the fermentation. Some wine-makers resort to heating red grapes before fermentation when colour and ripeness are deficient – this is usually applied to the produce of young vines.

With white wines, things are a little different. The stalks are not removed, as this makes quick and efficacious pressing easier. However, with automatic harvesters the stalks are removed, and care must be taken when pressing that blocks of the *marc* do not form. Luckily, the newest cylindrical presses (either pneumatic or screw-type) are very effective in making this fall to the 'carpet' at the bottom of the press. The juice is then run off, and usually goes through a cleansing process or *débourbage*, when it rests in a vat for twenty-four hours in order for the solid matter to fall to the bottom. Sometimes a centrifuge can be used for this purpose. A small amount of sulphur dioxide (SO_2) prevents fermentation from starting immediately, but when the *débourbage* is complete, fermentation will start with a cleaner must and probably result in fewer 'rackings' at a later stage. This is useful for light, dry white wines where minimum handling is advisable to guard against oxidation. White wine fermentation is usually between 15° and 20°C when elegant wines with strong bouquet are desired, but some very low temperatures are being practised in some parts of the world. After fermentation, red and white wine can be run off into barrels or kept in vat. With red wine which has only undergone fermentation but not pressing the correct term is 'free run' wine. This *vin de goutte* can be mixed with a proportion of *vin de presse* – the amount will vary with the characteristics of the year in fine wine regions, as *vin de presse* is not quite of the same composition as the *vin de goutte* – it is, for example, higher in volatile acidity and tannin, as well as mineral content.

In certain areas of the world carbonic maceration is practised in cases where red wine is intended for young drinking. Here the grapes are put whole into a closed vat in a carbonic gas atmosphere. The grapes undergo an intercellular fermentation, with a small quantity of sugar within the berry itself being converted into alcohol without the need of yeasts. Some of the grapes are crushed by the natural weight of the volume, and their normal fermentation also creates carbon dioxide. This maceration can go on for five to ten days, followed by pressing, with the *moût de presse* being added to the *vin de goutte*. The fermentation is then finished within forty-eight hours. Carbonic maceration wine is less rich in extract, acidity, colour and tannin than classically fermented wine.

Cellar Work – or Elevage
'Bringing up' a wine is precarious business, requiring particular attention when wine is aged before selling. Many wines for quick consumption (Beaujolais and many dry white wines) have a short stay in vat and are bottled a few months after their birth. Serious red and white wines will go into cask (usually oak) after their alcoholic fermentation.

This results in significant evaporation, and regular 'topping up' is necessary to prevent oxidation. This should be done under very hygenic conditions, with wine of top quality, itself kept in perfect conditions. However, the tendency seems to be leading to earlier three-quarter bung (the bungs to the side of the cask) – in Bordeaux this is often now in May after the vintage. The malolactic fermentation will take place either, in some cases, almost concurrently with the alcoholic fermentation, or usually a little time afterwards. Basically, this is the transformation of the rather green malic acid in the wine into the milder lactic acid. Malolactic fermentation nearly always takes place in red wine, sometimes in white.

If wines are stored in vat, they can be protected from the air by means of a covering of carbon dioxide or of nitrogen. Wines in cask are always subject to a small amount of oxidation through the wood, but this is desirable in the maturation process. If the casks are new oak, flavour and tannin will certainly be imparted to the wine. If a wine is big and solid, this can add a new dimension, but a light wine can be enveloped by new oak. Wines in cask must be racked, or periodically removed from the old lees of one cask to go into another, clean one. At all stages of cellar work, sulphur dioxide is used as a cleanser. A delicate wine should not be racked as much as a robust one, as it is a tiring process. In Bordeaux, during the first year of its life, a wine will be racked four times. No wine, even in vat, should remain in contact with old lees for too long, as the wine then begins to taste stale.

Wine also has to be clarified, or fined, removing the unstable elements in it. There are many products used to achieve this, including white of egg (for very fine wines), gelatine, fish glue (isinglass), and casein. For a wine to be stable, it should contain free and bound sulphur dioxide, but the free sulphur can be very low in certain types of wine. Heating, refrigeration, sorbic acid, ascorbic acid, metatartaric acid, citric acid, and bentonite (against excess protein) are other stabilizing treatments. Refrigeration is used to cause precipitation of potassium bi-tartrates. The temperature has to be lowered to $-3°C$ or $-5°C$ for table wines and $-8°C$ or $-10°C$ for fortified wines, and it is vitally important that this temperature should be held for an absolute minimum of five days, rising to twenty days in some cases. The addition of metatartaric acid (dehydrated tartaric acid) can only prevent tartrate formation for a limited amount of time, and thereafter can even aggravate the problem. It is a pity that a crystalline tartrate deposit is not acceptable to many consumers (probably because the crystal looks like sugar, or even glass), as it does not indicate that the wine is in any way impaired, and acceptance of a few crystals would mean that yet another wine treatment could be avoided.

In Germany, it has been noticed that in some years when there is a great deal of *Botrytis cinerea*, a slime acid called very unprettily *Schleimsäure* and which is a form of oxidized glucose, can occur. It can be tolerated up to 2 grams/litre in must, but above this it forms an insoluble calcium salt which tends later to throw a white opaque crystal deposit in bottle – again, nothing to worry about.

Choosing the right bottling time for individual wines is of paramount importance. This can vary from a few months after the vintage for light, fresh white wines, to two years for top red Bordeaux, or even three years for Yquem. Wines bottled too late for their particular composition and qualities can tend to lack vigour. Most wines now are bottled at their place of origin, although certain mass-market wines are transported in bulk and bottled by the customer. Certain grape varieties, such as Cabernet Sauvignon and white Chardonnay, need good bottle-ageing to reach their full potential and breed. Bottling should be carried out in conditions of great hygiene, and should be homogeneous – bottling from cask to cask is not advisable, for example. Wine is usually assembled in a bottling tank, given a light, final filter, and then bottled. In some areas of the world, notably California, there is a vogue for unfiltered wines from specialist wineries – the wines are meant to retain more character and fruit when unfiltered. If a totally sterile wine is desired (and this is usually not the case in fine wines intended to develop in bottle, but in wines sold for mass-consumption), pasteurization, flash-pasteurization, or hot bottling can be employed. If all this seems daunting, it is certainly meant to show that wine-making is not for the dreamy poet, surveying his vineyards glass in hand, but for the informed professional, alert to the dangers constantly threatening the ultimate quality of his wine, but perceptive enough to see the real and realistic potential of his wine and intelligent enough to develop it. Each region has its nuances in wine-making, and within each region there are people attempting different things. It should always be remembered that there are producers who are striving for the best, and others who are looking for the short-cuts. There are also areas which are not designed for top wines, and here the aims are for pleasant wines at accessible prices, with resulting modifications to 'classic' practice.

A really good cellar is almost as precious a commodity as a great wine; very often, the cellar is the rarer. The best advice is probably to look at what constitutes ideal cellar conditions, and then choose the best place in the house, flat or garden shed that most nearly corresponds to them. If no corner of one's abode is suitable, it is really better to keep only everyday wine to hand, and either share good cellar accommodation with someone luckier, or rent cellar space with a wine merchant. This obviously entails charges, but they will invariably be lower than ruined fine wine. The most dangerous thing for wine is a large fluctuation in temperature. Anything between 7°C and 12°C is ideal, the lower figure preferable for white wines (they can be put below the red wines, because heat rises). It would matter less for the temperature to be slightly higher than for there to be a considerable seasonal change. The higher the temperature, the faster your wine will tend to age. If wine gets too cold, it can throw tartrates – not in itself harmful to the wine, but worrying when people do not know what they are. Half bottles mature faster than bottles; and magnums more slowly. Choose a place that is dark, or make it dark, as light can harm wine. Clear bottles (Sauternes, some Champagne) are very vulnerable to sunlight. A damp atmosphere is preferable, as the corks stay in better condition. Wine matures more slowly in damp conditions which are totally beneficial, except sometimes to the labels. A humidifier can be used if excessive dryness is a danger, or sometimes a large bowl of water placed in the midle of the cellar can be sufficient. 16°C relative humidity is a good guideline, but you could go above this – I have seen a cellar with a humidity level around 25°C and there was no damage to the labels. Another solution to a lack of healthy humidity in a cellar is to put some small gravel on the floor of the cellar and sprinkle it with water occasionally – gravel retains humidity. Alternatively, this could be done with gravel in a wide tray. No storage place should be near a heating system, or have a strong smell, as this can eventually permeate the bottle. Reverberation should be avoided. Wine bottles should be stored horizontally so that the liquid is always in contact with the cork to prevent it from drying and shrinking and thus letting in air. You can stack bottles on their side in a small space or specially-made bin, or in a metal or wooden rack, which makes the bottles easy to remove. Sherry and Madeira can be left upright, as the spirit in the wines can eat into the cork over a long period, and if air does penetrate the drying cork, this is not harmful to a wine (with the exception of Fino Sherry, which should be drunk young and fresh and would not be stored anyway) whose production process protects it from oxidation. Vintage Port should be stored horizontally, with no change in the bottle's position so that the 'crust' or deposit can form evenly.

Many people worry about the journey from the cellar to the table – how should wine be carried. Should it travel in style in a basket, or should it go 'deck class', unadorned? The logical answer is that if the bottle is likely to have a sediment, it is best to draw the cork with it lying horizontally in the same position as it was in the cellar – standing upright and waiting for the wine to clear can take days, and in a few cases, the wine never completely clears. Therefore, a basket to keep the bottle in the same position is a great aid. Baskets in a restaurant, when the wine is either young with no deposit, or when the wine has already been carried around vertically, are just an affectation. First, remove the metal capsule to below the ring of the bottle-neck. Drawing a cork horizontally, from a bottle reclining in a basket, can be tricky. The patented, plastic

Screwpull makes even this easy, and has also proved its worth on old, crumbly corks. When a bottle is vertical, the kind of corkscrews with 'wings' are just as simple and again involve no strength on the part of the bottle opener. When decanting from your horizontal bottle, put a candle in a candlestick, lift the bottle out of the basket so that the shoulder is lit up by the candle behind it, and pour slowly and steadily until you begin to see cloudiness or sediment enter the neck of the bottle – then stop, and use the 'silt' for marinating or in a stew!

To decant or not to decant – a most complicated question. In Bordeaux, it is a common occurrence, in Burgundy a rare one, for Vintage Port it is a necessity. It is the best thing to do when a wine has thrown some sediment in bottle. The very action of pouring the wine from one receptacle to another aerates it and releases the esters and aldehydes, perhaps trapped in the bottle for years, to intoxicate your nose and palate. A young wine can soften with this contact with the air, an old wine will release its complexity. The general rule is that the younger a wine is, the longer time the wine should be decanted before a meal. A very old wine often needs to be decanted and then drunk almost immediately, before it 'dies in the glass'. However, there are exceptions, largley due to the character of certain years (the 1945s in Bordeaux, for example, usually need time in decanter to open out) and certain grape types are more fragile than others. When in doubt, 'under-decant' rather than decant too soon – if the wine has not had enough time since the cork was drawn and you suspect it can open out further, just leave it in the glass, coming back to it at intervals to see how it is getting on. On the other hand, a wine that was decanted too soon and literally dies in the glass before you, cannot be revived. The same rule applies to the temperature at which wine should be served. A red wine served too warm or *chambré* is unrecoverable – if it is on the cool side, put your hand round the glass and warm it a little and coax out the bouquet. A wine too warm is a tragedy – it takes the edge off the flavour and makes it go 'soupy'. Never drink fine red wine in hot weather, unless you have air conditioning. White and rosé wines should be served slightly chilled – a few hours in the door of the refrigerator (the warmest part) is usually ideal. Certain light, fresh red wines are delicious cool – some reds from Provence, some straight Beaujolais, young quaffing wines. When decanting, always smell the decanter first, to see if any off-odours have entered it. Unobtrusive checks on glasses in restaurants are also worthwhile, because wine for which one has paid dearly will hardly improve when mixed with unrinsed detergent. Ideally, water only should be used for washing all decanters and glasses. If a decanter becomes stained, the simplest remedy is to scatter some denture powder on the bottom of the vessel and fill it with cold water. After some hours, the water is usually pink, and the decanter can then be rinsed out and will be bright.

Ideal tasting glasses, and also ones which are suitable for drinking just about everything, are those designed and approved by the Institut National des Appellations d'Origine (INAO). They have a nice stem which can be held without contact with the wine, the bowl is sufficiently wide for a certain volume of wine, and the long glass tapers towards the rim, thereby 'trapping' the bouquet, and enabling one to swirl the wine, to release this same bouquet, without wine spilling. Variations of this tulip theme are always suitable, sometimes larger, wider versions for fine Bordeaux, and squatter versions for rich Burgundy, almost Cognac *ballons*. The traditional Sherry *copita* is a small version of the INAO glass, and an elegant Champagne *flûte* is narrower and longer. Never fill glasses more than two-thirds full.

The general order for both tasting and drinking wines is young before old, and dry before sweet. I, personally, do not like mixing very different types of wine at a meal (say, Bordeaux with Burgundy), but prefer a graduated escalation of quality, or wines of the same class of varying age. One can also mix countries, but stay with the same grape types – perhaps showing a Cabernet from California, followed by a Cabernet-dominated wine from the Médoc. But care must always be taken that too assertive a wine does not immediately precede a delicate one, otherwise the latter may not do itself justice.

2 *Guide to the Appellation System in France*

The *appellation contrôlée* system in France is an attempt to see that the wines come from the place they say they do, and gives basic viticultural and vinification instructions that are meant to lead to better quality. The laws do not guarantee quality, but they lay down specifications that are more conducive to making pleasantly drinkable wine than vinegar. The rules cover the area of production; the grape varieties permitted (sometimes divided into principal and accessory grape varieties); the minimum alcohol level of the wine (which should be achieved before chaptalization); the maximum yield allowed per hectare; the method of planting, pruning and treating the vines; the vinification of the wine; and conditions of ageing.

Vins Délimités de Qualité Supérieure (VDQS) have the same laws, but they are wider than Vins à Appellation d'Origine Contrôlée, i.e. greater yields, less strict conditions to the zones of production, sometimes less 'noble' grape varieties. However, in one way, the VDQS rules were tighter than the AOC laws, and this was in respect to tasting. Wines could only obtain the VDQS label after official tasting, while no such thing existed for *appellation* wines, unless local bodies set up their own forms of tasting. Now *appellation* wines must also go before a tasting panel, and although one cannot say that this has been completely set up all over France, it is undoubtedly on the way. Of course, no tasting panel is infallible, and the few wines that are refused, can represent themselves. Tasting panels are usually composed of a grower, a *négociant* and a broker, but there is, naturally, a certain reluctance to refuse wines when they are tasted blind in one's own region.

There is often the possibility of the wine taking a lesser classification if it fails to meet all the requirements for the higher one. However, this does not mean that the *cascade* system can operate – officially abolished in the *appellation* decrees of 1974. This involved making much more than the maximum allowed, obtaining the classification up to the limit, and a lesser classification for everything over that. This did not, obviously, improve the quality of the higher classified wine, it only maintained its high price. Now, the grower must opt for the classification he desires for the crop in its entirety at the time of his declarations of the vintage. With the best laws in the world, *and* the inspectorate to control them, it is impossible to follow every drop of wine in the cellar. The figures and papers must tally at the end of the day, but the cards can be shuffled *entretemps*. Perhaps not every vintage year is purer than pure, but who complains when a poor vintage gets a helping hand from a prolific, good one that had the intelligence to follow? Conversely, it is a pity when something very good becomes just good through being stretched by the addition of something that needed improving.

Vins de Pays do have approved grape varieties, but they are very wide, and maximum yield is set at 90 hectolitres per hectare. Some people making wine within this framework very much follow their own inclinations and set themselves far higher standards, and others take advantage of the greater freedoms, especially in prolific years. The Midi of France has a mass of Vins de Pays every year, but a Vin de Pays such as Jardin de la France in the Loire would be virtually unobtainable in a year of low yields. Below Vins de Pays, there are Vins de Table, which must conform to certain standards of palatability and say from whence they come. Vins de Table are at the bottom of the pyramid as far as classifications go. The EEC groups wines into two classes: Vins de Table and Vins de Qualité Produits dans une Région Déterminée (VQ-PRD). In France, each of these categories subdivides, with *appellation* and VDQS wines both falling into the European classification of VQPRD, and Vins de Pays and other Vins de Table both falling into the Vins de Table classification.

In 1983 and 1982, French wine production was broken down as follows: (figures given in hectolitres)

	1983	1982
AOC	17,175,715	19,841,583
VDQS	2,331,873	2,513,403
Vins de Pays	7,794,746	7,634,353
Wines intended for making into Cognac	10,719,549	12,549,922
Vins de Table	30,068,061	36,690,677
TOTAL	68,089,944	79,229,938

Like all laws, those of the *appellation contrôlée* work best when there is the will to see them work. Above all, they should allow the best possible wines to be made in each category, and marry tradition with innovation.

The four organizations listed below carry out between them the work of controlling the quality of and marketing French wines.

1. The INAO (Institut National des Appellations d'Origine)
2. The ONIVIT (Office National Interprofessionnel des Vins de Table)
3. The SRFCQ (Service de la Répression des Fraudes et du Contrôle de la Qualité)
4. The DGI (Direction Générale des Impôts)

3 Bordeaux

Bordeaux is a pivotal word for wine-makers and wine-drinkers all over the world, but it would never have been able to make this impact were it not for its size. It is the largest fine-wine producing area in the world, and that, in the vernacular, counts for something. Over 110,000 hectares are under vine, one-tenth of the Gironde, the largest *département* in France. In a good year, Bordeaux is now producing over two million hectolitres of *appellation* red wine and 1 million of white. It will also produce just under 2 million hectolitres of red and white *vin de table* or *vin de consommation courante*. 1979 produced a record quantity of red *appellation* wine: 3,315,124 hectolitres compared with 2,479,382 in 1973, an increase of no less than 33 per cent. It is noticeable that some of the largest increases are to be found in the Médoc and Haut Médoc *appellations*, while St Emilion and Pomerol are both below the 1973 level, an indication perhaps of the damage done by the 1977 frosts. With the decrease in the area under vine, similar results were hardly to be expected for the white wines. The total of white *appellation* wine was 1,124,048 hectolitres, which was the largest figure since 1974, but should be compared with the 1,313,553 made in 1970. This still brings the total of *appellation* wine for 1979 to the remarkable figure of 4,439,172 hectolitres, which is 17.5 per cent larger than 1973. This is not only the largest vintage since the Second World War, it is the first time since 1939 that more than six million hectolitres have been harvested in the Gironde, the total for *appellation contrôlée* and *vin de table* being higher than in that poor year, but still falling short of the prodigious 1934 yield. The 1979 record has since been beaten by the huge 1982 harvest.

It was during the 1850s that the disease of oidium struck the vineyards. No sooner was this blow assimilated than phylloxera and mildew followed, causing a viticultural depression throughout Europe. However, invention born of necessity triumphed, and with the vines grafted on to American root stocks, the nineteenth century ended with some fine vintages and the restoration of Bordeaux's reputation, if not her complete economic health. The fact that the troubled times of the beginning of the twentieth century, culminating in the First World War and its implications both for France and her customers (obviously still European), did not create a stable market for Bordeaux wines, only served to underline that economic difficulties for those in the wine trade were not over. The glowing vintages of the late 1920s might have heralded a new horizon, but the between-the-wars slump arrived soon afterwards and, as if to reflect the depression, the weather did not assist a series of vintages in the 1930s. The 1950s did see prices slowly rising and a more healthy chain of distribution forming, with a solid basis of Bordeaux-loving customers spread out over many countries, and a little more money in their pockets with which to indulge their predilection. The very serious frost of 1956 did affect the vineyard area and cost a great deal of money in new plantings and lost sales. After the excellent and prolific 1970 vintage, things seemed set fair for a successful decade for Bordeaux. People bought the 1970s and the small but good 1971s as fast as they appeared on the market, and wine changed hands rapidly and unseen (or untasted). Wine was regarded as a commodity, not for drinking, but for making a profit. For the first time substantial investment was being made by people outside the trade who alighted on wine from Bordeaux simply as another way to make money. No blame can be attached uniquely to any group of people in these transactions. It is easy to criticize the 'philistine' outsider, but the fact remains that while the going was good, both merchant and château-owner were quite willing to sell at ever spiralling prices. This would not have been enough in itself to bring about the dramatic slump in the Bordeaux wine trade of

31

1973/4. When prices continued to rise on a poor vintage, 1972, the danger lights were on. No one ever makes a bad buy on a really good vintage, especially if one is not pressed to sell. But buying bad vintages at all, let alone at high prices, is ill-advised. And some of the top, classified Bordeaux châteaux, which is where the heavy investment was taking place, were bad in 1972 and should never have appeared under their château names. At the same time, the oil crisis hit the Western world, and the 'advanced' nations, those who drink fine wine, came down to earth with a crash.

The recovery was slow, but lessons have been learned. The problem is essentially one of supply and demand, and the Comité Interprofessionnel des Vins de Bordeaux (CIVB) has done much work to stabilize prices and review stocks. It introduced a *fourchette* system of maximum and minimum prices for the basic *appellations* and, in prolific years, blocks some of the yield for release at a later date in order to keep prices steady. No one can say that all its efforts succeed, agreements are not always adhered to, and growers, brokers, and merchants or *négociants* do not always have the same aims or needs, but everyone is now aware of the problem.

The *négociants* of Bordeaux suffered a great deal from this unhappy period, and the newer ones, without reserves of stock and capital, crumbled under the blow – often rather unfairly, as some of them were not the worst offenders in encouraging the exaggerated prices. Some disappeared from the scene, and others became less of a *négociant* and more of a broker (*courtier*) – working on commission and eschewing stocks. The recovery was slow, both in Bordeaux and in the customer markets, as there was an immense amount of stock lying on people's hands, some of it 'dumped' by companies that fell by the wayside. The Bordeaux market is now on a more even keel. Prices can still go high, but they tend to do this on excellent vintages, such as, 1978, 1982 and 1983. The market has also had to come to terms with large vintages, the product of greatly increased plantings and avoidance of the worst disasters dealt by the vagaries of the weather. Large harvests are good for the consumer, and in the 1980s there is a great deal of reasonably-priced, good Bordeaux available.

However, the balance between the red and white wine in Bordeaux has changed, with many white vines being replaced by red. Dry white wine is now in demand all over the world, especially at a reasonable price, and this shortage could be felt in the future, now that Bordeaux has learnt how to vinify well this type of wine. There are also periodic shortages of Bordeaux Rouge at *négociant* level, as the small properties that used to furnish the merchants with this basic *appellation* now often prefer to bottle under their château name. Buying of generic wine, such as Médoc, St Julien, St Emilion, has certainly become more difficult and very much more expensive for this same reason, and well-chosen small properties are often better value.

The top twenty exporting Bordeaux Négociants are: D. Cordier, Barton & Guestier, C.V.B.G. (Maison Dourthe), A. Delor & Cie, Alexis Lichine & Cie, Sté Distribution des Vins Fins, Calvet, Castel Frères & Cie, Cruse & Fils Frères, A. de Luze & Fils, Maison Sichel, Gilbey de Loudenne, J. Lebègue & Cie, Schroder & Schyler & Cie, Dulong Frères & Fils, Les Fils de Marcel Quancard, Borie Manoux, Louis Eschenauer, De Rivoyre & Diprovin/Dubroca and R. Joanne & Cie.

Classifications in Bordeaux
The very word 'classification' can sometimes sound rather terrifying, as if Bordeaux wines are in rigid groups and failure to know by heart the exact placings of all the important growths will result in awful drinking mistakes. It will not. In fact, personal experience or reliable recommendation is the surest way to find the best wines. But, with all the reservations brought out below, the 1855 classification of top châteaux did produce a quality structure, at least a standard at which to aim.

This classification was not just decided upon overnight. It was based on the prices that these top châteaux had fetched for approximately a hundred years, and on previous assessments. It was largely the work of brokers who sold the wine *en primeur* or when very young. The fact that these châteaux consistently fetched high prices did establish that

FIRST GROWTHS

Lafite-Rothschild (Pauillac)   Margaux (Margaux)
Latour (Pauillac)   Haut-Brion (Pessac, Graves)

SECOND GROWTHS

Mouton-Rothschild* (Pauillac)   Gruaud-Larose (St Julien)
Rausan-Ségla (Margaux)   Brane-Cantenac (Cantenac-
                                     Margaux)
Rauzan-Gassies (Margaux)   Pichon-Longueville-Baron
                                     (Pauillac)
Léoville-Las-Cases (St Julien)   Pichon-Lalande (Pauillac)
Léoville-Poyferré (St Julien)   Ducru-Beaucaillou (St Julien)
Léoville-Barton (St Julien)   Cos d'Estournel (St Estèphe)
Durfort-Vivens (Margaux)   Montrose (St Estèphe)
Lascombes (Margaux)

THIRD GROWTHS

Giscours (Labarde-Margaux)   Palmer (Cantenac-Margaux)
Kirwan (Cantenac-Margaux)   La Lagune (Ludon-Haut-
                                     Médoc)
d'Issan (Cantenac-Margaux)   Desmirail (Margaux)
Lagrange (St Julien)   Calon-Ségur (St Estèphe)
Langoa-Barton (St Julien)   Ferrière (Margaux)
Malescot-St-Exupéry (Margaux)   Marquis d'Alesme-Becker
                                     (Margaux)
Cantenac-Brown (Cantenac-
Margaux)   Boyd-Cantenac (Cantenac-

FOURTH GROWTHS

St-Pierre (St Julien)   La Tour-Carnet (St Laurent-
                                     Haut-Médoc)
Branaire (St Julien)   Lafon-Rochet (St Estèphe)
Talbot (St Julien)   Beychevelle (St Julien)
Duhart-Milon-Rothschild   Prieuré-Lichine (Cantenac-
(Pauillac)   Margaux)
Pouget (Cantenac-Margaux)   Marquis-de-Terme (Margaux)

FIFTH GROWTHS

Pontet-Canet (Pauillac)   du Tertre (Arsac-Margaux)
Batailley (Pauillac)   Haut-Bages-Libéral (Pauillac)
Grand-Puy-Lacoste (Pauillac)   Pédesclaux (Pauillac)

Grand-Puy-Ducasse (Pauillac)

Haut-Batailley (Pauillac)

Lynch-Bages (Pauillac)
Lynch-Moussas (Pauillac)

Dauzac (Labarde-Margaux)
Mouton-Baronne-Philippe†
(Pauillac)

Belgrave (St Laurent-Haut-
Médoc)
de Camensac (St Laurent-Haut-
Médoc)
Cos Labory (St Estèphe)
Clerc-Milon-Rothschild
(Pauillac)
Croizet-Bages (Pauillac)
Cantemerle (Macau-Haut-
Médoc)

*Decreed a First Growth in 1973.

†Formerly known as Mouton Baron
Philippe.

this is what people were ready to pay for them – in short,
they were worth it. The proof of the general accuracy of the
classification is that, with few exceptions, the châteaux listed
are still the best in Bordeaux, largely because they occupy
the best sites. Obviously, the best site, the most ideal soil and
potential is not always well-exploited, and châteaux have
their good and bad epochs. Consistency is really the crux of
the matter – if a châteaux not in the classification regularly
makes very fine wine, it should be considered for entry
should it ever be revised, or in the case of a château already
in the listing, it should go further up the ladder.

There is no doubt that the price gap between the First
Growths and the others is extremely wide and entrenched,
and to some, inexplicable. If this is felt strongly enough,
there is nothing like 'voting with one's palate' – in other
words, desist from buying. Much depends on needs and
requirements – if you do not want to age wine before seeing
it at its best, do not choose a First Growth. There is no use in
denying that the classification is controversial. And certainly
it needs reviewing. Some châteaux have disappeared and
others have fallen too far by the wayside, or really do not
have the potential to be top flight – one must here put into
question at least two of the wines of St Laurent. There are
also some top *bourgeois* growths waiting in the wings.

The *crus bourgeois* are the step just below the classified
growths and in 1978 the Syndicat des Crus Bourgeois

du Médoc produced an up-to-date assessment of these properties, dividing them into *grand bourgeois*, with 18 *crus exceptionnels* amongst them, and into *bourgeois* growths. It is intended periodically to keep this under review, which shows admirable flexibility.

THE GRAPES OF BORDEAUX (RED)

Cabernet Sauvignon: Cabernet Sauvignon must take pride of place in the list of red grape varieties. It is the dominant grape variety in the Médoc and Graves and, combined with the gravelly soils and superlative drainage of the best sites, can produce wines of some of the greatest breed in the world. It is a grape variety that needs time to develop complexity, although it always has a depth of fruit. When young, it can be austere and tannic and for this reason it is nearly always blended with a proportion of Cabernet Franc and Merlot. Cabernet Sauvignon is a late ripener, but this can have its advantages at the beginning of the season when spring frosts can wreak havoc. It is, however, a strong grape, resistant to *coulure* and rot. The berries are small, with thick skins, resulting in a lowish yield. It is less successful and less used in St Emilion and in the cooler soil of Pomerol, where it is known as the Gros Bouchet.

Cabernet Franc: This grape variety is a slightly muted version of Cabernet Sauvignon, less tough in youth and less concentrated, but with a lovely 'grassy' perfume. It is an important part of Médoc and Graves; but much more widely planted in St Emilion, Pomerol and Fronsac, where it is, logically, known as the Bouchet.

Merlot: Merlot is a vital part of Médoc and Graves wines, and the dominant grape variety in St Emilion and Pomerol. Many small properties in other regions of the right bank, such as Bourg and Blaye, also have a good proportion of it. The yield is generous, and the Merlot gives more alcohol than both the Cabernets, varying between one and 1.5 per cent more. The grape flowers earlier than the Cabernet and is picked earlier. But *coulure* can be a problem and rot can race through Merlot if not checked in time. The grape is also prone to attacks from red spider. But the wines are very commercial, tending to mature earlier than Cabernet-dominated wines, and they are softer and rounder in character. The wines have good colour when young, but tend to brown earlier than Cabernet Sauvignon.

Malbec: The Malbec plantings are less than they used to be in Bordeaux, and probably no vineyard wants more than 5-10 per cent now. In St. Emilion, it is known as the Pressac. The wines from this grape variety can be very pleasant, if not really distinguished, but the dangers from *coulure* in the vineyard are considerable.

Petit Verdot: This grape variety has never had more than a tiny share of the Bordeaux vineyard, but a small proportion (especially in the Médoc) can add much-needed concentration to a soft wine. It needs a great deal of sun to ripen to its full degree, but can add real body to a wine.

THE GRAPES OF BORDEAUX (WHITE)

Sémillon: By far the most distinguished of the white grape varieties, when made in the proper way, the Sémillon is a vital component of great Sauternes and Barsac, and also in top Graves dry white wines. It is resilient and gives a good yield. However, in the right conditions, it is also a good recipient of *pourriture noble*, or noble rot. It is blended with the white Sauvignon for both the sweet and dry wines. When made into a sweet wine, it can impart great lusciousness and richness, and in dry wines this same richness can be a revelation – full, high in glycerine and smoothness, with wonderful, subtle flavours.

Sauvignon: This grape variety has taken an increasing hold on the Bordeaux area. As well as being a vital part of the blend in the above wines, it is also used alone, or as the most important part, in light dry white wines for early drinking, as in Entre-Deux-Mers. It is an aromatic grape variety, with a pungent smell and taste. The yield is moderate, and the sun is needed if Sauvignon wines are not to be too acid.

Muscadelle: This is a reliable grape variety, producing a great deal of lesser sweet wine in such areas as the Premières Côtes,

Bordeaux

Wine region   Appellations: 1 Médoc 2 Haut-Médoc 3 St Estèphe 4 Pauillac
5 St Julien 6 Listrac 7 Moulis 8 Margaux 9 Graves 10 Cérons 11 Barsac 12 Sauternes
13 St Macaire 14 Ste Croix-du-Mont 15 Loupiac 16 Premières Côtes de Bordeaux
17 Entre-deux-Mers 18 Ste Foy-Bordeaux 19 Graves de Vayres 20 St Emilion
21 Côtes de Castillon 22 Côtes de Francs 23 Pomerol 24 Lalande de Pomerol
25 Côtes de Canon Fronsac 26 Fronsac 27 Bourg 28 Blaye

but is found in smaller quantities in Sauternes and Barsac. It is scented and yields well, but has a tendency to maderize relatively early unless great care is taken. Too much can give a coarse flavour.

There are a few other peripheral white grape varieties which may feature in basic Bordeaux Blanc and in the Côtes de Blaye – Colombard, Merlot Blanc and Folle Blanche. Ugni Blanc can sometimes be grown in the lesser sweet white wine areas; it is a late-ripening grape that gives acidity, and when blended with Sauvignon, can also produce a pleasant dry white Bordeaux in areas such as Entre-Deux-Mers.

As an indication of what can be produced from a good quality red-wine château, a yield of between four to five *tonneaux* per hectare would indicate a policy of careful wine-making, aiming for high standards. Obviously, this can vary according to the age of the vines in the vineyard (old vines producing less than young ones) and the nature of the vintage. A *tonneau* is not an actual barrel, but is the traditional measure in which the Bordeaux trade buys and sells – it 'contains' 900 litres of wine. The Bordeaux barrel or *barrique* is what you see in all the *chais* – they each contain 225 litres, and four of them make a *tonneau*.

Which Wines to Drink When

It is essential to treat the different strata of Bordeaux wines differently. Basic Bordeaux Rouge is delicious in the year after its birth, capturing all the fruit and charm of the Cabernet family. This applies also to *appellations* like Premières Côtes de Bordeaux, with some of the St Emilion 'satellites' and red wines from Bourg and Blaye needing a year or two more. However good, a small château wine will not improve beyond about five years of age as a general rule. They can be excellent after eighteen months. However, a *cru bourgeois* of a good year will only really give of its best after five years, and a *cru classé* after ten to fifteen years, again, in a good to a very good year. Very good, balanced years have a tremendous life-span. Even a *cru classé* in a light year, such as 1973, will not benefit from extensive keeping, and may even be more delicious relatively young. So, when deciding when to drink one's Bordeaux, the intrinsic quality of the property must be considered, and its position in the hierarchy, as well as the individual composition of the wine in a given year.

With Bordeaux white wines, the simple dry white Entre-Deux-Mers and other predominantly Sauvignon wines are usually best in the eighteen months after vinification. Sauvignon here is not quite so well constructed as in, say, Sancerre, and is usually quite a bit lighter. Dry white Graves of a certain quality category, going on to the top Graves châteaux, benefit from bottle age, round up and become more interesting. Top Sauternes and Barsac, with classic noble rot, keep for a very long time indeed, and their luscious qualities can become more subtle with time.

THE MEDOC

The topography of the whole Bordeaux region differs widely, having a great effect on the individual micro-climates. Rivers dominate the area, with the majestic Gironde coming in from its wide estuary at the Pointe de Grave and dividing into the Dordogne and the Garonne rivers near Bordeaux itself. The Atlantic Ocean is a very real presence in the vineyard area, especially in the Médoc, more directly under the influence of its moods and changeability. The first thing that is striking about the Médoc is its severity, the main *appellation* area being bare and gravelly, not pretty and soft. Here there is no polyculture, and a very gentle slope slides down to the Gironde. The best plateau areas are only for the vines.

There are eight appellations in the Médoc, all for red wine: Haut Médoc, Margaux, Moulis, Listrac, St Julien, Pauillac, St Estèphe, and Médoc (formerly the Bas Médoc). Below, there is Bordeaux Supérieur and Bordeaux, the two basic *appellations*. Apart from the *appellation* Haut Médoc, which encompasses all the list aside from Médoc, near the estuary of the Gironde, the *appellations* are named from a south to north direction, with the city of Bordeaux in the south. It could be said that the wines in the south tend to have more delicacy and less body than those in the north, but there are other factors, such as wines from nearer the river generally having more finesse than wines further inland, which can be more robust. Everything in the Médoc depends on depth of gravel, and good drainage. The fertile, alluvial *palus* next to the river is not suitable for fine wines.

HAUT MEDOC

Haut Médoc was the first, basic *appellation*, along with Bas Médoc, before the six other *appellations contrôlées* were formed. Thus, a bottle of 1947 Château Margaux, for example, is labelled Château Margaux, Appellation Haut Médoc. Pauillac received its *appellation contrôlée* before this, however, as 1945 Lafite has the Pauillac *appellation*, not Haut Médoc. There are five classified châteaux that still have the *appellation* of Haut Médoc. La Lagune is the first classified château you come to, going north from Bordeaux. A Third Growth, in the village of Ludon, this is a more than worthy introduction to the fine wines of the Médoc. La Lagune is a very beautifully run property, with the vineyards and *chais* always impeccable. The vineyard was almost totally replanted in the late 1950s, and so the wine was light at first. Ludon has a good deal of the excellent gravelly soil of more northerly Margaux communes, and so one can expect, and will get, finesse here.

The present owners of La Lagune are the Champagne house of Ayala, and the remarkable Madame Boyrie is the manager. The 1970s began magnificently for La Lagune, with a 1970 of full fruit and good breeding. 1971, 1973, 1975 are all excellent examples of their respective vintages, and the 1976 is a most exciting wine, with almost exotic fruit. The 1978 is very perfumed, with a bigger structure than usual, beautifully matched by high glycerine. The wines of La Lagune are always marked by new oak when young.

Château Cantemerle, a Fifth Growth, is in the commune of Macau, just south of where the *appellation* Margaux begins. The château, managed by Cordier since 1980, has long associations with Holland, as it was owned by the Bordeaux négociants, Beyerman, who are of Dutch origin. The two men who will be forever associated with

Cantemerle are the great M. Pierre Dubos and, after his death, his son-in-law M. Henri Binaud. The vineyards are on good, gravelly soil in the Ludon direction. The 1953 is superlative and the 1959 very good. There is a resemblance to Margaux, but the wines are fuller and plumper. There were some nice vintages up to 1966, then rather a disappointing period followed, but now, under the Cordier team, the wines of the 1980s are right back to top form.

The other three Haut Médoc *appellation*-classed growths, Château Belgrave, Château de Camensac and Château La Tour Carnet, are all in the commune of St Laurent, inland from St Julien. At the moment, I cannot see at least one of them retaining this status if there was a reassessment.

Other wines to look out for with the Haut Médoc *appellation* are: Château d'Agassac, Château D'Arcins and Château Barreyres. Château Beau Rivage, in fact, only has the Bordeaux Supérieur *appellation contrôlée*, because it is on the alluvial *palus* near the river. Managed by the firm of Borie-Manoux, it is a nice, easy wine – the 1967 was most acceptable. Château Bel-Orme-Tronquoy-de-Lalande, north of St Estèphe, makes a very good wine, and there are some remarkable old vintages that I have been lucky enough to taste. A *grand bourgeois*.

Château Le Breuil, near St Estèphe, is a good *bourgeois* wine and Château Caronne Ste-Gemme in St Laurent is a very good *grand brougeois exceptionnel*. Château Cissac and its good solid wine is well known in the United Kingdom and the United States. The owner, Louis Vialard, made slightly lighter wines in the 1970s than in the 1960s, but the style may go towards the more powerful again. Cissac is always splendid value. Château Citran, inland from Soussans and Margaux, is generally dependable. Château Coufran at St Seurin-de-Cadourne makes pleasant, lightish wines and Château La Dame Blanche at Le Taillan makes dry, white Bordeaux. Château Dillon at Blanquefort is owned by the regional agricultural school and the wines of the 1970s have improved greatly. Other châteaux to look out for are: Château Lamarque, Château Lanessan at Cussac, Château Larose-Trintaudon at St Laurent, Château Liversan and

Château Peyrabon at St Sauveur Château du Taillan at Le Taillan. Château Villegorge at Avensan is now owned by Lucien Lurton and the wine can have up to 60 per cent Merlot in its makeup. The 1983, 1982 and 1981 are all excellent, as was the 1961. Château Sénejac at La Pian is a Cru Bourgeois owned by American Charles de Guigné and the wine is consistently good.

BAS MEDOC

This is the area north of St Estèphe, beginning at St Yzans in the south and running up to Soulac near the sea, but the vineyards stop before then between Lesparre and St Vivien. The *appellation* is Médoc, but it should be remembered that, when speaking, people often refer to the Médoc when they mean the whole of the Haut and Bas Médoc together. There are many cooperatives, supplying beefy, full wines to the négociants. The best areas are round Bégadan, Blaignan, St Christoly, Ordonnac and Potensac, St Yzans and St-Germain-d'Esteuil.

Château Loudenne is the Gilbey/International Distillers & Vintners property. A beautiful château is surrounded by vineyards on gravel, unusually going almost down to the river's edge. Vinification is modern and efficient, and there is now a wine museum. Wine of great character, with the best vintages ageing beautifully. A delicious, Sauvignon-based white wine is also produced. Credit for much of what Château Loudenne is today must go to the late Martin Bamford of Gilbeys, France. Loudenne is also the headquarters of Gilbey's Bordeaux *négociant* business which is responsible, amongst other things, for the selection and distribution of La Cour Pavilion. The red is an excellent blend of wines from the area of Loudenne itself, bearing the Médoc *appellation* and showing the marked character of the communes around St Yzans. The white is *appellation* Bordeaux and is dry and crisp. There is also a highly recommended *appellation* Bordeaux Rouge, rather delightfully called La Bordelaise. Château La Cardonne at Blaignan is owned by the Lafite-Rothschilds and makes wine with character. Château du Castéra at St. Germain-d'Estevil is relatively unknown but good. Château Greysac at Bégadan is a *grand bourgeois* of good standard and much distributed in the United States. Château Livran at St-Germain-d'Esteuil is a wine worth looking for. Other reliable châteaux are: Château Patache d'Aux, and Château La Tour de By at Bégadan, Château Potensac, and Château St Bonnet, Château La Tour Blanche and Château La Tour St Bonnet at St Christoly.

MARGAUX

Margaux is one of the great names of the Haut Médoc. The *appellation* includes wines from the commune of Margaux itself, as well as Labarde, Arsac, Cantenac, and parts of Soussans. Margaux wines can attain great breed and finesse, with an intense, poignant scent and a real silky texture. They are not as 'fleshy' or big, as say, Pauillac wines. The very best parts of Margaux are covered in white pebbly gravel, and these *croupes* or ridges give the wines with most delicacy. The village of Margaux is the kernel of the *appellation*, with its meagre soil so beloved of vines. Many properties in this *appellation* have small parcels of vineyards in several different places.

CHATEAU MARGAUX (Margaux)

This is a First Growth that, at its best, conjures up all that is most elegant, scented and refined in top Bordeaux. Apart from approximately eighty hecatares under vines, Château Margaux is also an important farm. Château Margaux was bought by M. and Mme André Mentzelopoulos in 1976. Determined that the property should regain the peak of its marvellous potential, M. Mentzelopoulos brought the same dynamism he applied in his business life to the resuscitation of both the wine and the beautiful neo-classical château. Sadly he died at the end of 1980. The celebrated and experienced Professeur Peynaud, who has done so much in consultancy work in improving the quality of many top Bordeaux wines, had been called in to oversee operations. The change has been dramatic. The 1978 and 1979 are splendid wines, while the 1980 is most honourable in the context of the year. The 1981, 1982 and 1983 are a trio of stunners, which rank in the top few for each vintage – for some, they could well turn out to be the best. Enormous care in selection is now shown and there have been changes in the cellar and vineyard as a result of the highest technical advice. The Mentzelopoulos family must be congratulated on their great achievement, together with M. Paul Pontallier, their estate manager. The 1975 is good, but not amongst the greatest in this context. The wines of the 1960s and early 1970s did not really show the best that Margaux can do, which is quite remarkable, although the 1970 and 1966 are very honourable. The 1971 is not for keeping. But the 1961 is fine, absolutely delicious, scented wine, not too tannic – not quite as luscious as Palmer, but showing great breed. The 1953 Margaux was probably the best wine of the vintage, incredibly elegant and distinguished. The 1950 was a great success, and the 1947 is still glorious.

The property also makes some white *appellation* Bordeaux, called Pavillon-Blanc du Château Margaux. Now entirely made of Sauvignon, the wine is extremely good, grown as it is on ten hectares of 'black sand' vineyard outside the Margaux *appellation* in the commune of Soussans.

Château Rausan-Ségla, a Second Growth, is now part of the international combine, Lonhro. Sometimes bottles from good vintages are rather disappointing from this property, lacking the breed they should have. The 1975, however, has very good fruit and is well-made wine, if not amongst the deepest in weight. The Second Growth 'twin' of Rausan-Ségla is Château Rauzan-Gassies. The wine can have the best qualities of Margaux and Cantenac, and take time to show at its best. However, too many wines show rather thin. The 1976 seems one of the best in recent years, with a very fruity nose, lovely silky texture and nice fullness. Château Durfort-Vivens is owned by M. Lucien Lurton, who also owns Château Brane Cantenac. The wine produced is very firm, partly due to a fairly small proportion of Merlot, but there are changes afoot, and a more elegant Margaux wine could be emerging.

Another Second Growth, Château Lascombes, is now owned by the brewery and wine and spirits group, Bass Charrington. Alexis Lichine did much to restore the vineyard in the 1950s and 1960s, after a long period of neglect, but since his sale of the property in 1971, the château perhaps lacks tight personal control. The vineyard area has been greatly increased, but this is a property where the plots are very scattered. The 1970 is full and plump, but other vintages in the 1970s have tended to dryness and are rather light for the class of wine. Château Brane Cantenac is a large property, possessing a magnificent plateau of very white, chalky-gravelly soil. This can produced Margaux *appellation* wine *par excellence*. The 1961 and the 1970 are both beautiful wines, appearing elegant and not too weighty, but with the balance to go on for a long time. M. Lurton is a very careful proprietor, and the Brane Cantenacs of the 1970s and 1980s are quite excellent. He has also revived Château Desmirail, and the 1982 and 1983 show Margaux scent and elegance. Château Kirwan does not really impress at the moment.

Château d'Issan is another Third Growth, and is owned by Mme Emmanuel Cruse. Unfortunately, the distribution of the wine is not very general, which is a pity, as d'Issan can produce big, rich, fruity wines, rather atypical Margaux. 1966 and 1970 both produced good wines, the 1964 is extremely good for the year, and 1979 and 1982 are remarkable. Château Giscours is a very important Third Growth, owned and managed by the energetic and conscientious Tari family. Although the area under vine is large, about 70 hectares, the estate is much bigger, and includes forest, farm and horses. The wine of Giscours is distributed by Gilbeys of Loudenne, and the reputation at the moment is justifiably high. The bouquet can often be aromatic, and the texture of the wine silky. The 1976 is rich and full, and the 1975 quite excellent, with an intense, fruity nose, real breed and a cedary flavour, married to good 1975 tannin – all pointing to a very harmonious future. The 1973 was very good for the year as was the 1980. Château Cantenac-Brown is not exceptional at the moment.

Château Palmer is a property at its zenith, on occasions

rivalling the First Growths in spite of its classification as a Third. Palmer is internationally owned by the firms of Mahler-Besse (with Dutch connections), Sichel (English) and the Miailhe family (French). Production is meticulous, both in the vineyard and in the *chais*, and every detail is known and followed by M. Chardon, the *régisseur*, whose family have a great hand in the reputation Palmer now enjoys. Palmer 1978 has a wonderful colour, richness and structure, perhaps following the 1961 style, but lighter in weight. Château Margaux's 1978 is bigger. The 1979 looks set on an excellent course. The 1977 is pleasant, although Palmer's Merlot grapes (of which there are approximately 40 per cent) were badly hit by the frost on the last two days of March. The 1976 is sweet and ripe, with the softness of Merlot, with depth of fruit and a lovely velvet texture. The 1975 wine is very fine indeed, with an almost exotic nose that Palmer can attain in its great years, great fruit and persistence, acidity and tanning – all the ingredients for a long life. One has to mention the 1973, 1971 (one of the best in the Médoc), 1970, 1966 (incredible depth of scent and individuality), 1962, 1961, 1960, 1959 (absolutely superb in magnum in January 1980, still youthful, and rich as a 1961), 1957, 1955 and lovely 1953. The 1961 is legendary, and is a quite glittering wine of immense opulence and beauty, a taste one recalls for ever.

Château Malescot-St-Exupéry is a Third Growth, very well managed by the owners, the Zuger family. The wine has delicacy and class, with the scent of Margaux and good balance, qualities needing time to show themselves. The 1970 and 1961 are very good. The 1975 has a classic Margaux nose and a lot of body, and the 1978 shows great promise. Owned by Alexis Lichine since 1952, Château Prieuré-Lichine, a Fourth Growth, is witness to what great care and personal pride can do in restoring a property. With 52 hectares now under vine, some of them are necessarily young. The 1978 has elegance and tannin, a medium-weight wine. The 1977 has a nice blackcurrant flavour and is full of fruit. The 1970 shows an exotic, blackcurranty nose, and is rich and high in glycerine. The 1967 is most successful, as are the wines of the eighties. The 1974 is well above average. Château Marquis-de-Terme, a Fourth Growth, has a high production but the wine is sound and ready to drink relatively quickly.

Château Le Tertre is owned by one of the well-known Gasqueton family, Médocains par excellence. The vineyard is in one parcel, which is unusual for the Margaux *appellation*, and there is a great deal of Cabernet Sauvignon. The wines thus have a great deal of body, but with the perfumed bouquet of Margaux.

Other châteaux of note are; Château Boyd-Cantenac, Château Marquis d'Alesme-Becker, Château Siran, Château La Tour de Mons, Château Bel-Air-Marquis d'Alegre, Château d'Angludet, Château Paveil-de-Luze, Château de Labégorce, Château l'Abbé-Gorsse-de-Gorsse, Château Labégorce-Zédé (particularly fine) and Château Ferrière. Château Martinens is a *grand bourgeois* in the 1978 classification, and Château Tayac is a *cru bourgeois*. A further twenty-five or so châteaux regularly make wine, none in very large quantities. Margaux is an expensive *appellation*, and no château with that on its label is ever going to be cheap. But good Margaux can give really refined and elegant drinking, and should be savoured.

ST JULIEN
The wine of St Julien represents very precious liquid. It is the smallest of the four great communes in the Haut Médoc, with a high proportion of properties in the top category, especially among the Second, Third and Fourth Growths. The very best sites are along the river slopes, gravel over clay outcrops, and attract all the available sun. Further inland there is more variety in the soil, which can include sand and silicate. St Julien might be the easiest to appreciate at all stages of its development of the four great Haut Médoc *appellations*. The wines can have great suppleness and lusciousness of fruit, and a generous, distinguished, tempting scent. They can be gloriously glossy. Perhaps they do not always have the sheer finesse of top Margaux, or the backbone of top Pauillac – St Julien could be described as a stepping-stone between the two styles. All St Julien

appellation wines are in the same commune.

Château Léoville-Las-Cases, a Second Growth, makes uncompromisingly excellent wine. The main part of the vineyard is a walled forty-hectare enclosure, aristocratic vine territory. The soil is such that the wines of Léoville-Las-Cases have weight combined with their St Julien fruit. There is also a high proportion of Cabernet Sauvignon, more reminiscent of neighbouring Pauillac than a classic St Julien vineyard make-up. The direction of the property has now passed to M. Michel Delon, whose wine-making intelligence and enormous attention to detail are second-to-none. Throughout this century, Léoville-Las-Cases has made magnificent wines, and with every vintage now this reputation is consolidated. There was, however, a transient period in the 1950s, following extensive replanting. The great 1928 is still, in 1980, outshining all else from that year, with its characteristic power, but with much more fruit than some of the tannic, dry examples of the vintage. The late 1940s produced fine wines, and then the 1959 marked the end of the young-vine stage. The 1961 is enormous, still with a distance to go, but the 1962 is a glorious wine that is now showing all its paces. The 1966 is the other great wine of the 1960s, but very honourable wines were made in 1964 and 1967, the former perhaps the best wine of the vintage in the Médoc. The 1970 is a classic, but it should be emphasized that this wine really needs time to come out. In the context of their vintages, one cannot fault 1971, 1973, 1976 (superb), a 1977 with charm, and a full, rich 1978. The 1979 is right up with the First Growths. The 1973 is a classic in the making, distinguished, intense, with a concentration of fruit and body that takes it into the very front ranks. It is this combination of unctuous fruit, breed, and weight that singles out Léoville-Las-Cases as top Claret. Clos du Marquis is a second label of the property, often exceptional in good years.

Château Léoville-Poyferré, a Second Growth, was a real rival of Léoville-Las-Cases during the 1920s and 1930s, and the 1928 and 1929 are rightly famous. There was a perfectly lovely 1961, sweet and ripe, with that St Julien lusciousness of fruit. The 1966 had a classic blend of fruit and tannin, so typical of this year. But then there is a very doubtful period, with great differences between bottlings; however, the 1973 is most pleasant drinking. Now, Didier Cuvelier is managing the property and the wines of the 1980s show real promise, with the 1982 top quality. Château Léoville-Barton is another of the fine collection of St Julien Second Growths and has been in the hands of the Barton family since 1826. The long era of Ronald Barton has seen some very fine vintages make their appearance, but now management has passed to his nephew, Anthony. In 1978, Léoville-Barton made a big, tannic wine, *charpenté*, and with almost a flavour of fennel. The 1977 very much follows the style of the property, but in lighter vein. The 1976 excels, with good youthful astringence for the year – much needed in a year of low acidity. The 1975 is a classic, with a *grand vin* nose, enormous flavour and tannin, a worthy successor to the glorious 1970, a great, glossy mouthful of wine, rich with enormous body. The 1961 has always showed as really fruity St Julien whenever I have seen it. In great years, one feels the Cabernet in these wines.

Château Gruaud-Larose is a large property, but that does not deter the Cordiers from running it with great attention to detail. A feature of all the Cordier properties is the presence of sixty-hectolitre wooden *cuves* or vats, alongside the normal 225-litre *barriques* or casks. The maturing wine spends time in both receptacles, and this is seen as especially beneficial in light years, when this type of vintage benefits from being part of a greater 'mass' of wine but the procedure is being phased out. The wines are now generous and fruity, showing well comparatively young, but having the balance to last with grace. There is a high proportion of Cabernet Sauvignon, and approximately eighty hectares are under vine. The 1977 has charm and more 'extract' than most, showing the effect of its time in large vats. The 1976 is really rich, and the 1975 has great *race* and style, with a juicy acidity balancing the great tannin. The 1974 is to be complimented for the year, the 1973 is admirable, and the 1971 good. The 1970 is a beauty, classic and showing good acidity and fruit and the 1969 is one of the best of a mean bunch. The 1967 has an excellent reputation in this charmless year, the 1966 is to be savoured, and the 1961 is superlative.

It is always with immense pleasure that one writes about Château Ducru-Beaucaillou, as when a man of integrity and modesty succeeds in what he intends to do, it is a cause for celebration. M. Jean-Eugène Borie owns and lives at Ducru-Beaucaillou, and he and his family have put the property at the forefront of Bordeaux wine. The vineyard is situated in the best ridge, not far from the river, near Léoville-Las-Cases and Beychevelle. Ducru's wines are 'breed' exemplified, the opposite of 'coarse', elegant and silky-textured. They usually do not have the weight of Léoville-Las-Cases (the soil changes even between neighbouring properties), but are refined, 'classy', and distinguished. In blind tastings and in good vintages Ducru can rival the First Growths. The property built up its redoubtable modern reputation throughout the 1950s, with 1953 a star in the decade (perhaps tiring now), and triumphed in 1961. This decade included many fine vintages, and the next began with a magnificent 1970. The 1971 is delicious in the Médocain context (a vintage where St Emilion and Pomerol usually eclipsed the Médoc), and the 1975 has great finesse, with harmony and breed. The 1976 is elegant rather than big. The 1977 looks charming, the 1978 rich, full and well-structured, and the 1979 totally consistent.

Château Langoa-Barton, a Third Growth in the Barton stable, can produce some quite remarkable wines. The 1974 is probably the best I have seen in the Médoc, quite leaving the rather dull standard of the main body of wines, and showing a deep, aromatic nose, with a flavour somewhere between cassis and mint, rich and fruity. The 1971 is also quite exceptionally good, a lovely fruity, 'chewy' wine, and the 1977 scores heavily and is remarkable drinking value. The 1975 and 1970 are on very good form, true to their respective vintages. Château Lagrange is a Third Growth that was for long solely distributed by one *négociant* and so was not seen everywhere. But now it is once again on the open market, and the excellent 1978 vintage heralds this new era. The wine always has body and backbone, perhaps a cross between St Julien and St Laurent style, and the 1978 represents good value. The owners are now the Japanese firm of Suntory. Château Branaire-Ducru is a Fourth Growth that would most certainly be classed higher in a new list. Owned by the dynamic M. Jean Tapie, the wine is often excitingly good, full of exotic flavours and nuances. Since 1952 when M. Tapie bought the property, the vineyard has been gradually replanted and innovations in the cellar have taken place. The wine is part-stored in new oak and part in old oak, and the final result is a judicious blend of the two. I always think Branaire has great individuality, with an almost chocolate flavour on the nose, great colour and depth, and strong body and richness. Branaire par excellence is the 1975 – a fantastic wine of enormous interest, a whole span of flavours, and a great future ahead of it. The 1979 and 1978 look outstanding, the 1976 is excellent, the 1971 is delicious, and the 1970 is a classic wine. The 1960s produced a very high standard throughout, with 1966 outstanding, although the poor vintages of 1963, 1965 and 1968 did not appear under the vintage label. A small part of the vineyard is on the plateau of St Laurent, but because of historic usage, all the wine is under the St Julien *appellation*.

Château Talbot is another Cordier property, this time a Fourth Growth. The same large oak vats have the same effect as at Gruaud-Larose. The attention to detail, and quality rather than excessive quantity for the area of vineyard, is followed throughout the properties. Larger than Gruaud-Larose, it can also afford to knock off some bunches about three weeks before the harvest, to give the remaining bunches more chance to retain real ripeness. Cordier also make a practice of removing the bottom leaves on the vine to let the sun get at the grapes for optimum sugar gain. Although a neighbour of Gruaud-Larose, the wines are always different when tasted side-by-side, with Talbot usually the lighter. The proportion of Cabernet Sauvignon is relatively high. The 1976 will make very supple drinking, and the 1975 will not take as much time to come round as some wines. 1973 is highly drinkable, and the 1970 has every quality in good proportions and is intensely perfumed. The

1959 and 1961 drink beautifully in the 1980s.

The production of Château Beychevelle is, luckily, large. Beychevelle makes supple, fruity wines that can come forward more quickly than comparable growths, but which offer a wonderful, ripe St Julien flavour. The 1961 is a great wine, so complex and scented, and showing beautifully from now on. 1962, 1964 and 1966 all really showed the very best that these respective years could offer, and this pattern has followed in the 1970s, picking out especially the 1971, 1975, 1976, 1978 and 1979. Amongst old vintages, the 1928 is still a great and pleasurable experience to drink. Beychevelle gives us wines that delight the nose and palate, and could be a wonderful introduction to top St Julien. Château St Pierre-Sevaistre and Château St Pierre-Bontemps, both Fourth Growths, are now one property. Château St Pierre is now being made by the team at Château Gloria and the 1982 and 1983 are both very fine wines in the making. The 1975 St Pierre is fruity and scented, a most rewarding bottle of Bordeaux while the 1978 is outstanding.

Château Gloria has been built up during the last thirty years, gradually acquiring very good parcels of land from classed growths nearby. M. Henri Martin is a man of immense experience, and he has established the solid reputation of Gloria on a very genuine basis. The wine is fleshy and fruity, and shows a very commendable consistency. One can safely say that, apart from the acknowledged poor vintages, Gloria has made good wines throughout the last twenty years. Personally, I find the 1978 and 1975 quite the best Glorias I have tasted, albeit at an early stage. Château Peymartin is a subsidiary *marque* that is used for the product of the less mature vines. There is also Château Haut-Beychevelle Gloria, usually lighter than Gloria itself. Château du Glana was built up during the twentieth century and has recently been classed as a *grand bourgeois exceptionnel*. Production is high, but the wines can be good.

In St Julien, there is not the mass of lesser châteaux that one finds in, say, St Estèphe. Château Terry Gros Caillou is worth looking out for, but St Julien is not a happy hunting ground for a 'good little château wine'. One needs to save up for the glamorous beauties. M. Meffre, at Château du Glana, makes very good generic St Julien. However, there is one very welcome addition to the list of St Julien properties, and that is M. Jean-Eugène Borie's Château Lalande-Borie. He bought eighteen hectares of land from Château Lagrange in 1970, and with the 1979 vintage, supple and fruity, but with good backbone, we have much drinking pleasure ahead.

PAUILLAC

To some, Pauillac is the king of the Médoc. It can often be magisterial, powerful and definite. Its fame rests on its great growths, which carry the weight of responsibility with honour. There is immense variety between the top châteaux, but they all have good body and firmness when young. Sometimes they do not have the intense bouquet of the other communes in the Médoc, nor the sheer flowery elegance of, say, Margaux, but they have flesh and great character, and age to perfection. It is perhaps more of a crime to drink top Pauillac too young than any other wine. There is a great deal of gravel in Pauillac, sometimes mixed with heavier soil, especially further away from the Gironde, and there is good mineral content below. Pauillac embraces quite a few sub-communes, all with their small differences of micro-climate and soil.

CHATEAU LATOUR (Pauillac)

Latour is only just in the area of Pauillac on the southern limit, bordering St Julien. The vineyard occupies some of the choicest sites of the Médoc, on marvellous gravelly outcrops near the river front, but there are parcels further inland. The site to see is not so much a handsome château, but a very impressive and modern *cuverie*. Huge, tall stainless-steel fermenting vats tower over the human beings below and minute attention is paid to temperature. Enormous care is taken with the raw material, and the grapes themselves are checked for every flaw before being allowed into the *fouloir-égrappoir*. A very well-planned underground cellar ensures ideal conditions for the wine during its life in cask.

For three centuries Château Latour was the property of connected families. In 1962, majority control of Latour was sold to the English, predominantly to a company headed by Viscount Cowdray, with Harvey's of Bristol acquiring 25 per cent, and the last French owners, the Beaumonts, maintaining an interest. Harry Waugh, then of Harvey's, became a director, and has done a great deal for the reputation of Latour. He was instrumental in bringing in both M. Henri Martin and M. Jean-Paul Gardère, two very knowledgeable Girondins, steeped in experience and pride in their work, and Latour has benefited enormously from their attentions.

The total *encépagement* of the vineyard is 80 per cent Cabernet Sauvignon, 10 per cent Cabernet Franc and 10 per cent Merlot, which includes some Petit Verdot and Malbec. It is certainly true to say that the wines of Latour bear the character of Cabernet Sauvignon in as much as they are slow to mature, and have firm body, and astringency, when young. But it is not only the grape variety that marks the wine – after all, Mouton Rothschild has almost the same proportion of Cabernet Sauvignon, and the two wines do not taste at all alike, especially when mature and 'nosed' and tasted side-by-side. The differences in soil, distribution of vineyard parcels, drainage and micro-climate are much more important. Latour wines of good vintages are very deep coloured, big and powerful, tannic when young, but fleshy enough to give lovely texture and flavour when smoothed out with bottle age.

I have drunk Latour 1928 in both half-bottles and bottles during the latter part of the 1970s, and it seems to keep its character very constantly – albeit a severe rather than soft wine, but lovely, deep and 'meaty'. The 1931 is an amazing example of what Latour can do in an 'off' year – in 1980 it had a beautiful, typically Latour nose, and intricacy of taste coupled with silky fruit. The 1944 is an unheralded delight, while the 1945 is still, in the 1980s, a veritable blockbuster.

The 1955 is very great, far more distinguished than the run of the vintage, and looking superb in 1979. Latour made a great success of the light 1960, probably the best wine of the year, but it should have been drunk by 1985. The 1929, a fabled wine, is showing marked differences in the bottle in the 1980s – the best are still sublime.

The 1961 is very top Claret, certainly in the league of the greatest one will see. In 1978, when I saw it twice, it had still not entirely opened out, but it is quite one of the most complete wines I have ever tasted, promising a long and glorious future. The 1962 is excellent and distinguished, while the 1964 is one of the most successful Médoc wines of the year. The 1966 is very fine Latour indeed, and although still tannic, might well head the list of the vintage in the end. The 1968 is light and pleasant, and still drinking well in 1980 – I much prefer it to the 1969. The 1970 is tight and dumb at this 'adolescent' stage, but the fruit will come through. The 1973 is satiny and has style. The 1975 is absolutely superb – not so massive as Mouton, but with a better finish at this young stage. It has an immensely interesting, complex, cedar-wood nose (but this can always close up again temporarily in young Latour), with great grip on the finish. The 1976 has class but is still tannic and 'hidden', the 1977 is very light indeed. From 1978 through into the 1980s, Latour has made splendid wine, rich, powerful and glossy.

The other wine of Latour, Les Forts de Latour, launched with the 1966 vintage, is made up of younger vines (generally speaking, those up to twelve years) and from the produce of certain sections of the property. Fermentation usually takes twelve days, whereas it is up to three weeks for Latour. In all cases, the individual blend of the year is the decision of M. Gardère, and it is based on sound experience. The 1970 is a great delight, the 1976 forward and delicious, and the 1978 superb. Since then Les Forts has really been made to the standard of a Second Growth.

CHATEAU LAFITE-ROTHSCHILD (Pauillac)

Probably the most magic name in the whole of Bordeaux is

right at the other end of Pauillac, on the northern limit, just across the Jalle du Breuil from St Estèphe and Château Cos d'Estournel. *Jalles* are streams in *bordelais* parlance, and much used as borders between the communes in the Gironde. Lafite became Rothschild property in 1868, when Baron James de Rothschild acquired it, and has passed down ever since. The shares are always divided in the family, with one member having particular responsibility for the running of the property. Between the end of the Second World War and 1977, this person was Baron Elie de Rothschild, but now Baron Eric de Rothschild has assumed responsibility.

Perhaps the previous regime was not the happiest time for Lafite, with some superb highlights, but too many disappointments. And with that potential, this was tragic, especially so for some who paid very high prices. In 1975 the ubiquitous Professeur Emile Peynaud was asked to advise at the château. In the same year, the extremely able M. Jean Crété, formerly *régisseur* of Château Léoville-Las-Cases, was appointed to the post of *régisseur* at Lafite. The results were immediate, even with the 1975 vintage, not controlled throughout by the new regime, but brought up by them. Since then, it would be difficult to find fault with anything. Much is made of the Merlot content of Lafite's wines, in an attempt to explain the extraordinary finesse of its great vintages. In fact, nowadays, an average of a sixth of the blend would be from the softer Merlot grape variety, with variations of anything from 10 to 24 per cent in recent years. Thus, the almost lyrical delicacy of flavour must be put down to other factors, by far the greatest of which being the unique *assemblage* of wines coming from forty different *parcelles* of land. These different plots of vines have different soil compositions, face in different directions, receive different doses of sunlight and experience different drainage conditions. When their produce is blended, the result can be fascinating complexity. The total land under vine is around ninety hectares. Fermentation is still in oak vats.

There has been a proliferation of tastings of old Lafites, and I shall not add to extensive notes on vintages that are largely academic. The 1940s produced a string of good Lafite years,

1945, 1947, 1948 and 1949, still superb. Some of the 1953s were wonderful, some were not, and this could be applied to the 1961s, 1959 is still, in the 1980s, an incredibly beautiful wine. 1962 was excellent at the château, but then one has to wait until 1970 for real First Growth Claret again. Then there is another gap until 1975 for really fine Lafite, which was followed by marvellous wines in 1978 and 1979. M. Crété has now retired, and in 1983 was succeeded by M. Gilbert Rokvam as technical director. 1981, 1982 and 1983 are all great successes for Lafite.

The second wine of Lafite was Carruades de Lafite but, to avoid confusion, this name was last used in 1967. There was an interim period when the property used an extremely discreet label 'Bordeaux Supérieur' with, in very small letters, 'Mise en bouteille au Château Lafite-Rothschild', but legislation changes stopped this. Now the label 'Moulin des Carruades' is used for the second wine of Lafite.

CHATEAU MOUTON-ROTHSCHILD (Pauillac)

Mouton was elevated to First Growth status in 1973, after long being at that level in price and quality. While one could have wished that this had been part of an overall reassessment, no one could grudge the need for Mouton's achievement to be recognized. Baron Philippe de Rothschild worked tirelessly for this honour, and the estate has been in his hands for nearly sixty years. The enhancement of Mouton has included the creation of a unique museum and the commission of famous artists to design the labels. Mouton is large, with about seventy-five hectares of vineyard, most of which is planted in Cabernet Sauvignon. The character is unmistakable, especially in comparative youth, and there is a deep, cassis-like concentration about the wine, broadening out as its gets older, but always retaining an intensity and almost exotic opulence about it. The nose is definite and impact-making, and the deep blackcurrant nature of its unadorned fruit can sometimes remind one of a forceful top Californian Cabernet Sauvignon, usually without quite that alcohol. No two First Growths taste less alike than Mouton and Lafite, and yet their vineyards almost touch in parts – proof of the finely differing soil types in the Médoc.

I have been charmed by the delicious 1933, and impressed by the harder 1934. The 1947 and 1949 are superb, and the 1953 one of the most beautiful bottles of mellow, opulent Claret I have drunk. The 1959 is excellent, and the 1961 has everything, enormous cassis flavour, wonderful youthful acidity, a wine to go on and on, not austere and tough, but fleshy and full and really distinguished. 1962 and 1966 are very fine, but the rest of the 1960s provided some poor or mediocre wines, and it could be argued that a First Growth should make wines of a certain standard, even with difficult weather conditions. One could say the same for the 1970s – when Mouton hits the bull's eye, it is terrific, but there are perhaps too many misses. However, the 1970 is a classic, with excellent fruit and acidity balance, the 1975 is vigorous and tannic, and the 1978 and 1979 very fine. But the 1982 and 1983 have another dimension, truly superlative wines. Mouton Cadet is in no way related to the First Growth but is a branded Appellation Bordeaux Contrôlée.

Second Growths are: Château Pichon-Longueville, often known as Pichon Baron, now belonging to the Bouteiller family of Château Lanessan. Pichon Baron makes big, beefy Pauillac wines, needing time to attain a fine bouquet and softer texture. There were some fine wines in the 1940s and 1950s, but in the last twenty years the property has perhaps not had either the intimate care or the consistent distribution that goes with top-class wine. 1962 and 1966 were solid and good, but many vintages were on the dull side – the material was there, but perhaps the direction was lacking. However, the 1979 is excellent, *fin* and distinguished, which is most encouraging. Across the road is Château Pichon-Longueville-Lalande, owned by the Miailhe family. Pichon Lalande has a beautiful, custom-built underground cellar, and a skilful *régisseur*, M. Godin, trained by M. Paul Delon of Léoville-Las-Cases. M. Godin has firm views, great enthusiasm and talent, and he is making excellent wine at Pichon-Lalande. About a third of the vineyard lies in St

59

Julien, but now the *assemblage* or final blend of the Grand Vin all has the right to the Pauillac *appellation*. There is no doubt that the St Julien contribution adds its share of finesse and fruit to the wine, with Pauillac backbone behind it. The vintages of the 1960s were admirable in the different conditions of the years, with 1961 outstanding, but the 1967 is a most successful example of this rather 'dry' year. Consistency in the 1970s is remarkable, with a run of vintages, 1975, 1976, 1977, 1978 and 1979 all showing what trained and devoted wine-making can make of nature's varying gifts. The 1980s have continued in this vein. Pichon-Lalande is a wine to recommend unhesitatingly.

There is quite a jump in dimension between the First and Second Growths of Pauillac, and the Fourth (Duhart-Milon) and Fifths – there are no Third Growths in the commune. In 1964, the Lafite-Rothschilds bought Château Duhart-Milon, a geographically logical extension to their first property, and have done extensive replanting. Some of the *croupes* or gravelly ridges are really fine vineyard, and the scene is now set for some excellent wine. Rigorous selection is practised and the wine-making is as well done as it is now at Lafite – the 1978 is very good and the 1982 shows immense promise. There is the opportunity to make a 'second' wine when necessary (when only the best selections will go into the Grand Vin), and this will be named Moulin de Duhart.

In the 1855 classification, Château Pontet-Canet was the first of the many Pauillac Fifth Growths. The property belonged to the Cruse family of owners and *négociants* for over one hundred years, but in 1975 was sold to M. Guy Tesseron of Château Lafon-Rochet, who is married to a Cruse. There were some legendary Pontet-Canet wines, such as the 1929 (and I have enjoyed the 1917, the balanced 1948 and a 1953 which is still excellent), but the latter part of the Cruse ownership saw some dull wines. The yield is probably the largest of the classed growths. The vintages made under the new ownership are good, without being exciting. The 1978 is nice, but seems a bit short, the 1977 is good for young drinking, with a very Pontet-Canet nose mixed with new oak, but the 1975 is very good, showing the high percentage of Cabernet Sauvignon in the vineyard.

Château Batailley is owned by the Borie family and very ably managed by a son-in-law, M. Emile Castéja. It is sold through the *négociant* Borie-Manoux. The wines are big, firm, fruity Pauillacs and the standard is consistent and high. Excellent wines of the past have included 1953, 1961, 1962, 1964 and 1966, with 1975, 1976, 1978 and 1979 very good. The 1981 and 1982 are remarkable. Château Haut-Batailley is another Borie property, but here M. Jean-Eugène Borie of Ducru-Beaucaillou is administrator and in charge of wine-making. The difference in style between Batailley and Haut-Batailley is as much due to the individual style of the wine-making as anything else, as both properties are 'inland' wines, towards the woods. The wines have elegance and charm at Haut-Batailley. The 1970 is a delicious example of these qualities. I liked the 1976 which was quite solid when in cask, and the 1978 is stylish. Cabernet Sauvignon in the vineyard is about 65 per cent.

Château Grand-Puy-Lacoste is another property that has now come under the wine-making control and part-ownership of Jean-Eugène Borie and his son Xavier, and the beneficial effect is immediate. The late owner was the legendary M. Raymond Dupin, a man of great stature, much loved in Bordeaux circles, and a great gastronome. Grand-Puy-Lacoste is predominantly Cabernet Sauvignon in style (we may see this gradually change, to give more finesse), and tends to be big, straightforward Pauillac. The 1979 is absolutely excellent, and the 1978 superb, with perfume and intensity. The area in production has increased to fifty-five hectares, as Léoville-Poyferré sold some of its Pauillac vineyard land to Grand-Puy-Lacoste. The 1953 was very good, not quite up to Grand-Puy-Ducasse when compared together in 1978. The 1960s produced very dependable wines, and the 1980s look very promising indeed. The wine of Château Grand-Puy-Ducasse has always been a personal favourite, with its glossy fruit and long-lasting flavour, and I am glad I have renewed acquaintance with its recent vintages, after a period of changing ownership and lack of availability on foreign markets. In 1971 it was sold by the Bouteiller family to a group in which the Bordeaux *négociants*, Mestrezat Preller, are involved. In youth, the 1978 had that lovely, thick purple colour of good Grand-Puy-Ducasse, an almost aromatic nose that reminded me of the wonderful 1961 and 1962 with great depth, but in the 1980s the wine is strangely disappointing. The 1977 has the same style of nose, and exceptional fat and length for the year. The 1976 has real richness and ripeness, married with backbone, and the 1975 was still extremely tannic in 1979, barely out of the embryonic stage. The 1974, not a favourite vintage, had good fruit and acidity and was most charming. The vineyard is now thirty hectares.

Château Lynch-Bages has one of the wines that are easiest to recognize on the nose alone, as usually there is enormous intensity of Cabernet Sauvignon (in spite of only 65 per cent planted in the vineyard) and an overwhelming 'blackcurrant' flavour. It has wonderful, tempting fruit, and is nearly always excellent drinking. The 1978 looks fine, the 1977 is too Cabernet and drying (95 per cent Cabernet, as the Merlots went with the frost at the end of March that year), and the 1975 displays the best qualities of the year. Between then and 1970 I have not been very impressed, but the 1970 is a very good wine for the future. The 1962 is nice, and the 1961 has body and power, and a lovely cedary flavour, without being complex – beware the English bottlings of this vintage, incidentally. Lynch-Bages is owned by the Cazes family, now run by M. Jean-Michel Cazes. Château Lynch-Moussas, a very small Fifth Growth, is a Castéja family property. The vineyard suffered considerably in the 1956 frosts, and new planting meant light wines for some years. The wines are, naturally, difficult to find, and perhaps difficult to place in the classified bracket. But the 1979 points to a big improvement.

Château Mouton-Baronne-Philippe belongs to Baron Philippe de Rothschild of Mouton, and has been called Mouton d'Armailhacq, Mouton-Baron-Philippe from 1956, and Mouton-Baronne-Philippe from the 1975 vintage, in honour of Baron Philippe's late wife. There is considerably more Merlot here than at Mouton-Rothschild and, with the differences in vineyard site, the wine is softer and matures a little earlier than the First Growth, but the family resemblance is there. I do not see it very often, but the 1962 and 1966 are very good indeed, and the 1975 is big, straightforward classic Pauillac. Château Clerc-Milon is under the same ownership.

Situated near Lynch-Bages, Château Croizet-Bages is owned by the Quie family. With a high proportion of Cabernet Franc, the wine has quite an assertive flavour, and maintains a good, consistent standard, usually maturing well. The 1960 had the most amazing deposit in bottle and the 1966 is very good. The classed growths of Pauillac end here, but immediately after them, and surpassing a few, must come Château La Couronne, another property ably managed by the indefatigable Jean-Eugène Borie. This is good fruity, balanced Pauillac wine – always a good buy. Châteaux Haut-Bages-Monpelou, Haut-Bages-Averous, Pibran and Fonbadet are also in evidence on foreign markets and are reliable. The Pauillac cooperative is called La Rose Pauillac, and it has a good reputation.

ST ESTEPHE

There is a wide variety of wine in St Estèphe, some great long maturing ones, and some *petits vins* from the backwoods. There are fewer classified growths here than in Pauillac, St Julien or Margaux, but a large number of *bourgeois* growths which, when selected carefully, can give great pleasure. Perhaps St Estèphe, at the northern end of the Médoc, needs really ripe years to produce wines of top quality – then they can have richness, class and style, with a bouquet of great definition when mature. They can have marked flavour and individuality which, in lesser wines, can be a real *goût de terroir*. The fault with some St Estèphe wines is sometimes a lack of flesh, leaving rather a dry, thin wine. The wines need time to soften, and the heavier soil, with a little more clay and less gravel than elsewhere in the Haut-Médoc top three communes, leads to a robust character rather than finesse. Châteaux of note are: Château Cos d'Estournel, a Second Growth, has probably given me more pleasure than any other in St Estèphe. The wines tend to be the fattest and most fruity, in good years even opulent, with a firm backbone. The 1970s have seen a run of fine vintages, including 1970, 1971, 1973, 1975, 1976, and a much finer 1977 than the standard for the year, especially in St Estèphe, where the wines were particularly mean. The 1978 and 1979 is very good. The 1961 is magnificent and rich, but the 1950s were on the whole better than the 1960s. Cos's (and the 's' is pronounced) return to making great wine thus can be dated from when the Prats family took over in 1971, and M. Bruno Prats put all his training and skill into the wine. The wonderful oriental exterior of the property's buildings does not, in fact, front a château at all, but masks the *chais*. The proportion of Merlot is high for the Médoc, which partly explains the rich, fruity taste of Cos. Maître d'Estournel is a non-vintage branded wine with only a Bordeaux *appellation*, which is slightly misleading. The quality, however, is good.

Château Montrose is the other St Estèphe Second Growth, owned by the Charmolüe family. It has a high amount of Cabernet Sauvignon which, when combined with the heavier soil, can make for rather hard wines in youth. The 1979 looks very good. The 1977 suffered from being almost entirely Cabernet, as the Merlots were, unusually for the property, hit by frost. However, the 1976 is a lovely wine, fruity and supple, and the 1970 is very good indeed, cedary, fruity and balanced. The 1966 is much harder, and needs to soften a bit more before the fruit comes out.

Château Calon-Ségur is a Third Growth of imposing history, part-owned and managed by a member of a very old Bordeaux family, M. Philippe Capbern-Gasqueton. There is a considerable amount of Cabernet Franc and Merlot in the vineyard, which contributes to its different character when compared to Montrose. The vineyard of sixty hectares is in one piece, almost surrounded by a wall, and the château is very handsome. The 1948 in 1977 was still lovely and rich, even improving all the time in the glass, a sure sign that a wine is still vigorous. I am afraid I have not been impressed by the 1961, but the 1970s have shown Calons of consistently high standard. 1970, 1971, 1973, 1975 and 1976 can all be thoroughly recommended, but the 1977 was very light. The 1979 is most elegant, while the 1982 and 1983 are very fine. The one St Estèphe Fourth Growth is Château Lafon-Rochet. Now owned by M. Guy Tesseron, who did much replanting during the 1960s, the wine is mostly very reliable and good Claret, if a bit on the light side. The 1978 is light, elegant and fruity, the 1977 is another unsuccessful St Estèphe in this year, the 1976 is a bit thin, but flavourful, for early drinking, the 1975 combines fruit and tannin, even if it lacks individuality, and the 1974 is good for the year. St Estèphe finishes its classed growths with one Fifth Growth, Château Cos-Labory. Opposite Cos d'Estournel, the wine is good without being extraordinary. The 1975 has fruit, but also youthful, austered tannin and, as so often with this château, the character is really St Estèphe.

The top *bourgeois* growths of St Estèphe command attention. Château Phélan-Ségur is a *grand bourgeois exceptionnel*, usually robust and satisfying. They made a particularly good 1964, but new ownership promises even better wines. Château de Pez is very well run by M. Robert Dousson, who has been making wine there since 1959. There is a huge, very good 1970, a delicious 1971 for drinking over the next years, an outstanding, concentrated 1975, and a lovely 1976. M. Dousson told me he never adds in *vin de presse*. The large Château Meyney belongs to Cordier, and produces very well-made wines. I have admired the 1976, an excellent 1975, a delicious 1973, a really interesting, fat 1971, and a big, full 1970. The wines have a backbone of good St Estèphe *terroir*, and should be drunk when reasonably young to get the full benefit of their fruit.

Other wines to be recommended are Château Marbuzet, Château Pomys, Château Beau Site (belonging to the *négociants* Borie-Manoux), Château Tronquoy-Lalande, Château Haut-Marbuzet, Château Capbern (a London-bottled 1962, drunk in 1973, still had some way to go) and Château Les Ormes-de-Pez (owned by the Cazes of Lynch-Bages). There is a good cooperative which sells its wines as Marquis de Saint Estèphes, or under individual château names.

MOULIS AND LISTRAC

Although Moulis lies north-west of Margaux and inland, the wines have their own *appellation*, and generally combine firmness and fruit, without being in the top bracket of elegance. The best is Château Chasse-Spleen: the 1978 is good and very true to the *appellation*, the 1977 is pleasant and forward, the 1976 quite tannic, and the 1975 very concentrated and still a bit rough at four years old. Other châteaux to look out for are Château Poujeaux-Theil, the tongue-twisting Château Gressier-Grand-Poujeaux, Château Dutruch-Grand-Poujeaux, Château Maucaillou (owned by the *négociants* Dourthe), Château La Closerie, Château Brillette, Château Moulin à Vent and Château Pomeys. Listrac in some ways resembles Moulis, just to the south, and if there is one property today making classified-standard wine, (although a *grand bourgeois exceptionnel*), it is not because the soil is the very best gravel of the communes near the river (it has more clay and sand), but because of perfect wine management and clever composition of the vineyard. This château is Fourcas-Hosten, since 1972 owned by a group of French and Americans, headed by M. Bertrand de Rivoyre, the well-known *négociant* and owner. With the exception of the 1974, every vintage since the new ownership has been really good of its kind. The body and fruit of Listrac have at last been married with some breed and finesse. Château Fourcas-Dupré, belonging to the Pagès family, is made with the same care, and this is another very good *grand brougeois exceptionnel*. Other châteaux are Pierre-Bibian, Fonréaud, Lafon and Lestage. Château Clarke, which belongs to Baron Edmond de Rothschild, has now been replanted and is making good wine, which will get even better as the vines age. The cooperative in Listrac produces very good wines under the name of Grand Listrac.

GRAVES

Graves is a huge area of vineyard land, stretching from the outskirts of Bordeaux southwards to round Langon, with two sweet white wine areas, like islands, lying within the region near its southern limit – Sauternes/Barsac, and

Cérons. Graves is not an area (like the Médoc) with a high proportion of classified châteaux – it is more a large region of small proprietors, many of whom sell their wine to Bordeaux *négociants* who will blend it for generic red and white Graves. Obviously, small 'châteaux', or properties selling their wine under their own name, are increasing, but those of importance are few. The communes producing the best wines are those of Pessac and Talence, but unfortunately these are also the communes nearest Bordeaux, and precious vineyard land has been, and is being, eaten up by houses, railway lines and roads. Some of this ideal wine-producing land (Graves implies pebbles, and it is here where they go deepest) has gone for ever, and fighting for what remains is a constant battle. Léognan also produces top quality wines, and happily this is further south and further away from urban marauders, although they have left their mark here too. Graves, not so long ago, was producing one-third red wine to two-thirds white, and rather indifferent white at that, but the gap has narrowed considerably. The communes round Bordeaux concentrate on really fine red wines, with a tiny amount of absolutely exceptional dry white wine. Many important properties throughout the region make both a red and a white Graves.

The style of top red Graves is rich, even slightly spicy, with a faint earthiness in the finish. The nose can be fruit mixed with a whiff of tobacco, and the wines can have a firm grip to them when young, developing to a mass of subtle flavours when mature. Some of the top wines can seem quite Médocain in character, particularly La Mission Haut-Brion, but often there is something that is more exotic and less 'classic' about the flavour – now and again, a mature Graves can even, mysteriously, look like a Pomerol, which is strange when one considers that the *encépagement* is more Médoc than right bank of the Gironde.

The basic white wines have improved out of all recognition in recent years. White Graves can be fairly sweet or completely dry, which is slightly confusing for the consumer. There could be a decision to put dry wines in green bottles and sweet in clear white bottles, which would make things clearer, but organization for the merchants more difficult. The combination of sulphur and residual sugar in Graves white wines was certainly far from attractive, but now drastic measures are being taken to ensure healthier wines. White Bordeaux has always had to fight *pourriture grise*, or grey rot, leading directly to oxidation. Advice is given as to the best moment to pick and the best equipment to use, such as less fierce presses. The importance of reducing contact with the air is stressed as well as better selection and cold fermentation. Growers are encouraged to seek advice and have samples analysed at all stages of vinification, and the wine has become both fresher and more stable, with markedly less sulphur dioxide. The 1855 Classification of the Médoc contained one Graves wine, that of Château Haut-Brion, classed as a First Growth. In 1953, Graves made its own classification, which was confirmed in 1959.

CLASSIFIED RED WINES OF GRAVES

Haut-Brion (Pessac)	La Tour-Haut-Brion (Talence)
Bouscaut (Cadaujac)	La Tour-Martillac (Martillac)
Carbonnieux (Léognan)	Malartic-Lagravière (Léognan)
Domaine de Chevalier (Léognan)	Olivier (Léognan)
de Fieuzal (Léognan)	Pape-Clément (Pessac)
Haut-Bailly (Léognan)	Smith-Haut-Lafitte (Martillac)
La Mission-Haut-Brion (Pessac)	

CLASSIFIED WHITE WINES OF GRAVES

Bouscaut (Cadaujac)	Laville-Haut-Brion (Talence)
Carbonnieux (Léognan)	Malartic-Largravière (Léognan)
Domaine de Chevalier (Léognan)	Olivier (Léognan)
Couhins (Villenave-d'Ornon)	Haut-Brion* (Pessac)
La Tour-Martillac (Martillac)	

*Château Haut-Brion Blanc did not present itself for inclusion in 1959, but was added to the list in 1960.

CHATEAU HAUT-BRION (Pessac)

Since 1935, Haut-Brion has had a very special link with the United States, as in that year Clarence Dillon bought the property. It is now owned by his son, Douglas Dillon, and the President of the domain is his daughter, the Duchesse de Mouchy. The vineyard sites at Haut-Brion are very good, often enabling them to vintage relatively early, as the grapes have already reached maturity.

The nose of Haut-Brion is of the most extraordinary intensity, really rich, somehow reminding me of damp earth and lush vegetation. The wine can be velvety and glycerine smooth, with great flavours opening out in the mouth. Apart from the 1921, I have only seen the vintages made after the Second World War, which seem gradually to be developing a lighter style, only really becoming apparent with the wines of the 1960s and 1970s. The 1953 was delicious, the 1955 good, and the 1959 a most honourable example. The 1961 is definitely more advanced than many other Second, Third and Fourth Growth wines. But a bottle drunk in 1978 had a wonderful, taut, 'tobacco' nose, and a taste of enormous richness and an incredible tobacco-wood flavour. There was great concentration, without overpowering tannin, excellent balance, and it 'packed a punch' – there was no doubt that this would last. 1962, 1964 and 1966 were all most successful, with the 1966 having a beautiful flavour, less opulent but tighter than La Mission, and terribly Graves.

The 1970s have, regrettably, seen some light, dull vintages disappointing for a First Growth. The 1975, however, had all the breed of Haut-Brion, with a concentrated, rich taste and great Graves flavour, but it was very forward in development in 1979. The 1976 is very developed, the 1979 is distinguished and the 1981 fine and elegant. The 1982 and 1983 both look outstanding. Haut-Brion produces more wine on average than the other classed growths of the Graves and, at its best, it is a revelation of bouquet and taste. Haut-Brion Blanc is rarely seen, made from 50 per cent Sémillon and 50 per cent Sauvignon and bottled after fifteen to eighteen months in barrel. The 1983 has a lemony character in extreme youth and lovely flavour – the wines always round up with time.

Only across the road from Haut-Brion lies Château La

Mission Haut-Brion, but you could not get more different wines in the same area. In reality, the vines lie in both Pessac and Talence. The Woltner family bought La Mission in 1918, and for fifty years M. Henri Woltner contributed both love and immense skill to the property, founding its unassailable position today in the hierarchy of fine wine. M. Fernand Woltner also played a valuable part in this work, and his daughter and son-in-law, M. and Mme Francis Dewavrin, then administered the property with the utmost care. But in 1983 La Mission was sold to the owners of Château Haut-Brion and M. Jean Delmas is making both wines. The 1983 is a true La Mission wine, with all the tannin of youth, but the 1983 white Laville Haut-Brion is markedly different from the Lavilles under the old ownership, due to its longer ageing in barrel.

The gravelly soil of La Mission is really exceptional, sometimes descending fourteen metres in depth. There is approximately 65 per cent Cabernet Sauvignon, 10 per cent Cabernet Franc and 25 per cent Merlot. I have tasted a great many vintages of La Mission, and what a repertoire it is. In 1978 and 1979 the 1919 was gone, but the 1920 and 1921 were still there. The following were magnificent: 1924 (rich and excellent), 1926, 1928, 1929, 1933 (light, but excellent balance), 1934 (unbelievably elegant), 1936 (interesting and spicy), with a remarkable 1940. 1945 was big, 1947 is supple and harmonious, 1948 is very rich and still young, 1949 has real elegance, and the 1950 is terrific for the year. The 1952 is surprisingly good, and the 1953 very fine, but perhaps tiring a bit, the 1955 is classic Claret, the 1957 is very Graves, the 1958 fragrant and deep, and the 1959 has wonderful complexity.

The 1960s gave us some more outstanding wines: 1961 is one of the greatest in Bordeaux, intense, with a concentrated kernel to it and enormous lasting power. 1962 is most drinkable, 1964 is fruity for the year, 1965 was light but remarkable for the year, and 1966 a superlative wine, with a wonderful, fully-blown 'tobacco' nose, a really exotic taste and still great youth. The 1970 has great power and richness and is for the long-term, the 1971 is not one of my

70

favourites, and the 1973 was caught by hail. The 1975 is very big indeed, with great fruit and a chewy, long finish. The 1974, 1976 (very deep and complex), and 1977 all make the most of their respective years, but the 1978 is absolutely magnificent.

Château La Tour Haut-Brion is the second wine made by the property, and as the selection for La Mission is becoming even stricter, the La Tour is looking more and more classy. It is a separate property, but there is movement between the two. I have liked the 1959, the 1962, 1964, 1966, 1971, 1974, a marvellous 1975, 1976, 1977 and a big, excellent 1978. On the whole, La Tour should be drunk earlier than La Mission.

Château Laville Haut-Brion is one of the most exciting dry white wines of the world. Its development in bottle to a great, unctuous richness, coupled with a panorama of tastes and subtleties, is a meal and a nourishment in itself, demanding your entire attention. It is tragic to think that many bottles must be drunk too young, remaining delicious, but lacking that great experience for the senses. The white wine area of La Mission, never big, has recently become a little smaller, as some old vines have recently been uprooted, and the construction of a railway line did not improve matters. The soil is slightly richer than the pure pebbly gravel for the reds. The grape variety mixture is about half Sauvignon and half Sémillon, but emphasis is moving toward the latter, as giving that wonderful richness and class.

Fermentation is, unusually, carried out in cask and not in vat, and this no doubt contributes to the final flavour. Only very basic filtration is used, thereby retaining maximum texture and taste in the wine. Bottling is relatively early – the 1978 was bottled in May 1979. The 1978 looks as if it will be very fine and beautifully balanced, the 1977 is more austere with more acidity, the 1976 is very ripe, very rich and lanolin smooth, the 1975 very youthful in 1979, but one sensed the alcohol and the need for time in bottle, and the 1971 and 1970 both very fine, with the 1971 perhaps the more elegant. The 1969 is very smooth, the 1967 needs time, the 1966 is lovely, the 1962 exceptionally beautiful, with that lovely lemony Graves nose, glorious balance and elegance, with 1961 much more concentrated and seemingly alcoholic. In 1979, the 1960 was full, round, and only *just* beginning to show age.

Château Pape-Clement is, to me, Graves *par excellence* – its bouquet and flavour are textbook red Graves, full, earthy rich, with that strange, almost exotic tobacco overtone. M. Montagne had completely to resurrect the property after he bought it in 1939, and the 1955 is the first great vintage here after its revival, still lovely in 1979. However, the 1950 has remained youthful and blackcurranty, and I have been very impressed by the 1962, the 1964 (quite one of the best Bordeaux wines of the year) and the 1966. The 1961 is outstanding, with great interest and spiciness, soft and ready when drunk from magnum in 1984. There were some good wines in the 1970s, but direction seems to be lacking in the 1980s and there have been poor examples..

Domaine de Chevalier is in more rural Léognan, the commune that produces the greatest number of fine red and white Graves in the whole *appellation contrôlée* area. It is modest in appearance, but produces a small amount of aristocratic wine. The Ricard family owned the domain for many years, but now ownership has passed to the Bernard family, although the wine-making is still in the hands of the brilliant Claude Ricard. When the wines are not from excessively tannic years, Domaine de Chevalier matures relatively quickly, and goes for breed and style rather than sheer power. There is 30 per cent Merlot in the vineyard, but this is not unusual for the Graves, where the proportion is usually slightly higher than in, say, Pauillac. Delicacy and softness are the keywords here, especially in the old Domaine de Chevalier red wines; the few I have tasted, from the 1920s, were ethereal. Frost damage in 1945 caused some replanting, and the 1953 was the first top vintage after this setback. There really have been few errors since then, and I particularly remember the 1964 and 1966 as showing the elegance of the property. The 1973 was delicious drinking at six years old, with the 1970 and 1975 more long term and exceptionally promising. The 1977 was a bit marked by oak, but the 1978 is outstanding. The 1976 is delicious, with the 1979 and the 1981 maybe the best wines in the Graves. The white Domaine de Chevalier is made much in the same way as Laville Haut-Brion, with the very big difference of bottling time – Domaine de Chevalier used to bottle about a year later than at Laville, but with the 1983 vintage, this difference has disappeared. The quantity is about half that of Laville, and so, unfortunately, one does not see it at all often. The intense bouquet and fruity, yet taut, flavour need time to open out and, up until 1983, there was more evidence of oak in Domaine de Chevalier Blanc than in Laville. The Domaine's 1976 and 1970 are marvellous, and the 1979 shows superbly. Château Haut-Bailly is hidden away in the backwoods of Léognan, but the gravelly soil is ideal for red wine. It is owned by the Sanders family, who are Belgian. The 1961 is, justifiably, famous, and the 1960s were successful for the château, which continued to make rich wines with a true Graves flavour about them. The 1970s were less consistent, and only the 1975 and the superb 1979 were of the class that Haut-Bailly should attain, but the 1980s look set on the right course.

Château Malartic-Lagravière, managed by the Marly family, presents some of the best value in Graves today, making wines which are marked by both regional character and oak. Both red and white wines are made, but only a small amount of the latter. The 1955 red has stood the test of time very well. The 1970s have produced very good wines in the good vintages, perhaps less hard than in the past; the 1979 looks good. The 1978 has great individuality, as indeed has the white 1978, an extremely interesting wine. It has an intriguing, slightly spicy nose, with a great freshness in the mouth and an almost cinnamon flavour. Normally, it is not as rich as Laville and needs a little less time to reach full maturity, but there is great elegance and breed in it. The 1979 white is equally well-made. Château Carbonnieux is a very large property in Léognan, producing good red and white wines, the latter predominating in terms of output. The white is predominantly Sauvignon, and tends to be light and straightforward, rather than rich and complex. This is in a dry, light, crisp style, for relatively early drinking, but this is the good commercial white wine that M. Perrin and his son are looking for. The red wine has fine regional Graves flavour and is usually a bottle for medium rather than long-term keeping. Château Olivier was until recently managed by the *négociants* Eschenauer, and white wine production is about eight times that of red. It has to be said that the château itself is more interesting than the white wine, which is sound, commercial white Graves, inclined to have too much sulphur showing through. The red of Château de Fieuzal is classified, but the white is not. The wines are well-made, aiming for lightness and elegance.

Château Larrivet-Haut-Brion is also in Léognan, producing dependable red and white wines – the red 1966 has lasted very well. Château La Louvière makes red and white wines, and for some time the white wines appeared much better than their stablemate but that is no longer true. M. André Lurton makes the wine here, as well as at the small Château Neuf. Château Le Pape produces good wine.

The commune of Martillac has some good properties, with the wines not quite in the top rank. Château Smith-Haut-Lafitte is owned by Eschenauer – the red is classified, but the white is not, but then production of white only started in the late 1960s. The red wines tend to be solid and to age quite well, without having much breed. The 1959 was still young in 1972, the 1962 was very tannic, but rich and earthy in 1974, and the 1967 combined fruit and tannin when drunk at the same time. Château La Tour-Martillac is owned by the Kressmann family, and both red and white wines are classified – white wine production is very small. The 1978 red La Tour-Martillac looks good, although I was not impressed by the 1976. The white wine, from very old vines, is most interesting, when you can get it. Château La Garde is owned by Eschenauer, and is better known for its red wine. Château Ferran, distributed by Dourthe, should be mentioned, and I have heard good reports of Domaine La Solitude.

At Villenave d'Ornon, Château Couhins makes only white wines. M. André Lurton also manages this property, and now the wine is lighter and earlier maturing than in the past. Château Baret makes red and white wine, both good but the white especially so. I would also highly recommend

Château Pontac-Monplaisir – the white wine has real distinction. Château Graville-Lacoste in Pujols also makes very good dry white wine.

The commune of Cadaujac possesses Château Bouscaut, very well-known in the United States due to its American ownership for more than a decade. However, in 1980 this passed to M. Lucien Lurton. The style of both red and white wines is fresh and fruity, rather than distinguished, but Bouscaut is nevertheless a good bottle. At St-Morillon, there is the excellent dry white Graves of Château Piron. In the commune of Portets, Château de Portets and Château Rahoul are interesting, particularly the latter, which was under Australian ownership in the 1970s. The vinification improvements introduced then have continued and the results are most honourable. Both Portets and Rahoul make red and white wine. Other recommended properties include Château Le Tuquet in Beautiran and Château La Tuilerie in Illats. Château Magence in St-Pierre-de-Mons makes a fair amount of good red and white wine; the white is really pleasant and reliable, very Sauvignon in character. Château Archambeau at Illats deserves special mention. Philippe Dubourdieu here makes excellent dry white Graves, perfumed and flowery with a preponderance of Sémillon which gives depth. Illats is, of course, within the *appellation contrôlée* area of Cérons, itself an enclave in the larger area of Graves. Proprietors within the communes of Cérons, Illats and Podensac call their wines Cérons, Graves Supérieures or Graves for white wines, and Graves for red. In reality, owners do not keep changing, but opt for one of the white *appellations* according to what type of wine they are making – Cérons if it is sweet (weather permitting), and Graves or Graves Supérieures if it is dry. The minimum alcoholic level for Graves is 11 per cent and for Graves Supérieures 12 per cent – the latter would be more likely to have a small amount of residual sugar. Cérons itself is indistinguishable from Barsac, although lacking its top properties.

SAUTERNES AND BARSAC
Sweet white wines can be wonderful or dreadful, just like

red wines, only perhaps more so. Some of the greatest in the world come from Sauternes and Barsac, and if you have never appreciated them to the full, it is probably because they were not drunk at the right time or with the right food. Barsac and Sauternes are small, adjoining areas and *appellations* within the larger *appellation* of Graves, at the southern end of the latter, near the town of Langon and on the left bank of the Garonne. There are five communes entitled to the *appellation* of Sauternes: Sauternes, Barsac, Preignac, Bommes and Fargues. If you have a property in Barsac, you may call it 'Sauternes' but not vice-versa, and there is even provision for the description 'Sauternes-Barsac'. Occasionally, Haut Sauternes or Haut Barsac can be seen, but this does not mean that the wine is any 'higher' than the others – it is just a relic of the past. Barsac is the flattest of the communes, and the soil is gravel mixed with clay or sand. The other four communes are hillier, with more pebble, gravel and calcareous soil. Bommes and Sauternes have some beautifully exposed, pebbly hills, ideal for catching maximum sun in the long autumns.

Classic Sauternes and Barsac is not just sweet, luscious white wine – it should have the unique smell and taste of *pourriture noble* – noble rot or *Botrytis cinerea*. Unfortunately, this natural phenomenon does not happen every year, and a simply sweet wine from this area without noble rot is not particularly special. Equally unfortunately, it is still made and sold as Sauternes and Barsac, when to my mind, it would be better to 'cut one's losses' and make a dry or dryish 'Graves', never using additional sugar. (At the moment, a dry white wine from this area can only carry the cheap *appellation* Bordeaux Blanc.) This is quite logical, since Sauternes and Barsac are within the Graves area, there is a good, strong market for well-made white wine, more quantity could be made in this way, and economically it would be much more sensible for the owner. Then, all Sauternes and Barsac made would have a chance of being as great as its potential even if it could not be made every year. The weather conditions of heat and humidity in the autumn that give noble rot, and very small yields, are not conducive to healthy economics in wine-making. Some owners have given up, and others have compromised with quality. Some finance their Sauternes and Barsac with other ventures, which is all too precarious. It must always be remembered that *Botrytis* or rot is disastrous in other areas, and it is only when it attacks *ripe grapes* that the right conditions prevail for making classic top sweet white Bordeaux. This amazing fungus or mould can run rampant in humid weather, but if it does not start until the grapes are already full of sugar and ripe, it imparts an intoxicating flavour and smell to the resultant wine. The fungus gradually attacks the grape skin, finally piercing it, evaporating the water in the grape, and thereby increasing the sugar ratio. The grape shrivels (and looks most unappetizing), and the sugar concentrates.

All this produces wines of unctuous body, immense flavour, with essence-like aromas and concentration. But, even if nature is kind, minute care has to be given to the picking to obtain grapes at the optimum point – in the top vineyards, they go through the vineyard again and again, hardly an inexpensive process. Vinification problems are immense, with high sugar content often demanding a considerable amount of sulphur, although with the high alcohol of Sauternes, this is not as fragile a product as *Beerenauslese* and *Trockenbeerenauslese*. The grapes themselves must be in perfect condition when picking takes place, and it is also important that they are not overripe – a must should be somewhere between 20° and 22° Baumé for the fermented wine to stop naturally at 13.5 per cent or 14 per cent leaving sugar of about 5° Baumé. This is balanced, luscious Sauternes. Oxidation is an ever-present problem in wines that are kept for some years in wood, but with the exception of Yquem, this period is generally down now to between eighteen months and two years (a few even less), and the sheer alcohol of a Sauternes is an additional protection against oxidation. The grape varieties permitted are Sémillon, Sauvignon and Muscadelle, but the best vineyards concentrate on the first two, as Muscadelle can have a slightly vulgar taste. Sémillon is the key grape variety in Sauternes and Barsac, and its wonderful style, fat and lusciousness when really ripe and attacked by *pourriture noble* is one of the world's great tastes. Top wine from a good year needs time to marry all these qualities – an optimum point for drinking would probably be between twenty and thirty years, with some pleasant experiences on either side of this. The wines from hot, really concentrated years (1945, 1961) tend to darken very early, but this looks a healthy amber-brown colour.

In 1855, there was a classification of the best properties of Sauternes and Barsac. As there have been important changes since then, both in the names of châteaux and in sub-divisions, the full table of 1855 is given below, with the current names of the classified châteaux beside it.

1855 Classification of Sauternes and Barsac

Name of classed growth in 1855   *Name of classed growth today*

SUPERIOR GROWTH

Yquem (Sauternes)	d'Yquem

FIRST GROWTHS

Latour-Blanche (Bommes)	La Tour-Blanche
Peyraguey (Bommes)	Lafaurie-Peyraguey, Clos-Haut-Peyraguey
Vigneau (Bommes)	Rayne-Vigneau
Suduiraut (Preignac)	Suduiraut
Coutet (Barsac)	Coutet
Climens (Barsac)	Climens
Bayle (Sauternes)	Guiraud
Rieussec (Sauternes)*	Rieussec
Rabeaud (Bommes)	Sigalas-Rabaud, Rabaud-Promis

SECOND GROWTHS

Mirat (Barsac)	Myrat
Doisy (Barsac)	Doisy-Daëne, Doisy-Védrines and Doisy-Dubroca
Pexoto (Bommes)	Part of Rabaud-Promis
d'Arche (Sauternes)	d'Arche
Filhot (Sauternes)	Filhot
Broustet-Nérac (Barsac)	Broustet and Nairac
Caillou (Barsac)	Caillou
Suau (Barsac)	Suau

de Malle (Preignac)	de Malle
Romer (Preignac)†	Romer and Romer du Hayot
Lamothe (Sauternes)	Lamothe and Lamothe-Bergey

* The château of Rieussec is in the commune of Fargues.
† The château of Romer is in the commune of Fargues.

CHATEAU YQUEM (Sauternes)

Château Yquem stands on its own, in both price and quality, and sets the standards for everyone else. Of course, being able to command high prices brings with it the possibility of affording extra care and nurturing of the wine, but the property first had to attain this position at the summit before being able to rise significantly above the rest when it came to selling. Here, Yquem was helped by a wonderful situation of sloping vineyards, and the fact that the same family, the Lur-Saluces, has owned the property since 1785. The present owner, Comte Alexandre de Lur-Saluces, directs with aplomb and flair. Only about ninety hectares of vineyards are used for production, although more is entitled to the *appellation*, and the final amount of wine made is about eighty *tonneaux* on average, more than three times less than a top red-wine producing château in the Médoc would be producing.

The grape variety proportions at Yquem are 80 per cent Sémillon and 20 per cent Sauvignon. Enormous care is taken at all stages, from rigorous pruning and the use of organic manure in the vineyard, to picking in ten or eleven stages, often until late November. This carries its own risks, and in 1964 the whole crop was lost through autumn rain. The grapes are first crushed and then undergo three pressings – the immensely concentrated must is then fermented in new oak casks. Yquem still stands by its principle of keeping the wine three years in cask before bottling, which involves meticulous topping up and racking work.

Great Yquems were 1921, 1928 and 1937, but in the 1980s it is safe to say that their greatest moments are past, albeit remaining splendid. The 1945 is great Yquem, in the style of the 1961 – both are highly coloured, with slightly volatile noses and huge concentration. The high alcohol is evident in both, but the flavour of the 1961 is lighter and has more balance. The 1955 is big, with a luscious nose, but not the elegance of the best years; in 1980 it was still splendid drinking, but just beginning to go 'raisiny'. The 1959 is very volatile, but the 1962 has lovely balance and elegance. 1963 and 1968 were disasters, and should never have appeared under the name of Yquem – a trap for the uninitiated, which is hardly fair at very high prices. The 1967 is the ultimate in finesse married to luscious fruit, and will last for many a day. The 1970 is big and deep, and the 1971 is superb, with the elegance of 1967 but its own character. The 1975 is way out on its own at the top of this massive, alcoholic, overripe vintage – a wine of sheer class and great, tight flavour, with exotic overtones. Yquem also sometimes makes a dryish white wine, Ygrec. Made from 50 per cent Sémillon and 50 per cent Sauvignon, the nose is unctuous and resembles the 'true' Yquem, but the taste is a surprise, full but dry.

First Growths:
Château La-Tour-Blanche is now under the auspices of the Ministry of Agriculture, and is run as a school for viticulture and vinification. As such, there is continual experimentation, and this has sometimes perhaps not led to consistent quality. Sémillon predominates, and the wine is good rather than distinguished. The attractive château and vineyard of Lafaurie-Peyraguey are now owned by the important *négociants*, Cordier. The vineyard is composed of three-quarters Sémillon, a quarter Sauvignon, and the wine spends half its time before bottling in cask, half in vat. The whole style is much lighter than Lafaurie-Peyraguey of yore, and many of the vintages bear no trace of botrytis characteristics. The 1970 was pleasant but no more, and the 1975 immensely sweet without seeming to have balancing acidity or real style. However, I have been lucky enough to taste some superb older vintages, amongst them (in 1978) the 1922, which had a very dark colour and not a great deal of nose, but immense fruit in the mouth. The taste was like a bouquet of flowers, and the marvellous acidity, after all this time, kept the wine in perfect condition with terrific

balance. In 1977, I also greatly admired the 1928, 1929, 1945 and 1947 – some of which were better than their counterparts at Yquem at the same stage. At Clos-Haut-Peyraguey production is small, predominantly Sémillon, and the wine is bottled after two years, with time in cask and vat beforehand. It is not often seen, but now and again can produce very pleasant surprises. Château Rayne-Vigneau is now owned by a group and, although the site is one of the best in the whole region, wines are not being made to their true potential here. It is a very large estate, producing a fair amount of wine – an aspect of the management that shows in the style of the end product. 1976 is, however, quite excellent, a true Sauternes, luscious, but with lovely acidity – not heavy, but balanced. The 1975 was too alcoholic, and did not seem to have that magic *pourriture noble* nose. I have been fortunate enough to taste a still sweet and interesting 1900, and some halves of the 1923, which is still excellent and harmonious – unlike some 1921s which, because of the great heat, coloured up tremendously and eventually lost some of their sweetness through the effects of volatile acidity. There is also some dry Raynesec.

Château Suduiraut is capable of making some of the very greatest wines of Sauternes, and if rigorous selection and care continue, we will have some splendid drinking ahead of us. The vineyard is almost entirely Sémillon. The 1970s brought a few lapses – notably the 1971 and the 1975, which were not as good as they should be, when judged at the highest level. The 1970 is splendid, and the 1976 is quite excellent. I like the elegant 1969, the stylish 1967 and 1962, and the bigger 1961. The 1959 is absolutely classic and rich. The 1899 was quite outstanding and amazingly youthful, sweet and gentle in 1985. Château Coutet is always 'twinned' with the other great Barsac property, Climens, and they vie with each other to top the vintage in the commune. Coutet 1975 is exceptionally big, rich without being really luscious (anyway, in youth), but with lovely length and good balance. The 1973 has a nose of apples and peaches, with a surprising amount of concentration on the middle palate – most successful for the year. 1962 and 1971 are outstanding in their years. Château Climens is making superlative wine at the moment, combining finesse with luscious fruit. M. Lucien Lurton now owns Climens – perhaps the losses of some years at Climens are offset by his ownership of Château Brane-Cantenac. Mme Janin is the experienced *régisseur*. The *encépagement* is Sémillon, on chalky soil, and the wines are generally bottled at two and a half years after maturation in cask. I remember the 1962 with great pleasure, and the 1970s have given some classic Climens: a 1971 with some way to go, but an amazing finish, with a great opening out of flavours and esters; a wonderfully elegant 1975, with real *pourriture noble* character, perfect weight and balance; and a 1976 of distinction. The 1980 and 1981 show great promise.

Château Guiraud is a very large property, which was bought in 1981 by an enterprising Canadian, Hamilton Narby. He has made great technical improvements which are immediately evident in the excellent wines being made. The 1981 and 1983 have great potential. (He also makes dry white wine known as G.) The 1975 is somewhat heavy and alcoholic, but the 1976 is much more balanced. The 1966 is better here than the 1967. Château Rieussec is actually in Fargues, but as the vineyards are mostly in Sauternes, this is how the 1855 classification settled it. It always used to be amongst the 'drier' of the top Sauternes, but since new ownership in 1971, there is a certain overripeness and lack of balance, and the elegance seems to have been sacrificed. The 1975 at first seemed to have recaptured this, but in 1979 it was dark and ageing fast. The 1976, also, is much too dark at this early stage, too advanced, with some lovely lusciousness, but without balancing acidity. The 1971 is superb, richly flavoured and smelling of apricots. The 1970 is very fruity and the 1969 combines elegance with richness. In 1984, Château Lafite took a majority holding in Rieussec, but M. Vuiller, the previous owner, is remaining to make the wines. Château Sigalas Rabaud is predominantly Sémillon, and the wine matures in cask and vat. The 1975 is an excellent wine, balanced and stylish and the 1955 superb.

The list of the *deuxième crus classés* includes the good, the bad, and the totally disappeared – sadly, Château Myrat has been uprooted. However, the trio of Doisy châteaux are very much in existence. Doisy-Daëne, owned by the talented M. Pierre Dubourdieu, is renowned both for its sweet white Barsac and for its stylish dry white wine. Doisy-Védrines is administered by M. Pierre Castéja and is a fuller Barsac than Doisy-Daëne, resulting from more 'traditional' methods of sweet white wine-making. There is also a small amount of red Bordeaux Supérieur made, Château Latour-Védrines, a predominantly Merlot wine. Château Doisy-Dubroca, the second wine of Château Climens, is small, but under M. Lucien Lurton it is producing very fine wines.

Château d'Arche in Sauternes made great vintages in the early part of this century, and with the 1982 and 1983 is right back on form – Château d'Arche-Lafaurie is its second wine. Château Filhot in Sauternes produces carefully made wine, not quite in the top class. The 1975 is immensely fragrant, delicious and soft, while the 1976 has the same floweriness, sweetness – both have a hint of tar on the finish. But the sheer elegance of past years is missing.

There are four more *deuxième crus* in Barsac: Châteaux Broustet, Nairac, Suau and Caillou. Broustet's 1975 was good in this second category. Château Nairac, under Mr Tom Heeter, is predominantly Sémillon, and going from strength to strength; the 1975 is excellent, lighter than most. Château Caillou is not sold much to the trade. Château de Malle in Preignac is an enchantingly beautiful property, and the Comte Pierre de Bournazel is making his wines with immense attention to detail. The wines are not really rich and luscious, but intriguing and elegant. There is also a good, lightish red wine called Château de Cardaillan, and a dry white Sauvignon wine, Chevalier de Malle – the red has the Graves *appellation contrôlée* as the vineyards are in the commune of Toulenne. There are, in fact, two Châteaux Romers, of which the most important is now known as Château Romer du Hayot. The 1976 is exceptionally good and elegant. There is also Château Lamothe, and Château Lamothe-Guignard, with excellent wines in 1981 and 1983. Formerly, much property wine in Sauternes and Barsac found its way into *négociants'* generic blends, but nowadays more châteaux are known individually. The 1975 of Château Haut-Bommes and Château Saint-Amand are recommended – the latter has another wine, Château de La Chartreuse, with a very good 1971. In Barsac, there is the very good Château Liot, and Château Cantegril and Château Piada are reliable. Château Guiteronde produced an extraordinary 1967, marvellous when drunk in 1984. Château Bastor-Lamontagne in Preignac, Château Raymond-Lafon (owned by M. Meslier, the manager at nearby Yquem) and Château de Fargues (owned by the Lur-Saluces family) are also strongly recommended. Château du Mayne and Château Roumieu, both in Barsac, are usually good buys.

STE-CROIX-DU-MONT AND LOUPIAC

These are very small *appellations*, just across the river Garonne from Barsac and Sauternes. The lovely, hilly countryside is worth a lingering visit, even if you do not like sweet white wines. The wines are very similar to Sauternes and Barsac, with lusciousness in years of noble rot, and a sugary, cloying quality in poor years. The best are excellent, and these would include Domaine de Fonthenille, Châteaux Ricaud and Loupiac-Gaudiet in Loupiac, and Loubens, Terfort and de Tastes in Ste-Croix-du-Mont. Côtes du Bordeaux St Macaire is a diminishing *appellation*, next door to Ste-Croix-du-Mont. The wines are white and semi-sweet, often suffering from liberal doses of sulphur dioxide.

CERONS

Cérons is next door to Sauternes and Barsac, on the same side of the river. Here again, the wines resemble those of their neighbour, and good value can be found here – however, the sweet wines are not classy, and probably do not have the marked character of the best Ste-Croix-du-Mont and Loupiac wines. But Cérons has the luck of being able to make dry white wines under the label of Graves, and this gives them more commercial advantage.

PREMIERES COTES DE BORDEAUX

This is a large *appellation* on the right bank of the Garonne, producing both red and white wines. The red wines are at their nicest drunk young when they can be very quaffable indeed. Those sweet wines produced in the communes closest to Loupiac can have the name Cadillac added to the *appellation*, but this is rarely used nowadays. Most of the whites are medium-sweet to sweet, and form a good base of reasonable wine for the Bordeaux trade.

ENTRE-DEUX-MERS

This is a huge *appellation*, covering only white wines. The red wines produced in the area become Bordeaux or Bordeaux Supérieur. During the 1970s, Entre-Deux-Mers replied to the demand for dry white wine, and concentrated more on Sauvignon-based, light, fresh wines, made by modern methods. Some of these are extremely palatable, especially when there is some Sémillon, and perhaps Ugni Blanc, in the blend. The wines are bottled young and fermented cold in the best establishments – cooperatives are important here, and the brand name of La Gamage is one to look for. Now it is not possible to find sweetish Entre-Deux-Mers, as in the past, because a maximum residual sugar limit was set for the *appellation*. Entre-Deux-Mers is now the second largest *appellation* for white wine, after Bordeaux Blanc itself, and it must be admitted that the quality of the individual wine being tasted is more important than the difference between the *appellations*. This applies also to the Bordeaux Rouge produced here and elsewhere, in that a well-made wine with this simple *appellation* can be better than a wine carrying a classier title.

To the north of Entre-Deux-Mers there is the tiny *appellation* of Graves de Vayres, producing both red and white wines. I have liked Château Cantelaudette here. In the northeast corner of Entre-Deux-Mers there is another small *appellation*, Sainte-Foy-Bordeaux. The whites are better known, being traditionally sweet from Sémillon, Sauvignon and Muscadelle, but the Sauvignon and dry wines are now taking over. The reds are mostly Cabernet and Merlot mixtures.

ST EMILION

If Médoc wines can sometimes be haughty, austere and aristocratic, St Emilion wines are more attainable, more warm and welcoming. The best of them have immense breed, tempered with luscious accessibility and generous fruitiness. Lesser wines are giving from the start, a seductive invitation to Claret drinking. We are in quite different land in St Emilion. There are no huge, imposing châteaux – the properties are more country manor-houses or even farms. Now, St Emilion trade has prospered to a point where the wines are not channelled through Bordeaux – the bustling town of Libourne serves them just as well.

The range of wines is very wide indeed. Firstly, there are two distinct groups of wine within the St Emilion *appellation* itself – the Côtes area around the beautiful old town, and the Graves area on the plateau bordering Pomerol. Both soil and site differ, the Côtes vineyards naturally enjoying some kind of slope, with the plateau Graves exactly what it says. As well as the gravel here, there are pockets of much more sandy soil, while the Côtes vineyards are a mixture of silica, clay and chalk. In both areas every spare centimetre is covered with vines. The rocky nature of the land round the town has provided some magnificent natural cellars, like rabbit warrens in the hillside. Archetypal Côtes wines are Ausone, Magdelaine, Belair and La Gaffelière, with great scent, breed and style, intense but also delicate when mature. Archetypal Graves wines are Cheval Blanc, Figeac, and the Figeac 'family' – bigger, fuller, richer. The soil differences account for differences in weight, flavour and character, with fascinating nuances within each area.

Eight communes, including that of St Emilion itself, enjoy the right to call their wine St Emilion *appellation contrôlée*. There are also a few outlying communes, now reduced to four, who have the right to add the magic words 'St Emilion' to their name. Thus we have: Lussac-St Emilion; Montagne-St Emilion; St Georges-St Emilion; and Puisseguin-St Emilion. However, it must be admitted that, in the main, the wines from the other seven communes entitled to the St Emilion label are really no better than the 'satellite' communes – the *appellation* should really reflect the more accurate picture of the wines of the commune of St Emilion itself, and the rest. Tasting certainly makes this division. On the whole, these wines are delicious when drunk relatively young, generous and fruity and without much complication.

In St Emilion, the Merlot and Cabernet Franc grapes predominate, and there is also some Malbec – the Cabernet Franc is traditionally called the Bouchet here and the Malbec, the Pressac. Cabernet Sauvignon does not do so well on this side of the river, and there are ripening problems mostly due to colder soil. Its relative absence makes for less tannin in the wine, but it is wrong to assume that for this reason the top St Emilions do not last as well as top Médocs. The same rule applies here as elsewhere – if there are class and balance, wines live to great ages, provided they are nurtured at all stages of their life. But Merlot contributes a full character, a richness and seeming softness, and a respectable amount of alcohol – all of which serve to make good St Emilions seem rounder, sooner, than Médocs. Merlot ripens before Cabernet Sauvignon, and thus the vintage in St Emilion usually begins a week to ten days earlier than in the Médoc. Exceptionally, in 1978, the two vintages began together. The Merlot is, however, highly susceptible to rot, and three terrible vintages in the 1960s (1963, 1965 and 1968) led to improved vigilance in the vineyard and to a more perfect spraying technique. Its viticultural precocity, too, makes it vulnerable to spring frosts.

The best St Emilion growths offer an immense life-span of drinkability, opening out earlier than Médocs, and retaining their richness and charm for considerable time. The nose is often rather heady, exciting, more difficult to pin down than a pure, classic St Julien, for example. You are almost enveloped in fruit and ripeness, the whole backed up with a vinous softness that is distinctly 'more-ish'. The classification of St Emilion also has its own individuality. This was not achieved until 1955, with a slight modification in 1969. At least, this shows flexibility in comparison with the Médoc, but perhaps in the future one could wish for the occasional downgrading to match the promotions. This came in the new classification of 1985, which allowed eleven First Great Growths, with Château Ausone and Château Cheval Blanc set apart at the head of this section. The number of grands crus classés was reduced to sixty-seven at the same time. Naturally, these growths vary considerably both in quality and general availability. Both categories are subject to tasting. Below this, there is the somewhat amorphous category of *grand cru* which, to the uninitiated, can sound grander than it is. The title of *grand cru* is only awarded after tasting and for that particular vintage – so one year a château might have it, the next it would disappear from the label.

List of Classified Growths in St Emilion

FIRST GREAT GROWTHS

1.

Ausone	Cheval-Blanc

2.

Beauséjour (Duffau-Lagarrosse)	Figeac
Beauséjour (Société-Bécot)*	La Gaffelière
Belair	Magdelaine
Canon	Pavie
Clos Fourtet	Trottevieille

* denoted in reclassification of 1985.

GREAT GROWTHS

L'Angélus	La Clotte
L'Arrosée	La Clusière
Balestard-la-Tonnelle	La Dominique
Bellevue	Lamarzelle
Bergat	Laniote
Berliquet	Larcis-Ducasse
Cadet-Piola	Larmande
Canon-la-Gaffelière	Laroze
Cap-de-Mourlin	La Serre
	La Tour-du-Pin-Figeac (Belivi‹

Chauvin
Clos des Jacobins
Clos la Madeleine
Clos St-Martin
Corbin (Giraud)
Corbin-Michotte
Couvent-des-Jacobins
Croque-Michotte
Curé-Bon
Dassault
Faurie-de-Souchard
Fonplégade
Fonroque
Franc-Mayne
Grand-Corbin
Grand-Corbin-Despagne
Grand-Mayne
Grand-Pontet
Grand-Barrail-Lamarzelle-Figeac
Guadet-St-Julien
Haut-Corbin
Haut-Sarpe
La Tour-du-Pin-Figeac (Moueix)
La Tour-Figeac
La Châtelet
Le Couvent
Le Prieuré
Matras
Mauvezin
Moulin-du-Cadet
l'Oratoire
Pavie-Decesse
Pavie-Macquin
Pavillon-Cadet
Petit-Faurie-de-Soutard
Ripeau
St-Georges-Côte-Pavie
Sansonnet
Soutard
Tetre-Daugay
Trimoulet
Troplong-Mondot
Villemaurine
Yon-Figeac

CHATEAU AUSONE

This is the top *premier grand cru classé* of the Côtes area, with vineyards on a steep south-east escarpment below the town of St Emilion, looking out over the plain. There is something very miniature about Ausone, and the compact nature of its seven hectares producing under 3,000 cases of wine a year on average makes it appear quite manageable! The vines look gnarled, showing their average age of forty years, and the calcareous, crumbly soil is much in evidence, allowing the roots for the vines to reach down as much as six metres. Deep-rooted vines gain the maximum from the soil, all possible minerals and trace elements greatly contributing to the ultimate interest and subtlety of the wine. Ausone has the potential of being perhaps the most exciting wine of Bordeaux – a wine like the 1928 demonstrates the point admirably. The soil and site are perfect, only the right management was missing. Owned by the Dubois-Challon family and M. Alain Vauthier, the firm of J.P. Moueix has long sold part of the crop. After some really disappointing years since the Second World War, during the 1970s there was a dramatic change in the fortunes of Ausone. A new *régisseur*, Pascal Delbeck was installed, and there were immediate differences with the marvellously complex and exciting 1975 vintage. Certainly the very damp cellars in the rock at Ausone posed problems for the maintenace of casks, and the wine seemed to suffer from its time in wood, often losing that heady flavour and richness of Ausone and beginning to lighten, and even dry out, far too rapidly. The wine is now kept under impeccable conditions, and the results have been immediate. The vineyard is also run with great attention to health of the vine and optimum picking-point at vintage time – always easier to stage-manage in a small property like Ausone. The grape variety balance here is slightly more Merlot than Cabernet Franc. Ausone at its best recalls both opulence and finesse and the vintages of the late 1970s and early 1980s exemplify this. The 1978 and 1979 make a splendid pair, and with the 1981, 1982 and 1983, there is a remarkable trio.

CHATEAU CHEVAL BLANC

Cheval Blanc is put on a par with Ausone at the top of the classification, and this greatest wine of the Graves area of St Emilion provides a fascinating contrast in style and definition. The wines of Cheval Blanc are bigger and fleshier than Ausone, for me often characterized by a slightly 'roasted' nose of super ripeness and richness. On the Graves plateau adjoining Pomerol, the surface is gravelly with irony clay beneath it. This is a very large property for St Emilion, thirty-five hectares, but unfortunately this does not seem to have much steadying influence on the price!

The predominant grape variety is the Cabernet-Franc (two-thirds), but it is the complexity of the soil that gives the wine its unique stamp. A magnificent new, white *chais* built in 1974 permitted far better control over the whole wine-making process and also enabled Cheval Blanc to château-bottle – before that it was allowed to take place at

Libourne. The descendants of the Fourcaud Laussac family own the property, and M. Jacques Hebrard is co-proprietor and manager. The 1921 and 1947 Cheval Blanc are legendary. The grim February 1956 frost hit the St Emilion and Pomerol plateau with enormous ferocity, and only the 1961 marked a return to top form, if not exquisite Cheval Blanc. In 1978, I wrote of the 1961: 'Particularly dense colour, very tight, almost "roasted" nose to be found in Cheval Blanc of dry, hot years; totally different from other wines, a lot of grip and backbone and underlying hidden flavours – almost "oriental" and very far from straightforward, Médocain fruit.' The 1966 in the same year had a deep brown colour, and was big, rich and sweet – a weighty wine, classic of its type, slightly one-dimensional. This wonderful Cheval Blanc sweetness was also present in massive quantity in the 1970, with its lovely acidity and fruit, while the fabulous 1964 had opened out to real opulence in 1980. Really good wines have also been made in 1975 (lusciously fruity), 1976 (incredibly rich and exotic), 1978 and 1979. The standard has been maintained in the 1980s, and the 1982 must be one of the greatest Cheval Blancs ever.

Châteaux of Note in the Côtes Area of St Emilion are:
Château Belair shares ownership and management with Ausone, and also the same steep vineyards near the town of St Emilion with their clayey-calcareous soil, but facing southwards rather than south-east. There are also vineyards on chalky plateau. The wine is no longer kept in the cellars of Ausone, but in another very beautiful old cellar. Belair can sometimes be a bit 'thin', often with a light colour, but its breed and elegance is most evident. The 1976 is very fine indeed, and sweetness and elegance are both present in the 1970, although the length did not indicate a great keeper. A 1947 drunk in 1974 still had enormous fruit and life. The grape variety composition is 50 per cent Merlot and 50 per cent Cabernet Franc on thirteen hectares of vineyards.

Château Magdelaine is another property on the slopes of St Emilion, adjoining Belair on one side and facing south.

The exact composition is five hectares on the clayey slope, which gives depth to the wine, and six hectares on chalky plateau, which contributes finesse to the final blend. Owned by M. Jean-Pierre Moueix, it enjoys the same attentions as the rest of their properties. The vineyard includes a high proportion of Merlot, 70 per cent, with 30 per cent Cabernet Franc, and those ripe years for Merlot, such as 1971, obviously show Magdelaine at its best. Intelligent wine-making helps give Magdelaine the little bit more body that it sometimes needs – vines of between twenty-eight and thirty years' average age, a small proportion of stalks included in the vinification, picking as late as possible. I have been very impressed by the wines of the 1970s, which all show scent and delicacy.

There are now two Châteaux Beauséjours, one belonging to the Duffau-Lagarrosse heirs, and the other to M. Michel Bécot. The vineyards adjoin, and the tasting qualities are not dissimilar. They are typically full St Emilion wines, and improve greatly from ageing in good years. M. Bécot has extended his property considerably and is very forward-looking. Château Canon, now admirably run by Eric Fournier, is going from strength to strength, with the wines of the latter part of the 1970s, and 1981, 1982 and 1983 showing the sheer class and staying power of the legendary 1929 and the famed 1947. The 1966, 1964 and 1953 are very good indeed.

Owned by the Lurton family, Clos Fourtet has some remarkable cellars in the calcareous rock near the town. There is both Cabernet Franc and Cabernet Sauvignon in the vineyard, as well as over 50 per cent of Merlot. The wines are perhaps a little lighter now than they were, but the real tasting characteristic of Clos Fourtet was a certain toughness when young, but with remarkable ageing potential, when it developed an exceptionally delightful bouquet. The 1970 is good, and the 1979 looks promising. Very much the family château of the Comtes de Malet-Roquefort, Château La Gaffelière was known as La Gaffelière-Naudes until the 1964 vintage. Fuller and rounder than some wines of the Côtes, the wine can be superb and latterly has been really consistent. Past fine vintages include 1945, 1966 and 1970. Château Pavie is a large property, owned by the Valette family and very well-managed by Jean-Paul Valette (with advice from Professor Peynaud). The 1970 is lovely, full and plummy and the 1971 rich, but the 1978 and 1979 are much better than the 1975. The 1980s herald very good things for Pavie. Owned by the family firm of Borie-Manoux, Château Trottevieille's wine is generous and full, rather than elegant. There were some excellent wines in the 1960s, and 1979 and 1981 look promising.

There is a mass of *grands crus classés* in the Côtes area of St Emilion. Amongst them, Château L'Angélus is very well-known, both for its large production and the consistent pleasant wines it gives. Château Curé-Bon, or Curé-Bon-la-Madeleine, has something of the character of Belair about it, a wine of breed, often with a light colour; the 1979 is lovely. Château Balestard-La-Tonnelle is making excellent wine at the moment, with really careful vinification by the owners, the Capdemourlin family. Sometimes, in years of small production, the quality is exceptional. Nearby, at Château Villemaurine, the wine has finesse and ages well. Château Cadet-Piola is a real Côtes wine of breed and elegance, at its best ageing admirably, but unfortunately not always living up to this. Château Soutard is very well run, and the wine is of good, dependable quality, even if it does not show its breed in every year. Château Fonplégade has both generosity and class, and is beautifully sited. Further down the hill below St Emilion, there is Château Canon-La-Gaffelière, a property of some size, producing consistently pleasurable St Emilion wines of charm. Right beside the town, Château La Clotte is a particular favourite, sometimes giving wines of immense generosity and fruit, full and deep and memorable – the 1970, 1966 and 1959 are examples. Château Fonroque, to the north of St Emilion, is a Moueix property, with a marked character of the soil in the wine, giving it great individuality.

Château Grand Pontet is now owned by M. Bécot of Beauséjour. It is very honourable wine, grown in the vicinity of the Châteaux Beauséjours and Clos Fourtet. Château Laroze is quite easily found and extremely dependable; the 1979 is delicious. Château Moulin du Cadet is Moueix-owned, and near to Soutard and Cadet-Piola. It has the Côtes elegance, with pronounced flavour and definition. Château Pavie-Macquin, near Pavie, makes wines of some style, as befits its situation. Château Tertre-Daugay, now owned by Comte de Malet-Roquefort of La Gaffelière, is making splendid wines in the 1980s, while Château Troplong-Mondot is important both for its size and consistent quality. The excellent Château Larcis-Ducasse is not far away, but in fact lies outside the commune of St Emilion and in that of St-Laurent des Combes. This is also the case with Château Haut-Sarpe, which lies just inside St-Christopher des Bardes. Clos des Jacobins now belongs to the *négociants* Cordier, and makes softish wines of charm, with the exception of a remarkably tannic 1975.

The St Emilion Graves area has only two First Great Growths; Château Cheval Blanc has its place right at the top, but the other is a worthy partner indeed.

Although adjoining Château Cheval Blanc on the gravelly plain near the border with Pomerol, Château Figeac's wines have a very different taste. The *encépagement* is obviously partly responsible for this, since there is about 70 per cent of the two Cabernets, equally divided between the two types, with 30 per cent Merlot. This high amount of Cabernet Sauvignon is very unusual for St Emilion and is part of Figeac's individuality. The owner is M. Thierry Manoncourt.

I do not find that Figeac has the slightly *rôti* bouquet that Cheval Blanc can sometimes demonstrate. It usually has gloriously velvety elegance, rich without being over-powering. Throughout the 1960s and 1970s the wine has been consistently excellent, with a remarkably good, balanced 1970, and what looks like a very fine, classy 1978. The 1975 has a fascinating, scented, exotic nose, still dry and tannic, but a distinguished wine. The 1976 has intensity and depth. The 1980s promise great things.

There are not many *grands crus classés* in this Graves area of

St Emilion, but a few of note. Five of them inclue ne name 'Figeac' in their names, but they are certainly not of the class of the pivotal château. During the 1970s, the two properties in this group that impressed me most often were Château Grand-Barrail-Lamarzelle-Figeac and Château Yon-Figeac. The others are Château La Tour-du-Pin-Figeac (one part is owned by the Belivier family and the other by A. Moueix), and Château La Tour Figeac – I have found a casky taste in some of the latter's wines of the 1970s.

Corbin is another word that crops up again and again in St Emilion. By far the most famous property is Château Corbin in this Graves area of St Emilion. It is well vinified – an excellent *bourgeois* wine. Château Croque-Michotte, Château La Dominique and Château Ripeau are all worth finding and drinking, all capable of making exceptionally good wines in certain years. Following this, there is a mass of St Emilion *grands crus*, from both the main *appellation* area and the 'satellite' communes. Any château can aspire to *grand cru* status if it passes the annual tasting and has a minimum of 11.5 per cent alcohol. Many of these properties practise a flourishing direct sale trade to private customers in France, others such as Château Fombrauge and Château Lyonnat are regularly seen on export markets. Château Haut-Pontet has much impressed me. There are also important cooperatives.

POMEROL

The wines of Pomerol should not be linked with those of St Emilion as right-bank wines, as even though some of the greatest vineyards of the two districts are contiguous, the tastes are very different and totally individual. This is mainly due to soil fluctuations and the fascinating bearing they have on the final product. The soil of Pomerol is predominantly clayey gravel – a mixture of quite deep clay and a superficial layer of gravel giving the best wines. The proportion of clay and gravel changes with the growths – thus, Château La Fleur Pétrus, which is almost entirely gravel, gives a much lighter wine than some of the other great Pomerols, but is very elegant, while Château Pétrus has about 80 per cent clay and 20 per cent gravel, giving a much deeper, more powerful wine, at the same time as being supple and full. Château Trotanoy is somewhere between the two, mixing equally clay and gravel, and combining elegance with body.

Pomerol is Merlot land *par excellence*. Perhaps even more so than in St Emilion, the Cabernet Sauvignon does not do well here, due to colder, more acid soil, preventing good ripening. Clay holds cold, and it is significant that the growths with the most clay specialize almost entirely in Merlot. This high proportion of Merlot, inter-related with the soil, helps give Pomerol that full, luscious, almost exotic flavour. Pomerol is important for quality and its special taste, not for its quantity, which is the smallest of the main Bordeaux regions. This small production has certainly prevented some of the finest wines attaining the reputation and recognition accorded to the top Médoc wines – so few people can see exactly what is meant by supreme class in Pomerol terms. Ownership is also very split up – 110 owners possess less than one hectare and ninety proprietors between one and two hectares. This limited production has also contributed to the system of direct sales to the French public which many small Pomerol properties practise.

There is no official classification for Pomerol, so any hierarchy has to be made on informed opinion and experience. Pomerol trade is channelled through the market town of Libourne, and the firm of J.P. Moueix on the quay there has always been a monument to integrity and quality, and a rich source of fine wines at all levels. The best growths are on the plateau between the church of Pomerol and the St Emilion Graves area. Here is all vine-growing, the actual châteaux or manor houses are often very modest, and the atmosphere is very rural. To the south-west and west there are some bigger properties, good but not with the finesse of the greatest.

CHATEAU PETRUS

Pride of place must go to Château Pétrus, the epitome of all that is exciting and exotic in Pomerol. First launched into the international arena when it won a gold medal at the Paris

Exhibition of 1878, Pétrus is now considered a First Growth, even in the absence of anything official. The prices are certainly in the First Growth stratosphere. The peculiarity of the soil at Pétrus has already been discussed, and there are certainly traces of iron deep down in the clay, lending its mineral influence to the wine. The other critical factors of this small vineyard (average output is forty *tonneaux*) are the forty-year average age of the vines, and the 95 per cent Merlot – 5 per cent Cabernet Franc grape variety combination. Another insight into the immense ripe, super-mature taste of Pétrus is the late picking. The vintage is always as late as possible at Pétrus, usually mid-October.

The joint Loubat/Moueix ownership of Pétrus has over the years ensured proper recognition for this highly individual wine. Rigorous selection takes place for the final *grand vin*, which is all the more astonishing in such a small property. The taste of Pétrus is perhaps more difficult to describe than any other Bordeaux growth, encompassing as it does a massive range of flavours and nuances, combining the exotic with traditional power, and fining down to elegance with maturity.

The 1947 and 1949 were Pétrus at its most exciting, and there is no reason to suppose that either are not still showing this class. The 1946 was surprisingly good, if unfashionable, and the 1950 is magnificent. The 1960s produced very fine wines indeed, but I have had the opportunity to study the 1970s more closely. The 1970 has the property's big colour, with a bouquet that was still closed in 1978, a deep, herby flavour and an obvious very far distance to go before maturity. At the same time I tasted the 1971, which was even more crimson than the 1970, wonderfully developed and *épanoui*, with extreme ripeness and almost vegetal fruit. Already there were lovely subtleties and complexity – Pétrus at its most opulent. However, in 1980 I had the wine again, and it seemed rather overpowered by its enormous ripeness and had temporarily lost its balance – something that can happen at an intermediate stage. I have felt that this wine is potentially the best 1971 in the Bordeaux area. The 1975 has big colour, very great depth of fruit on the nose, and is complex and many-layered, but still very tannic and tight. The 1976 is very aromatic and fine – in 1975 and 1976, no chaptalization was needed, a not uncommon occurrence at Pétrus. The 1977, when very young, had a slightly salty taste and lots of dry extract, and the 1978 in cask had immense, purple colour, great character, and a wonderful ripe, almost cassis-like after-taste. The 1979 had twenty-four days of fermentation, tannin, and 12.6 per cent of natural alcohol, and it needs years in bottle. Both 1982 and 1983 are massive, minerally wines, with exotic ripeness.

CHATEAU TROTANOY

On current showing, and intrinsic merit of the property, this could be the best wine of Pomerol after Pétrus. Trotanoy is a sumptuous wine of quite dazzling quality. It is owned by the family of Jean-Pierre Moueix, and the vineyard is unfortunately small – nine hectares. The taste of the wine is of intense fruit with a velvety texture, backed by firm body, richness and fat. Sometimes it does not smell of Pomerol at all, but more of the Médoc, which is astonishing when one considers its proportion of grape varieties – 80 per cent Merlot and 20 per cent Cabernet Franc. The whole composition of the wine does not seem to fit our idea of the right bank. The vines are as old here as at Pétrus – with an average age of between thirty-five and forty years. 1961 Trotanoy is immense and amazingly good, 1962 is delicious, and 1966 very good indeed. 1970 is big and straightforward, with 1971 outstanding. 1975 is very classic, 1976 has class, ripeness and a long aftertaste, and 1978 is big, full and tannic – a huge wine. The 1979 is also big and rich – the result of long vatting.

CHATEAU LA CONSEILLANTE

I would put La Conseillante on the same level as Trotanoy, a wine of immense breed, perhaps without the glossy fat of Trotanoy, but nevertheless the wines can age with the utmost elegance. Owned by the Nicolas family, the vineyard is superbly placed on the plateau, opposite Cheval

Blanc. Here the Merlot is balanced by an equal amount of Cabernet Franc, with a small amount of Malbec. There are some fabled vintages of the past, but unfortunately I only started to see La Conseillante regularly with the vintages of the 1960s, which were consistently fine, although the one time I saw the 1961 it appeared dull and dry. 1970 is incredibly good – one of the really big La Conseillantes. There is a wonderful depth and intensity of fruit, almost tactile, quite stunningly good. I found the 1971 a bit thin, the 1973 exceptionally good, and the last years of the 1970s are all unmitigated successes, with a 1976 of great finesse and distinction, and a 1979 that looks a winner.

Other Châteaux are:
Vieux Château Certan makes some of the wines that last the longest in Pomerol. It is owned by the Belgian Thienpont family and lies near La Conseillante. There is Cabernet Sauvignon as well as Franc here, but half the total is made up of Merlot. There is distinguished breed at Vieux Château Certan, and the wines have a pronounced, individual bouquet. For the last twenty years, there has been great consistency here, and I have particularly admired a very flavoury, spicy 1970, a superb 1971, and a 1978 with ripeness, 'attack' and character. Again, near La Conseillante, the wines of Château l'Evangile can often require some time to age. Unfortunately, the wines do not often come my way (or I theirs), but the 1970 and 1971 are impressive. It is a predominantly Merlot wine. Château Lafleur is a little gem of a property, only four hectares of it, and should never be missed if an opportunity for tasting presents itself. The Robin sisters own it, and the wine is of exceptional quality, full and ideally suited to ageing. Château La Fleur-Pétrus is confusingly nearby, on what is known as the Graves de Pomerol. The wine has finesse and breed and nobility. I have never had anything less than a superb bottle, and will long remember the magnum of 1961 drunk at the generous Moueix table, as well as a remarkable 1948. Both the 1970 and 1971 are excellent, while the 1976 is for much earlier drinking. The 1977, with greatly reduced quantity because

of frost, has a lovely scent and balance, and the 1978 is aromatic, but does not appear to have the body to be a great keeper. Merlot predominates here, and therefore showed very well in 1979 – a great year for this grape variety. Château Petit-Village has wines of great quality, but unfortunately the few I have seen have not lived up to this potential. However, the 1945, drunk in 1980, was quite outstanding. Bruno Prats of Cos d'Estournel now manages the property. Owned by Madame Lacoste-Loubat who part-owns Pétrus, Château Latour-Pomerol wines can be both *gras*, or fat, and solidly constructed, with good penetration of taste. The 1970 has good fruit combined with a fair amount of tannin, and the 1978 has a projected nose and good character. The 1979 is very powerful wine. Château Certan de May made some splendid vintages before the 1956 frost, but suffered since then. However, the excellent site has huge potential. The 1978 had body and tannin, but perhaps could have been made in a way so as to give more finesse. Château Gazin's wine has a good reputation and is well known on the British market, but I have to say that I have never tasted a really distinguished Gazin – the breed always seems to be sacrificed to a certain coarseness. However, it ages well, and the 1945 was deep and remarkable in 1980. I have preferred the 1966 in more recent years. The 1970 is rather forward but very ripe tasting, the 1964 I found a bit 'jammy' and plummy, and the 1957 had a fragrant nose and fruit, but rather a short finish. The 1976 has good depth of fruit. The site of Clos L'Eglise is excellent, but the wine-making sometimes did not live up to expectations. At its best, it is delicate and fine, epitomized in the 1979, and it is evident that now the two Moreau sons are vinifying with great care. The wine of Château L'Eglise Clinet is very well made, and the taste full and charming. Worth finding, but production is small – about twenty *tonneaux*. Château Lagrave is now owned by Christian Moueix, and the wine is elegant and has breed, with less body than some so can be appreciated to the full earlier. I have found the 1976 delicious and glossy, with an enticing minty flavour, and the 1979 will be beautiful, fruity wine.

Château Lagrange makes wine that is more powerful, perhaps with less finesse. But it is beautifully situated on the plateau of Pomerol, and the wines have a delicious flavour and are of remarkable quality. Situated on the boundaries of Pomerol and St Emilion, the wines of Château Beauregard have breed and a supple character, and are very highly regarded. The wines often show well when comparatively young. Château Nenin is a wine that is often seen in the United Kingdom. It is good, but I have never seen a Nenin of ultimate finesse or breed, although with time very high quality bottles emerge. I have admired both the 1967 and the 1961, which both needed time to soften the tannin in them. Château La Pointe is a large property that produces wines with a lovely bouquet and great charm. The 1970 should last well, the 1971 has a delicious, intense Pomerol nose, but the last time I saw it I felt it was drying up a bit.

There are other properties in Pomerol that have good distribution and are really worthwhile. Clos René made a fruity, but rather light 1970, but excellent 1976, 1978, 1979 and 1982. Château Rouget has given me a lot of pleasure, particularly a stunning 1964 and a still lively, rich 1959. The largest property in Pomerol, Château de Sales, makes reliable wines, not in the top flight. I have liked the 1961 and 1962, and the 1976 shows promise. Château Plince is really rewarding Pomerol – the 1947 is fabled, and the 1971 could well turn out like that, warm and rounded, with a nose of truffles that I have also noticed at Lagrange. Château Moulinet is most honourable, and the 1970 and 1971 are both fine examples. Château Le Gay is a personal favourite, with wines of the 1960s outstanding, especially the 1964 and 1966 – the 1970s continue the good work. Château La Croix-de-Gay is also very good drinking, as is Château Vraye-Croix-de-Gay. Château Lafleur-Gazin is also recommended.

There is also the neighbouring *appellation* of Lalande de Pomerol. The wines of the commune of Néac can now use this *appellation*, which is certainly more advantageous for them.

FRONSAC

Fronsac has quite one of the most beguiling tastes of Bordeaux, extremely marked by the Cabernet Franc, with that lovely grassy, 'sappy' freshness about it which almost jumps out of the glass. These red wines have a slightly earthy finish, and when young can be quite tannic – although much less so nowadays, with a slightly less *artisan* approach to wine-making in the area. There are two *appellations*, Fronsac and Côtes de Canon Fronsac. Given time, good châteaux can develop real interest and finesse with six years or more of age – providing, of course, the vintage is good. I have particular admiration for the really tempting Canon de Brem from Canon-Fronsac, but I have also seen really good wines from La Dauphine and Rouet, both in the Fronsac *appellation*. Mention must also be made of Châteaux Canon (Canon-Fronsac), du Gaby, Junayme, Vrai-Canon-Bouché, Vray-Canon-Boyer, Mayne-Vieil, La Valade, La Venelle, Toumalin and Bodet.

BOURG AND BLAYE

Both these right-bank regions give wines that are a great standby for those who like to drink reasonable Claret on a regular basis. Uncomplicated red wines, for the greater part made of the Cabernet Franc and Merlot grapes, give much pleasure when drunk relatively young. The best growths of Bourg come from slopes near the Gironde, and have the most weight and character of this area. They have more body than the lighter Blaye wines, which are nevertheless full of fruit and charm. There is a mass of small properties in both regions ('château' would be too grand a word), and although they produce good base material, it is sometimes safer if a reliable *négociant* does the bottling. Bourg produces more wine than Blaye. The white wine of these areas tends to be somewhat common, although there are good Côtes de Blaye. The countryside is pretty, green and hilly, with mixed farming and an unspoilt feeling of rustic France. Cooperatives play a large part in wine-making, selling a great deal of their produce to the Bordeaux *négociants*.

There are some properties that are large enough to have

made their mark, and every good Bordeaux merchant has a good choice of *petits châteaux* from Bourg and Blaye. In Bourg, mention must be made of the excellent châteaux of de Barbe and Guerry, both of which have good ageing properties. Du Bousquet is also most reliable, and others of note are Coubet, de La Croix-Millorit, Guionne, Mille-Secousses, Poliane, Rousset and Tayac. In Blaye, Haut Sociondo and Le Menaudat have given really pleasant drinking, as have Segonzac and Mondésir-Gazin. Taste any small châteaux offered to you from these regions – they often provide a lesson in what Bordeaux can produce at a reasonable price. You can also find Bordeaux or Bordeaux Supérieur Côtes de Castillon, from around the small town of Castillon-la-Bataille – Château Lardit is a good example. These wines resemble 'satellite' St Emilions and can be very good wine to quaff. There is also a small amount of Bordeaux Supérieur Côtes de Francs, which is again Merlot-type wine. However, the overall *appellation* of Bordeaux Supérieur is now usually used alone. The wines from around St André-de-Cubzac are only entitled to be called Bordeaux or Bordeaux Supérieur, but there are important properties here – Château de Terrefort-Quancard, Château Timberlay and Château du Bouilh.

Bordeaux Vintages
Nowhere else in the wine making world are vintages more relevant than in Bordeaux. This Atlantic-influenced region is at the mercy of the weather, and although man can mitigate its ravages, spray in hand, he cannot provide what is not there. Vintage characteristics are not there by accident – they are the direct result of the weather prevailing during the growing and ripening season. Above all, in Bordeaux, the month of September is all-important – September can make or break a vintage. 1977 was an example of a vintage 'made' in September, 1963 an illustration of a vintage 'killed' by rain in September. Even when events are not so dramatic, sun, warmth and dry conditions can make the difference between good and great.

The Bordeaux vintages that are most likely to be drunk

now are those from the last two decades (some older wines are described under individual châteaux):

1960: A light vintage, with some pleasant wines that should have been drunk by now.

1961: A very great vintage indeed, which will certainly prove to be one of the best of the century. A tiny, concentrated vintage – the product of perfect summer and autumn weather. Wonderful balance, fruit and extract, with intense bouquet and flavour. The wines have great individuality, even in lesser growths and are an experience to drink at all stages of their life. Some of the top wines will last for ever, but at over twenty years of age, most are already superb. The sweet white wines are famous, but are perhaps not the most elegant of their kind – alcoholic and concentrated rather than honeyed finesse.

1962: A large vintage of wines that have given more and more pleasure over the years. High acidity gave the best wines the ability to age and all are now ready to drink, displaying a classic flavour and great interest. Wines were good from all areas, with most of the St. Emilions and Pomerols now fully recovered from the 1956 frost. Lovely wines of breed in Sauternes and Barsac.

1963: Terrible wines that should never have been sold under illustrious labels.

1964: Unfortunately, over a week of continuous rain in the Médoc during the vintage took its inevitable toll, and some wines are rather dry and short, either because the whole crop was not picked before the rain started, or because careful selection of the grapes did not follow. However, the good wines are very worthwhile, and many St Emilions, Pomerols and Graves are superb – the right bank wines, picked well before the rains, can be really full and luscious. It is certainly not worth keeping Médoc wines any longer. The October rain demolished nearly all the sweet white wines.

1965: A miserable year, and the grapes never ripened. *A oublier.*

1966: A very classic vintage – in the Médoc, the best of the decade after the 1961s. The wines are beautifully constructed, deep-coloured with ample fruit and tannin. The best are splendid keeping wines; it is difficult to find any fault with the 1966s. There are some really good Sauternes, even if not quite top class.

1967: Some worthy wines from a large vintage, but there are many with a characteristic dry, somewhat hard finish, especially as they get older. Even the best will not benefit from further keeping. St Emilion and Pomerol tend to be fruitier. There were really outstanding Sauternes and Barsac, rich wines with great style and elegance.

1968: Rain did much damage again, but with careful selection there were a few light, drinkable wines, all of which should have been drunk. Sauternes was ruined.

1969: Happily, this was a small vintage, as the wines turned out to be exceptionally mean, dry and charmless. The best 1968s gave more pleasure! Light, not very consequential Sauternes.

1970: An exceptional year, combining abundance with quality. The grapes everywhere were perfectly healthy – many wine-makers said they had never seen such ideal conditions. From the start, the 1970s had wonderful colour, and all the qualities of fruit, acidity and tannin. The top wines went through a rather dumb stage of adolescence, but in the 1980s they are opening out and showing their full potential. A few giants need longer (Latour, for example). Although this vintage does not have the sheer beauty of 1961, it has richness and depth that reward keeping. The Sauternes are good and consistent.

1971: A much smaller amount of wine made, with the wines possessing a very different structure. They have ripeness and fruit, with a seductive bouquet, but the low acidity indicates a far shorter life for them than the 1970s. A few Médocs can be slightly dry, and some took on a brown colour relatively early. More selection has to be exercised in 1971 than in 1970, but the St Emilions and Pomerols are superb, rich and fascinating. White Graves, Sauternes and Barsac were all magnificent, with wines of the utmost finesse and distinction.

1972: There is a nasty, unripe, greenish quality about the 1972s that completely obliterates charm and makes most of them singularly unattractive to drink. Age has brought no improvement – maturity cannot change basic faults, it usually accentuates them. It was a pity that many classified châteaux bottled under their own name – more modest properties often made better wine than the big stars.

1973: A large vintage with many wines of immense charm – on the light side, but with a flowery attractiveness that made delicious Bordeaux drinking. Some were too weak, or too heavily chaptalized, results of a high yield. Only the top properties are lasting well into the 1980s – in general, it was a vintage to drink young and enjoy. Rather an ordinary year for Sauternes.

1974: A poor September ensured that these wines would not be anything special. They are very dull, with neither districts nor châteaux possessing individuality. Apart from the odd exception, this is a vintage that lacks charm and fruit and any form of complexity. Really poor for Sauternes.

1975: A very good vintage, stamped with the heat of the summer and ideal conditions in September. The wines are concentrated and tannic. In some cases, this tannin is too heavy for the fruit, and the effect can be dry or clumsy, but other wines have a better balance of fruit and they have the best potential. The greatest wines will be complex and fascinating, and really repay cellaring, if you have the patience. The Sauternes were very rich and alcoholic.

1976: The vintage was very early, after an extremely hot and dry summer, but it rained during picking. The wines combine as much tannin as 1975 (although of a riper, softer kind), but with very low acidity – a point always worth bearing in mind when projecting length of life. Lesser growths were ready very soon, and the top wines show all their ripeness and fruit in the 1980s. St Julien and Pomerol seem particularly favoured. Some exquisite white Graves and Sauternes, with finesse rather than sheer power.

1977: September saved this vintage from disaster, and there are some pleasant wines for relatively young drinking. Others are somewhat mean and thin (northern area of Haut Médoc and Médoc), and the warmth of the Merlot (hit by the frost at the end of March) was missing. With careful selection, there are some good buys, but these are not wines for cellaring. No real Sauternes, although a few nice dry whites.

1978: A splendid autumn imbued the wines with some extraordinary qualities. They have great depth and structure, and a velvety texture, full of 'fat' and glycerine. All the wines are stamped with class, at their respective levels, and the top wines are the stars of the future. There is great consistency of quality throughout the region. No wine lover should be without them. The Sauternes were picked very late, as the weather was superb and the grapes ripe, but the lack of humidity precluded any *pourriture noble*.

1979: The second largest vintage ever, picked in October for the third year running. The Merlot was splendid, which especially favoured Pomerol and St Emilion, but as the wines have matured in bottle it has become evident that it is a superb vintage everywhere. The top wines have breed, opulence and structure and are set for long keeping. It is worth remembering that the vineyard area increased tremendously during the 1970s and this accounts for the size of the vintage – the top châteaux made good, but far from excessive, yields. Fine Sauternes of style.

1980: A very late vintage, saved by the weather in September, although it was cold and wet for much of the picking. Châteaux which made careful grape selection have produced highly drinkable wines, and this is the year to try classed growths sold at a more modest price than usual and which will mature relatively quickly. Even the grandest wines will probably be at their best during the decade. Good white wines, both dry and sweet.

1981: The fourth largest vintage ever made. A vintage created by fine weather, with only a few days of rain during picking. There are many wines of classic structure, marrying fruit with concentration, and although such high quality is not universal, this is a very good year with copybook Bordeaux, and it would be a great pity if it was overshadowed by the following 1982s. Good white wines, and the sweet ones will keep. Overall, 1981 has elegance.

1982: The biggest vintage ever, and that is not the only thing which is great about these wines. Glorious summer weather ensured exceptional ripeness, and the only problem was the heat during the vinification. Most of the better châteaux are now equipped to cope with this, but obviously there were "accidents". In the main, however, exceptional wines were made all over the region, with masses of concentrated fruit, ripe tannin and super-luscious opulence. They look like being wines which will taste superb throughout their lives, in youth, middle-age and when really mature. These are 1947-type wines, but with better technical know-how in the vinification, so they are more balanced, less overpowering. White wines will probably evolve quite quickly.

1983: This was the third largest vintage ever, and the third splendid vintage in a row for Bordeaux. The weather was wonderful throughout the vintage, with very ripe grapes giving high natural alcohol. The wines are majestic, in the classic mould. There is more forceful tannin than in the 1982s and the top wines look like being great keepers. The white wines are very good, with the prospect of great Sauternes.

1984: This is a Cabernet year, as many Merlots were lost through *coulure* (when the fruit does not set) and *millerandage* (uneven development of the berries). As a result St Emilion and Pomerol were not favoured, crops were disastrously small, and the wines tend to be empty and mean. The Médoc, however, is a different story, with some really good wines, especially amongst the Crus Classés. If there is a fault, it is a short finish. There will be some successful Sauternes where properties picked before the rain. Delicious dry white wines.

4 *Burgundy*

Good Burgundy is difficult to make – it is also difficult to buy. There are probably more pitfalls in Burgundy for both the amateur and the professional buyer than in any other fine wine area of the world. It has to be remembered at the outset that, for red wine, Burgundy is at the very northern limit of feasible production. Certainly, neither England, with its attempts at a pale red wine, nor Germany with its 'curiosity' red wine of Assmannshausen, would claim to be in the fine wine league. The problem, here, when so far north, is largely one of colour (*véraison*) and ripeness. But the special slopes that make up so much of Burgundy help to counteract this by attracting all the sun there is available, and the continental nature of the climate ensures drier weather than, say, in southern England. Eastern France becomes very cold in winter, often freezing with a dusting of snow, but the summers and autumns can be very warm.

One is talking in very general terms when one talks of 'Burgundy', as the word encompasses such disparate wines as Chablis, Romanée-Conti and Beaujolais. The worst climatic hazards occur, naturally enough, in the most northerly vineyard area, Chablis – a viticultural 'island' in the *département* of the Yonne, about 175 kilometres southeast of Paris. Continuing southeast, one arrives at Dijon, the start of the kernel of Burgundy, the Côte d'Or. This Golden Slope encompasses the Côte de Nuits in the north and the Côte de Beaune in the south, stretching for sixty kilometres down to Chagny. This town marks the beginning of the Côte Chalonnaise, which ends at Buxy and Montagny. Here the vineyards merge into the Mâconnais, they in turn give way to the Beaujolais, and the Burgundian road comes finally to an end above Lyon. The Burgundian area is elongated, but

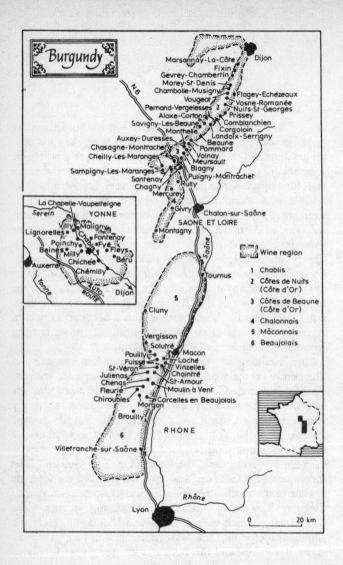

Burgundy

Marsannay-La-Côte
Fixin
Gevrey-Chambertin
Morey-St-Denis
Chambolle-Musigny
Flagey-Echézeaux
Vougeot
Vosne-Romanée
Pernand-Vergelesses
Nuits-St-Georges
Aloxe-Corton
Prissey
Savigny-Les-Beaune
Comblanchien
Monthelie
Corgoloin
Auxey-Duresses
Landoix-Serrigny
Beaune
Chasagne-Montrachet
Pommard
Cheilly-Les-Maranges
Volnay
Meursault
Sampigny-Les-Maranges
Blagny
Santenay
Puligny-Montrachet
Chagny
Rully
Mercurey
Givry
Chalon-sur-Saône

SAONE ET LOIRE

Montagny

Tournus

N 6

Serein

La Chapelle-Vaupelteigne
YONNE
Villy
Maligny
Lignorelles
Fontenay
Poinchy
Fyé
Fleys
Beines
Milly
Chichée
Béru
Auxerre
Chémilly
Chablis
Yonne
AUTO ROUTE
Dijon

Dijon

Cluny

Vergisson
Solutré
Pouilly
Macon
Fuissé
Loché
St-Véran
Vinzelles
Julienas
Chaintré
Chenas
St-Amour
Fleurie
Moulin à Vent
Chiroubles
Corcelles en Beaujolais
Morgon
Brouilly

RHONE

Villefranche-sur-Saône

6

Rhône

Lyon

Saône

Wine region

1 Chablis
2 Côtes de Nuits (Côte d'Or)
3 Côtes de Beaune (Côte d'Or)
4 Chalonnais
5 Mâconnais
6 Beaujolais

0   20 km

not wide, and unfortunately the narrowest point, the Côte
d'Or, is also the finest. Total production can be only
one-third of that of Bordeaux, and by far the greatest part of
the Burgundian figure is made up of Beaujolais. The figures
for 1983, a generous year, show how the *appellation contrôlée*
total is broken down:

	White (in hectolitres)	Red and Rosé (in hectolitres)
Regional Appellations	102,524	114,035
Chablis	141,567	—
Côte de Beaune + Grands Crus	39,418	114,771
Côte de Nuits + Grands Crus	147	138,584
Chalonnais	9,316	32,704
Mâconnais	175,140	60,989
Beaujolais	5,817	1,264,256
TOTAL = 2,199,268	473,929	1,725,339

The comparable 1982 figure was 2,582,000 hectolitres, but it
is still not a great deal of wine to supply world demand. To
complicate matters, not all of this wine is good, and
although this is true of any wine area of the world, the
problem is particularly acute in Burgundy due to the
distribution of the vineyards and their fragmented
ownership. Unlike Bordeaux, the Church played an
enormous part in the development of the Burgundian
vineyards and its importance cannot be enough stressed.
Unfortunately, what remains of the Benedictine Abbey of
Cluny can give no idea of its former magnificence and size.
However, the Revolution put an end to both Church and
noble ownership, and the parcelling out of vineyards
literally changed the face of Burgundy, particularly in the
Côte d'Or. But the Burgundian *négociants* were already
established, and began to build up their businesses and
domains. Vineyard ownership multiplied, with single
domains being divided into little plots. In many cases, this
splintered still further owing to the French inheritance laws,
where property is divided amongst all the children equally.
When a single *appellation*, often not large in size in

111

Burgundy, is in the hands of many different owners, there is an obvious variation in quality, and only careful and experienced tasting will prevent buying accidents. There is also the practical problem of vinifying very small amounts of wine. It is extremely difficult, if not impossible, to do this well with only a *pièce* or two – wine needs a certain 'mass' to ferment and develop smoothly. (A *pièce* is a hogshead of 225 litres.) Another contributory factor to variable quality in Burgundy is the comparative lack of experience in *élevage* and bottling on the part of some growers. Growers are just that, people who grow and tend vines, and most of them do it very well. But that does not mean they are automatically expert in the difficult art of cellar work.

For various socio-economic reasons, more growers are bottling their own wines than ever before in Burgundy – it is estimated that 30 per cent of the wine produced is now domain bottled and sold direct to the consumer. This is partly due to the depression of the market in 1973/4, when the *négociants* did not require so much wine from growers, who thus had to devise other means of selling their production. Direct sale to the public filled a large gap, and had the added advantage of being highly profitable – the grower took the *négociant*'s margin, as well as his own. The development of this type of selling has obviously made the *négociant*'s life more difficult, with more limited choice, especially in years where there is a small crop, and those *négociants* who are also domains owners are better placed to ride this particular change in market conditions. There are also many vineyards *en métayage* in Burgundy. This is the system, still very much alive in France, whereby a vineyard owner has an arrangement with a grower who undertakes to 'farm' his vines in return for what is usually half of the crop. This further complicates the issue, as legally the same wine from the same plot can be sold estate bottled under the name of the *vigneron* and under the name of the owner.

Much is made of the changed yields in Burgundy, and the effect of this on the style of the wines. It is certainly true that for the first twenty or thirty years of this century yields were much lower (fifteen hectolitres to the hectare were considered good generally), and this contributed to a more concentrated, bigger wine. And it is also true that some *appellations* tend to overcrop. But often Grand Cru owners do not make the maximum allowed under the *appellation contrôlée* laws, and if they are aiming for high quality and keep a good proportion of old vines in their vineyard, could not hope to. It could be said that the *appellation contrôlée* limits are not properly adjusted to what is really feasible in Burgundy: normally, a Grand Cru of real class on the Côte d'Or will not produce the maximum production per hectare of thirty hectolitres, a Premier Cru at thirty-five hectolitres might be right, but a straight village wine with a limit of thirty-five hectolitres in a healthy year could easily be lifted – there is too little difference between the great and the pleasant. However, in 1982 (no doubt inspired by the huge crop), the Institut National des Appellations d'Origine increased all the *appellations* of Chablis, the Côte d'Or and the Beaujolais by between 10 and 30 per cent. Thus, red Grands Crus like Corton can now make thirty-five hectolitres to the hectare, while the whites have jumped further, Chablis Grand Cru from thirty-five to forty-five hectolitres to the hectare and Montrachet from thirty to forty hectolitres to the hectare. But there are also annual adjustments to the basic quantity permitted. Thus, Montrachet in 1982 was allowed to make sixty hectolitres to the hectare plus a further 20 per cent under the *plafond limite de classement* (plc) system, giving a total of seventy-two hectolitres to the hectare, and in 1983 the comparable figures were fifty hectolitres to the hectare plus 20 per cent, giving sixty hectolitres to the hectare. High production affects white wine less than red, especially when the latter is made from the Pinot Noir, but it could be argued that yields are now too generous for these very expensive wines. Not everyone, however, takes advantage of these extravagant permitted yields, and Bouchard Père et Fils, for example, only made thirty-two hectolitres to the hectare in their part of the Montrachet vineyard in 1983. The vintage will be seen at its finest in instances like this.

What has certainly changed for everyone is the nature of

the grapes themselves. Clonal variations in Burgundy are very marked, and these have a direct impact on the taste of the wine. In one experiment alone at Echevronne in the Hautes-Côtes-de-Beaune the following clones of Pinot Noir were being studied: type fin; type moyen; type droit; type Jura; type Côte Chalonnaise; and type Champagne. The Pinot Noir of old was smaller, with a thicker skin and less flesh in relation to the skin. This meant less water in relation to solid, colouring matter, and the resultant wine was tougher, deeper and more concentrated. The grape has evolved, and does not make wine of the weight of yore, but tends to make wines of a more supple character. In the white wines, the Chardonnay has developed local characteristics that entirely suit the soil it is in. The grape is not the same in the Mâconnais, on the Côte de Beaune or in Chablis – in fact, if you transplanted the slightly muscat-flavoured Chardonnay of Mâcon to Meursault, your Meursault would taste very different. In Chablis, the Chardonnay is referred to as the Beaunois, the same word, incidentally, as one would use to describe a citizen of Beaune. With the exception of the modest Bourgogne Passetoutgrain (two-thirds Gamay and one-third Pinot Noir), the wines of Burgundy are made of a single grape variety. The red wines of the Côte d'Or and the Côte Chalonnaise are made from the Pinot Noir, while the reds of the Mâconnais and Beaujolais are made from the Gamay. The Pinot Beurot, or Pinot Gris, is still permitted and occasionally used in very small proportions. The Chardonnay is responsible for all the white wines that are not named Bourgogne Aligoté – the Aligoté is a more lowly grape variety making a simple white wine, delicious in ripe years, much too acid in sunless years.

The Chardonnay has shown itself beautifully both in California and in Australia, and only the very best wines of the Côte de Beaune and Chablis have something individual, a sheer class, that makes their drinking not just another dimension of a varietal taste, but a distinct, inimitable addition to the repertoire. The Gamay is an amazing grape, capable of being so common on the wrong soil, and so very delicious on its chosen territory. This happens to be the granite of northern Beaujolais, the home of the nine Beaujolais *crus*. It also does well on more chalk-based soil, as in southern Beaujolais, but it does not rise above a very ordinary level in rich, more fertile soil. The Gamay is a much more productive plant than the Pinot, and pruning should be quite severe. The Gamay is grown in bushes round a single stake, with no wire – *à gobelet*. The Pinot Noir and the Chardonnay (as well as some Gamay in basic Beaujolais) are trained along low wires – *taille guyot*. In the Mâconnais, it is the *taille à queue du Mâconnais*, where the fruit-bearing branch is bent over and attached to the lower wire. Frost is an ever-present risk in the Burgundian vineyard, especially on the plain, and growers always have this in mind when pruning – unfortunately, as this takes place long before the latest spring frosts can occur, the tendency is to take the risk into account and accordingly prune less severely. Hail is much more of a danger in Burgundy than in Bordeaux. It is usually patchy and localized, as in parts of the Côte de Beaune in 1971, parts of Mercurey in 1976, and in 1979 when there was a June hailstorm which seriously affected Nuits-St-Georges and Vosne-Romanée, and in July another attack which touched Gevrey-Chambertin. In spite of rockets and aeroplanes disturbing cloud formations so that rain falls instead of hail, it can be seen that there is no 'cure' for hail.

How Burgundy is Classified

Classification is perhaps a misleading word, because in Burgundy it in no way resembles the 1855 classification of Bordeaux châteaux. Burgundy now has Grands Crus and Premiers Crus, followed by the village wines, e.g. Volnay, Nuits-St-Georges. A First or Fifth growth in Bordeaux will only have one owner, but a Grand Cru in Burgundy, e.g. Bonnes-Mares, can have several owners. In Burgundy it is the plot of land that is classified, and even if an owner is negligent, his mediocre wine will still be Grand Cru. A Grand Cru is the *appellation* itself, and does not have to show the name of the village it is in, e.g. Clos de la Roche does not have to be followed by the village name of Morey-St-Denis.

With Premiers Crus, however, the name of the village must appear with similar-sized letters, e.g. Pommard les Epenots. If two or more Premiers Crus are blended together, the wine is simply known as a Premier Cru, e.g. Beaune Premier Cru. Sometimes this is also done because the name of the village *appellation* carries a great deal of weight and the name of a slightly unknown Premier Cru would mean little outside the region. Beneath Premier Cru, a grower is permitted to put a *clos* or vineyard name, provided it is not more than half the size of the lettering of the village *appellation* name.

The ladder begins with the basic *appellation* wines of Burgundy, such as Bourgogne Grand Ordinaire (rarely seen on the export markets, probably because of the pejorative sound of *ordinaire*), Bourgogne, Bourgogne Passetoutgrain and Bourgogne Aligoté. Then there are *appellations* such as Beaujolais, Beaujolais Villages, Mâcon, Bourgogne Hautes-Côtes de Beaune and Hautes-Côtes de Nuits, Côte de Beaune Villages and Côte de Nuits Villages. Then there are the village names, such as Fleurie, Chassagne-Montrachet and Gevrey-Chambertin. Finally, Premiers Crus and Grands Crus top the ladder. For red wines, Grands Crus should attain 11.5 per cent alcohol minimum, without chaptalization, Premiers Crus 11 per cent, and village wines 10.5 per cent. For white wines, the figures are 12, 11.5, and 11 per cent for straight commune wines.

The 1974 legislation (see page 28) did decree that within five years all wines wishing to have *appellation contrôlée* status should be analysed and tasted. In Burgundy this was regarded as a near impossible task, with the mass of different owners and wines, but in 1979 the mechanics of these analyses and tastings were set in action. Before presenting his wines, a grower may have the option of choosing which *appellation* to ask for, but he has to make this decision for his *whole* crop. For instance, in a poor year a grower may decide that his wine is not up to Beaune standard, and decide to declassify his entire crop to Côte de Beaune, but this would be a last resort, when a wine was really inferior to its true *appellation*, as there would be an inevitable loss of revenue. A

Grand Cru *could* declassify right down the scale, to Premier Cru, or to village status, Bourgogne, or finally to Bourgogne Grand Ordinaire. The need for it is rare, however. It must be said clearly that the classification of Burgundy, the choice of Grands Crus and Premier Crus, is extremely accurate. These are really the vineyards with the best potential, capable of producing the most distinguished wines. Of course, occasionally a very well-made village wine, sometimes beautifully blended from various vineyards by an experienced shipper, will surpass a badly made Premier Cru from an unskilled producer, but this is the same thing as a really good Cru Bourgeois sometimes surpassing a *cru classé* in decline. The basically marlstone soil of the Côte d'Or, mixed with calcareous soil, with more limestone where the white wines are grown, has many nuances within a very short space – sometimes a tiny track in the vineyard can mark a change of emphasis in the soil. All this has been noticed in the classification of the vineyards, together with the exact angle of the slope and the micro-climate. The Grand Cru vineyards tend to be in the middle of the Côte, facing southeast, neither near the scrubby top of the hill, nor in the fertile 'plain' near the Route Nationale that runs the length of the Côte d'Or. There are a few Premiers Crus that could be elevated to Grand Cru status, based on their sheer, persistent greatness – such as Clos St-Jacques and Les Véroilles in Gevrey-Chambertin, Les Epenots and Les Rugiens in Pommard and Les Caillerets in Volnay.

There are certain discrepancies in Burgundian spelling of place-names (Dominode and Dominaude, Véroilles and Varoilles), but these are usually self-evident, especially when pronounced out loud. The word *climat* means 'vineyard'.

Which Wines to Drink When
Burgundy offers a whole range of wines, those to keep for many years, or as long as you can hold out, and those to drink while waiting. You can start drinking Beaujolais a few weeks after the grapes are picked from the vine, but Beaujolais Villages have more to offer in the following year, and the Beaujolais *crus* have a longer life altogether. Mâcon

wines are usually best with the fruity freshness of youth, and this could be said for most of the basic *appellations*. On the Côte d'Or and Côte Chalonnaise, village red wines vary with the year and the commune, but three to ten years would be a generalization. Premier Cru and Grand Cru wines, when superb examples of their kind, often prove to have limitless lives when they are from excellent vintages, but it would be a pity to guzzle them at under five years, even in the lightest of vintages.

Many top white Burgundies are drunk far too young, and much of their glory is thus missed. The Chardonnay takes some time to develop in bottle, especially in a northern clime. Young Grand Cru Chablis is as nothing beside a mature ten-year-old, and Corton Charlemagne remains very closed for the first four to five years of its life. However, white Mâcon and the Pouilly family are meant for relatively young, fresh drinking.

COTE D'OR: COTE DE NUITS

The Côte de Nuits makes the most majestic wines in the whole of Burgundy, wines of great breed and structure, often of great richness and opulence. They are almost entirely red. The complexity and depth of flavour in the best is a reflection of the mineral-rich soil, the geological deposits of ages past, and the exposure of the slopes. The Côte de Nuits is both narrower and steeper than the Côte de Beaune. The slopes are mostly east-facing, with variations of east-south-east or east-north-east, and therefore the weather is less southwest orientated than the Côte de Beaune and is more under the influence of the continental weather type, with its extremes of a drier cold in the winter and hotter summer. Some of the alluvial deposits are near the foot of the slope, and generally the best growths are lower down in the Côte de Nuits than they are on the Côte de Beaune, from mid to lower slope. Some of these deposits also gather in folds in the slope. Geological debris, silt and scree, blend with marl over calcareous soil to make the perfect combination. Marl (clay and carbonate of lime) would be too rich and fertile on its own, and needs to be mixed with poorer soil for high quality wine production. On the other hand, thin limestone soil on its own really is too meagre for the best wines, and in some parts of the Côte de Nuits there have been earth additions. However, the structural aspect of the slope is all important. Parts of the marl-rich soil of the Côte de Nuits appear almost red in colour, indicative of the exciting shades and tints in the wine to come. Production in the Côte de Nuits is smaller than in the Côte de Beaune. Starting from Dijon and working southwards down the Côte, these are the main villages.

Marsannay-La-Côte: This is a real Burgundian village, with some fine houses (and fine cellars) nestling away in their unshowy manner, solid and reassuring behind their walls. Marsannay should be one of the villages producing Côte de Nuits Villages, but the matter is still under discussion, hotly opposed by some growers from villages which already have the right to this *appellation*. Some red Bourgogne Marsannay is produced, but the commune is particularly known for its Bourgogne Rosé Marsannay, a pleasant curiosity, rather than a 'must', on a drinking itinerary. The famous grower, Bernard Clair, who lives in Marsannay, also has a small amount of Bourgogne Aligoté in the commune.

Fixin: This commune marks the southernmost part of what was the Côte Dijonnaise. Fixin is entitled to use the *appellation* Côte de Nuits Villages (and, exceptionally, can be declassified into that *appellation*), but the best *climats* are much more likely to be sold as Fixin itself. Fixin also includes neighbouring Fixey, and with true Burgundian individuality, the 'x's are pronounced as double 'ss'.

There are six Premier Cru vineyards in Fixin, of which the most distinguished is certainly the Clos de la Perrière – it is also the largest. The other Premier Cru wines are Clos du Chapitre, Les Hervelets, Les Arvelets, Aux Cheusots (more often known as Clos Napoléon) and Les Meix-Bas. I have always found Fixin wines deep in colour, slow to mature, and somewhat rustic if you compare them to the top wines from the Côte de Nuits. However, Clos de la Perrière can certainly share many characteristics with a Premier Cru from Gevrey-Chambertin. These robust wines are always

119

well-made by the Domaine Pierre Gelin and, outside the Premier Cru category, Domaine Marion. Charles Quillardet, Bruno Clair and Philippe Juliet are also recommended.

Gevrey-Chambertin: Where does one begin in a village capable of making some of the greatest wines on the Côte de Nuits and some of the most sad. The village *appellation* of Gevrey-Chambertin extends over the Nationale road, well into the plain, where the soil is vastly different from that of the slope, and the wine considerably more common. Some of the produce of this area has not done a great deal of good to the name of Gevrey-Chambertin, and one hopes the new tasting commissions will be courageous and will throw out wines not worthy of the name.

Gevrey-Chambertin is a typical example of a Burgundian village that enhanced its status by tagging on the name of its most famous vineyard (Chambertin) to the name of the village – Gevrey. It has done it no harm. Chambertin and Chambertin-Clos de Bèze are the two most prestigious vineyards in the commune, Grands Crus in a special, outstanding category of their own. Production is limited to thirty-five hectolitres to the hectare, but rarely reaches that quantity. Chambertin-Clos de Bèze can call itself Chambertin, but Chambertin *tout court* cannot become Chambertin-Clos de Bèze. Both should be majestic, the essence of the Côte de Nuits, beautifully constructed, generous and perfectly balanced. Bottles of these Grands Crus should not be broached within a few years of their birth – much will be lost if they are drunk at too embryonic a stage.

With more than two dozen owners, Chambertin and Chambertin-Clos de Bèze will not produce wine of a uniform quality. But there are some very meticulous owners in these magic 'fields', and their wines are worth saving for. Domaine Clair-Daü used to make some of the biggest wines – its Clos de Bèze always needing years to show at anywhere near its best. This was partly explained by old vines, and partly by more length vatting than some growers. The Clair-Daü Clos de Bèze 1978 was a typical example, firm, big and rich. But at this level of *cru*, there should always be breed and elegance beneath the structure – top wines should never be clumsy. Unfortunately, there has been family disagreement and Bernard Clair is no longer at the Domaine Clair-Daü. Drouhin-Laroze is also known for his Clos de Bèze, but this is quite a different style. This grower makes delicious flowery and fragrant wines, very pretty when young – perhaps tailing off a bit when older in light years. But when youthful, it is like having a mouthful of flowers on the palate.

Other owners in Chambertin and Chambertin-Clos de Bèze are: Domaine Armand Rousseau (M. Charles Rousseau makes superb wines); Pierre Gelin; the *négociant* Louis Latour (whose Chambertin 1971, Cuvée Héritiers Latour, is all silky elegance); Marion; Trapet; Camus, whose wines have disappointed recently; Domaine Pierre Damoy (with greatly improved wines in the 1980s); and Tortochot. There are six other Grand Crus, which differ from the 'top two' in that they are allowed to produce up to thirty-seven hectolitres to the hectare. Latricières-Chambertin must be considered on the same level as Chambertin itself – it is indeed on the same level on the slope. The 1978 Latricières from Bouchard Père et Fils is a gem of a wine, concentrated, with a mass of ripe Pinot Noir in it. I remember having a 1952 from Jules Régnier in 1973 that hardly showed any signs of age, had a beautiful bouquet and was balanced, lightish and elegant. This finesse is very typical of Latricières, and Trapet also makes perfect examples of the *appellation*. The other Grands Crus are Charmes-Chambertin (or Mazoyères-Chambertin), excellent at Domaine Dujac and Domaine B. Bachelet, and the 1969 of Bouchard Père is wonderful, Chapelle-Chambertin, Griotte-Chambertin, Mazis-Chambertin (or Mazys or Mazy) and Ruchottes-Chambertin. Mazis-Chambertin is the only lot of Côte de Nuits wine appearing at the Hospices de Beaune sale (this began in 1977), and although the first year's offering was poor, the 1978 and 1979 Hospices wines were superb.

There is a magnificent array of Premiers Crus in Gevrey-Chambertin, at least two of which stand out as being on a par with the Grands Crus: Clos St-Jacques and Les Varoilles (or les Véroilles). One of the best Burgundies I have ever experienced was the Clos St Jacques 1969 of Fernand Pernot. Nowadays, the Pernot Fourrier domain only makes good wines. Clair-Daü's Clos St-Jacques 1976 is very dense in colour, has a deep bouquet, and is huge and tannic, full of scent and flavour. Overall, the Domaine Clair-Daü is the largest private domain in Burgundy – all the larger domains are owned by *négociants*. It owns over forty hectares of vineyards, and no fewer than eighteen hectares of these are in the Grands Crus and Premiers Crus, nearly all in the Côte de Nuits. The Domaine des Varoilles part-owned and managed by Jean-Pierre Naigeon is highly respected. This is a relatively small domain of twelve hectares, nearly all of which is Premier or Grand Cru. It takes its name from the most important holding, the Clos des Varoilles – the whole six hectares is owned by the domain. Varoilles has a micro-climate, which enables picking to take place up to eight days later than elsewhere. The Clos des Varoilles 1976 is big and tannic, with a spicy nose – here, M. Naigeon had only vatted for one week, as given the conditions of the year, a normal vatting would have produced altogether too much tannin. The very good 1972 was perfect drinking at twelve years old, while the 1978 Varoilles is outstanding and the 1979 and 1980 very fine. Amongst the other Premiers Crus, look out for Cazetiers, Etournelles, Fonteny, Combe-aux-Moines, Clos-Prieur and Champonnets – Leclerc produces delicious examples.

Straight village Gevrey-Chambertin should be warm and generous, with a lovely scent. Much depends on the maker and where the vineyards are. Some parts of the commune of Brochon are entitled to the Gevrey-Chambertin *appellation*. Respected domain names are Louis Rémy, Henri Rebourseau, Philippe Rossignol and Joseph Roty.

Morey-St-Denis: Here, the modest village of Morey opted for the addition of St-Denis, from the name of its famous Clos. The four Grands Crus of the commune are comparatively little vaunted, when put against the other big names of the Côte de Nuits. Apart from the Clos St-Denis, there is the

Clos de la Roche, bigger in area and body, Clos de Tart, and a small part of Bonnes-Mares – by far the greater part is in the commune of Chambolle-Musigny. A maximum yield of thirty-five hectolitres to the hectare is permitted for these *appellations*. The Clos de la Roche and the Clos de Tart tend to be the biggest wines of the commune, the Clos St-Denis combines charm and *mâche*, and Bonnes Mares has much of the character of the neighbouring commune.

M. Jacques Seysses of Domaine Dujac lives at Morey, and in his cellars you can see the fine differences between the growths. The domain has eleven hectares of vines, comprising ten *appellations* – an indication of the 'parcelling' in Burgundy.

In November 1979, the Morey-St-Denis Premier Cru 1978 had already been bottled, and had a fine strawberry nose, a long finish and silky texture, almost a Chambolle character. The 1978 Clos St-Denis was deceptively charming, but with firm backbone behind it (as it should have at this young stage), while the Clos de la Roche filled the mouth with luscious fruit. A Clos St Denis 1969 was very *racé*, full of breed, stylish, fruity and elegant. At this domain, bottling is done entirely by gravity, as M. Seysses is convinced that pumping oxidizes and tires the wine and, when in vat, the wine is kept under nitrogen gas. The entire domain is vintaged in a week, thereby managing to pick all the different parcels of vineyard more or less at the optimum moment. The Dujac 1982s are exceptionally good.

The Clos de Tart, exceptionally in Burgundy, has one owner, the Beaujolais *négociants*, Mommessin. The wines are good, and a 1964 and 1923, drunk in 1984, were superb. The Clos des Lambrays, or Les Larrets, was made a Grand Cru in 1979, the same year that ownership changed from the Cosson family to a group founded on Lazards Bank. Under Mme Cosson, there were some amazingly good wines up until the 1950s, but thereafter there were lapses. A third of the Clos was replanted in 1980, and a good wine was made in 1982, but obviously complete vineyard renovation will take time. The Premiers Crus most likely to be seen are Les Sorbés, Le Clos-des-Ormes, and Clos-Bussière; Roumier makes a good example of the latter. Important domains include Amiot, Ponsot and Georges Lignier.

Chambolle-Musigny: Le Musigny is a great wine, in the right hands. A Grand Cru of enormous elegance, subtle, with a hidden, almost 'irony' backbone, Le Musigny should have a sorcerer's bouquet when mature. Comte de Vogüé's wines have this magic. The 1976 Musigny of Louis Latour has real class, and their 1971 is absolutely impeccable, with restrained breed that opens out, great ripeness, and ultimate elegance. I have also tasted a Musigny 1969 Vieilles Vignes from Remoissenet, but although this had interest, there was a trace of clumsiness at the end which one should not find in this Grand Cru. Owners of note in this Grand Cru include Domaine Jacques Prieur, Domaine Comte Georges de Vogüé, Domaine Mugnier, Joseph Drouhin, Roumier and Hudelot. A tiny amount of white Musigny is made.

Bonnes-Mares is the other Grand Cru of Chambolle-Musigny, and I have never seen a classier example than that of Bouchard Père in the 1969 vintage – with a scent which permeated the whole taste, and an almost 'irony' flavour and backbone which characterizes Bonnes-Mares. This wine has a great future, and must be admired as a feat of buying and *élevage*, as Bouchard Père do not own in Bonnes-Mares. A Bonnes-Mares 1970 from Drouhin-Laroze, tasted at the beginning of 1980, was deeply scented and very consistent and still solid. Comte de Vogüé, Clair-Daü and the Domaine des Varoilles make outstanding Bonnes-Mares. Most owners of Musigny have a plot in Bonnes-Mares. I have also admired a 1976 Bonnes-Mares from the shipper Louis Jadot. The Domaine Roumier is important. The Premiers Crus of Chambolle can be silky, satiny, elegant wines. Les Amoureuses and Les Charmes must be considered at the top; the rest are nearly always sold as Chambolle-Musigny Premier Cru.

Vougeot: With the fifty hectares of Clos de Vougeot (or Clos Vougeot), Burgundy has a Grand Cru of Bordelais proportions! Unfortunately, the wall-enclosed Clos does not have one owner, but around eighty, and one does not have to be psychic to see that this means variations in quality. These variations are not only due to where exactly in the Clos the owner has his plot, but also to the amount he has, because it is much more difficult to make fine wine with just a tiny quantity. However, exact vineyard site is of paramount importance, and it has to be admitted that were it not for the historical creation of the Clos by the Cistercians, by no means all of the area would be classified as Grand Cru, especially those vineyards bordering the Route Nationale 74. In fact, one of the choicest parts of the Clos slope is occupied by the famous Château du Clos de Vougeot, but I am sure no one would consent to its destruction to make way for more vines, especially if they were in the habit of attending the boisterous Chevaliers du Tastevin dinners within its walls.

The name is certainly illustrious enough to encourage some high yields within the Clos, and it is comparatively rare to taste a Clos de Vougeot of real distinction. At its best it should be a big, rich wine, with a complex, scented nose. Just about every owner from the neighbouring communes has a slice of Clos de Vougeot, as well as many of the shippers, such as Morin, who has Château de la Tour de Clos Vougeot, Faiveley and Joseph Drouhin. The Domaine des Varoilles which now vinifies its wine with another owner in order to get a better 'mass' of wine, has made an outstanding 1978 and a 1976 of immense *ampleur* and richness. The 1977, 1979 and 1980 are all *Tasteviné*, which seems to happen with remarkable regularity with the wines of this domain. A 1972 Clos de Vougeot from René Engel, tasted in December 1979, had a rich smell, great concentration and a lovely flavour – perhaps it could have been even better had it been picked a little later, in this unripe year, but it was still a fine bottle. Other owners are Drouhin-Laroze, Charles Noëllat, Jean Grivot, Jacques Prieur and Henry Lamarche.

The Confrérie des Chevaliers du Tastevin is a brotherhood of wine which has done a miraculous feat of promotion for Burgundy, its wines and its *joie de vivre*. Many other *confréries* have followed, but none have the world-wide influence and impact of the Chevaliers du Tastevin. The Confrérie also awards its label to wines submitted and found to be truly good and representative examples of their *appellation* and vintage. The wines are tasted blind by a panel consisting of different aspects of the wine trade and consumers, and there is no doubt that the award of a Tastevin label adds *cachet* to a wine. There are occasional lapses in judgement here, as there are everywhere, and certain tastevine wines have had a tendency to go on for ever, but generally it is an indication of a wine that is honourable, and often very good indeed. The *tastevin* itself is a shallow, fluted cup, often silver, which is traditionally used by Burgundians, to look at the colour and clarity of a young wine. It is, however, more difficult to judge the bouquet of a wine in a wide-surfaced container, and many wine professionals like to use a classic tasting glass, even if it looks less picturesque.

The commune of Vougeot consists of nearly thirteen hectares, and so is naturally overshadowed by the great Clos. But its Premiers Crus can produce very fine wines, such as the Vougeot Clos de la Perrière 1962 from Domaine Bertagna, perhaps then making more outstanding wines than nowadays, partly because there was new planting later in the 1960s. The other Premiers Crus are Clos Blanc, Les Petit-Vougeots and part of Les Cras; the Clos Blanc makes white wine from Chardonnay.

Flagey-Echézeaux: The village of Flagey-Echézeaux is stranded on the wrong side of the Route Nationale 74, far from its main vineyards, which are up behind the Clos de Vougeot. Flagey-Echézeaux is not a commune *appellation*, and if the great vineyards of Grands Echézeaux and Les Echézeaux are declassified, they become Vosne-Romanée, the neighbouring commune. Grands Echézeaux is a Grand Cru of enormous quality, full and rich and complex. Les Echézeaux is more than three times the size, and therefore more variable – it does not have the sheer class of Grands Echézeaux, but can be very fine wine. It is made up of a number of vineyards, including Les Rouges, and Les Champs Traversins. Owners are the Domaine de la Romanée-Conti, René Engel, the Gros family, Henri Jayer and Domaine J.

Jayer, both of whom made particularly fine wine in 1982. Well-chosen Echézeaux can be at a relatively good price for a Grand Cru.

Vosne-Romanée: The Grands Crus of this commune are the greatest names of Burgundy, mostly justifying their reputation, if not always their astronomical price. This kind of price spiral is difficult to avoid when the quantities are tiny and the *renommée* is international, but there should always be some relation between the two. Romanée-Conti is just under two hectares of red-earthed grandeur. It is solely owned by the Domaine de la Romanée-Conti (the de Villaine and Leroy families), who market the wine with vigour. At its best, Romanée-Conti is an unrepeatable drinking experience. The 1971 is a vintage like this, a scented wine, with beautiful balance, big with lovely fruit, almost chewy in its body and texture. Now, the Pinot Noir vines are on American, phylloxera-resistant root stocks, but until 1945 the Romanée-Conti owners persevered with French root stocks, in spite of a severely deteriorating yield.

The Domaine de la Romanée-Conti is also the sole owner of the six-hectare La Tâche. The 1971 La Tâche was exquisite, soft and scented in 1974, with a glorious ripe finish; the 1962 is as great. Romanée-Conti can age even more splendidly than La Tâche on occasions. A comparison between the two was made with the 1952 vintage, but here La Tâche was the easy winner, a great and noble wine in 1979, for this was the first vintage, made with young vines, from Romanée-Conti after the replanting. The 1970 La Tâche seemed to me good, but not great. The 1969 had a deep colour in 1974, was much racier and nervier, and seemed set to last to perfection. However, five years later the wine was browning and seemed clumsy and unbalanced. Occasionally, the domain grapes seem to be picked too late, giving a slight taste and smell of over-ripeness to the wine, almost a roasted flavour or imbalance of alcohol. La Tâche 1979 looks harmonious and deep-scented. Apart from being sole owners of Romanée-Conti and La Tâche, the Domaine also owns in Richebourg, Grands Echézeaux and Echézeaux, as well as in Le Montrachet. In addition, the Domaine produces and sells about half of Romanée-St-Vivant, the part which forms the Domaine Marey-Monge; the 1979 is all truffles and richness.

Richebourg can be big, fat and velvety, a most seductive Grand Cru. The 1971 Richebourg from the Domaine de la Romanée-Conti was massive and concentrated. I tasted this against a 1971 Grands Echézeaux from the Domaine, which has a big 'masculine' style, and the rather delightful rich, minerally earthiness that I often find in top Vosne-Romanée wine – almost a spiciness on the nose. The 1978 Richebourg of Bouchard Père is really *gras*, rich and full, with immense backbone, and their 1971 is a great wine now and for the future, enormous and spicy. I have also been impressed by the Richebourg 1971 of Remoissenet, which has class – again, a big wine, with a lot of scent, power and strength, with the opulence of the *appellation*. Remoissenet had as well a very good Grands Echézeaux 1969, Cuvée Jacquinot de Richemont, with some tightness and concentration as befits this great year.

Romanée-St-Vivant is under ten hectares and has a monastic background. Part of the vineyard is called Les Quatre Journaux and belongs to the *négociant*, Louis Latour. The 1971 shows immense class and breed, a beautifully made wine from this very ripe vintage. Magnums of the 1966 drunk in 1979 were superb, as is the 1978.

La Romanée is the smallest *appellation* in area in France, producing an average thirty hectolitres of wine per crop. Lying just above Romanée-Conti, it is inevitable that the wines should be compared, but really they are very different. This difference is attributable to nuances in the soil and to different ownership, and therefore to varying methods of vinifying and *élevage*. La Romanée is entirely owned by the family of Liger-Belair, but the distribution and *élevage* is now effected by the Beaune shippers Bouchard Père et Fils. This has been the case since the 1976 vintage, as with Vosne-Romanée Les Reignots. The 1978 La Romanée is top-class, with a vast range and depth of flavours and great silkiness.

Commune Vosne-Romanée wines can give immense

pleasure, and their heady perfume and generous nature are very individual. There is a very respectable list of Premiers Crus: Aux Malconsorts (I remember a magnificent 1935 from the Barolet collection), Les Beaux-Monts, Les Suchots, La Grand'Rue, Les Gaudichots, Aux Brûlées, Les Chaumes, Les Reignots, Les Clos-des-Réas and Les Petits-Monts. The wines of Lamarche and Noëllat often look better in cask than in bottle but Mongeard-Mugneret and Henri Jayer are highly recommended. The Domaine Daniel Rion makes very true wines, with both Beaux-Monts and Chaumes.

Nuits-St-Georges: There may be no Grands Crus in Nuits-St-Georges, but it is rich in Premiers Crus. If the name is full of imagery, the taste is no less so, incisive, earthy and plummy. There is a kind of irony backbone about good Nuits that is extremely evocative, and the flavour lives long in the mouth. Nowhere is Nuits better than at the Domaine Gouges. The late M. Henri Gouges was one of the very first growers to bottle his wine himself. The domain is over ten hectares, which is less than it sounds when one calculates that this is spread over many *climats* and must satisfy the world. Gouges own in Les Vaucrains, Les Saint-Georges, Les Porrets (they have the Clos des Porrets, which is the best part of the first growth), Les Pruliers, Aux Chaignots, and have white wine in La Perrière (made from a white mutation of the Pinot Noir), as well as straight village Nuits.

The vineyards north of Nuits, towards Vosne-Romanée, are not quite as famous as those Premiers Crus south of the village, but remain very good sites – they tend not to be so big and are more supple than those *climats* to the south. The best of this group of Premiers Crus are probably Aux Boudots, Aux Murgers and Aux Chaignots (Alain Michelot always makes an excellent example). South of Nuits there is a succession of very fine Premiers Crus: Les St-Georges, probably the wine with the most finesse – there is a little sand in the soil; Les Vaucrains, the most solid of all and the slowest to mature; Les Cailles; Les Porets (or Les Porrets); La Perrière and Les Pruliers. Les Hauts-Pruliers of the Domaine Machard de Gramont and the Domaine Chantal Lescure are strongly recommended.

The neighbouring commune of Prémeaux can also use the *appellation* Nuits-St-Georges, and there are Premiers Crus here too, notably the Clos de la Maréchale (sold by Faiveley), Les Didiers, Clos-des-Forêts, and Clos des Corvées. Faiveley is a big owner throughout Nuits, as is Lupé-Cholet – they have the Château Gris. Commune Nuits-St-Georges is, unfortunately, expensive, but at its best you are promised a bottle of considerable interest – the wine is bound to have a pronounced nose and a strong flavour coupled with a velvety texture.

Bourgogne Hautes-Côtes de Nuits: Up behind this southern part of the Côte de Nuits, from the hills behind Nuits-St-Georges itself down to south of Corgoloin, a considerable revival has taken place in the vineyards and some pleasant wine is being made under the Bourgogne Hautes-Côtes de Nuits *appellation*. These Arrière-Côtes are very charming, with small Burgundian villages dotted around on the rolling hills amidst mixed farming. Pinot Noir, Chardonnay, Gamay and Aligoté are planted in these hills, and the wines have to pass a Commission de Dégustation (tasting panel) before achieving the *appellation*. The problem in these Arrière-Côtes is lack of sun, as many of the slopes do not face in the right direction. Much of the wine is made at the Cave Coopérative des Hautes-Côtes just outside Beaune. The house of Geisweiler own seventy hectares of Pinot Noir and Chardonnay round the village of Bévy. There is much less Hautes-Côtes de Nuits than Hautes-Côtes de Beaune, and it could hardly be called cheap. But sometimes bottles can be surprisingly good and fruity; especially those from Delaunay and Bernard Hudelot.

The Côte de Nuits peters out with the three communes of Prissey, Comblanchien and Corgoloin, all of which can produce Côte de Nuits Villages. Much of Comblanchien and Corgoloin seems to be eaten up by marble quarries, but Corgoloin has a single vineyard of some note, the Clos des Langres. The vineyards of the Côte de Nuits run almost straight into those of the Côte de Beaune but there is a clear division in the two slopes, and it is not one continuous Côte.

Ladoix-Serrigny: The first commune on the Côte de Beaune is Ladoix-Serrigny, an *appellation* in its own right, but not often seen on labels. Most of the vineyards are very good, but they have the right to the Grand and Premier Cru *appellations* of the neighbouring commune of Aloxe-Corton. What is left is more often than not declassified into Côte de Beaune Villages, thereby incorporating the magic name of Beaune. Red and white wines are made. I have admired the Ladoix Côte de Beaune 1976 of the Prince de Mérode, who makes wines with real Pinot Noir character.

Aloxe-Corton: The *appellations* and vineyards within this commune are some of the most confusing (and confused) in Burgundy. The wine of the commune can be soft (like the sound of the 'x' in Aloxe), but full and ripe. The nub of the whole area is the impressive hill of the Grand Cru Corton. Here are the best and most magnificent red wines of the Côte de Beaune, and some would argue that the best whites are also made on these slopes too – about 30 per cent of the production is in white wine. The *appellation* of Corton is made up of several vineyards which can add their name to that of Corton itself, e.g. Corton Bressandes. Any wine with a label that features the name 'Corton' is a Grand Cru. But some of these vineyards are only in part classified as Grand Cru, and the other part is Premier Cru, therefore becoming an Aloxe-Corton-Maréchaudes, for example. The part of this vineyard that is Grand Cru would be labelled Corton-Maréchaudes, or just simply Corton. Le Corton is just one of these vineyards making up the Grand Cru of Corton. It, like any other, can be sold separately, or blended with other vineyards within the Grand Cru, but of course two vineyard names would not appear – it would just be Corton.

The great red wines of Corton have some of the majesty of the Côte de Nuits, taking time to soften and open out, but eventually combining body with enormous seduction. Probably the Corton Clos du Roi wines need the greatest time to reach their apogee, with Corton Bressandes often showing lovely fruit earlier. The wines of M. Daniel Senard are excellent, as are those of M. Antonin Guyon at the Domaine de lay Guyonnière – his Corton-Bressandes 1971 has a wonderful, ripe, Pinot nose, and is rich and completely balanced. Bouchard Père have splendid Le Corton and Tollot-Beaut is reputed, with a very good 1976 Bressandes. Louis Latour also make excellent wine in Corton, namely their Château Corton-Grancey, their domain wine which is not named after a vineyard but after their Château de Grancey. Loùis Latour's Clos de la Vigne au Saint produces superb bottles. A Corton-Bressandes 1969 from Joseph Drouhin had a ripe nose, and was rich and full with good length – a Burgundy for cold climates. On the other hand, a Corton Clos du Roi 1971 from Michel Voarick was really very light, but most flowery, which proves that the hand of the wine-maker can prevail over the intrinsic character of the respective *climat*. The Prince de Mérode has Corton-Maréchaudes and Clos du Roi, and makes commendable wine. Some very good Corton-Pougets come from Louis Jadot. A white Corton Vergennes 1976 Hospices de Beaune from Chanson looked superb in 1979.

The great white wine, Corton-Charlemagne, comes from round the bluff of the Corton hill, facing the little road going into Pernand-Vergelesses and below the tree-line of the hill-top. These upper slopes have more limestone in the soil, and lend much to the splendour of the bouquet. Corton-Charlemagne owes nothing to anyone; it is aristocratic, subtle wine that will take its time to show its full beauty. So often it is drunk too young, when all the complexities of nose and taste are still hidden. There is a wonderful firmness, even a tautness, about Corton-Charlemagne when young, breaking out into glorious Chardonnay scent and elegance when mature. The best sites are not those nearest Pernand, but to the south of the slope. One of the most famous owners is the *négociant* Louis Latour – it was the great-grandfather of the present Louis Latour who started planting white grapes at Corton. The 1978 already has that mysterious, unmistakable slightly peppery nose that is Corton-Charlemagne, and a waxy texture that makes for a great future – the 1976 drunk in 1979 had a lot of body behind it. The 1974 when young was already scented, but not really developed, with many flavours and that Chardonnay-almondy finish, but in the background the firmness of the *appellation*. The 1973 was obviously much more forward, crisp and utterly drinkable relatively young. The 1972 had more acidity and firmness, and the 1971 had an overwhelming nose, very big and 'giving'. The 1961 was superb in 1980. Other important owners are the shippers Louis Jadot and Bouchard Père, and the Domaine Bonneau de Martray, the latter also having red Corton. Corton-Charlemagne can, in fact, be produced from part of the *climat* called Corton, and vice versa, but note of the exact composition of the soil will indicate whether Pinot Noir or Chardonnay is most suitable. With the demand for top white Burgundy, there has been, perhaps, a tendency to plant Chardonnay in plots more suited to red-wine production. 1983 was a splendid year for Corton-Charlemagne.

Pernand-Vergelesses: The village of Pernand lies in a fold of the hills, in the shelter of the great Corton hill. Where the vines end, the woods begin, and there are some lovely walks into the Arrière-Côtes from here. The wines of Pernand can have a lovely, flowery bouquet, delicate and subtle – some say of violets. Nowadays they tend to be light, and their charm lies in their youthful fruit. I even drank a straight village 1977 in 1979 with much pleasure, although one would obviously not take this course of action with the 1976s and 1978s. Although there are five Premiers Crus in Pernand-Vergelesses, one stands out – Ile des Vergelesses – which generally has more body and elegance than the others. Louis Latour makes a good example of this Premier Cru, as do Dubreuil-Fontaine, the Domaine Chandon de Briailles, and the Domaine de la Guyonnière, whose 1973 was a memorable wine. The Rapet family are big owners in Pernand and the shippers Chanson own in another Premier Cru, les Basses-Vergelesses, although the word *Basses* is dropped on the label (following a tendency in place-names all over France – gone are the Basses Pyrénées and the Basses Alpes). Chanson also produce a little white wine from the Caradeux vineyard, and I can recommend the Pernand Vergelesse (the final 's' is sometimes dropped) Blanc 1976 from Guyon which, at the beginning of 1980, was excellent, with a very perfumed nose. The whites in Pernand tend to be soft but full, totally without the nervy class of Corton. Good Aligoté comes from Laleure-Piot.

Chorey-Lès-Beaune: The flat vineyards here are not particularly favoured, and much of the wine is sold to the Beaune shippers for Côte de Beaune Villages, a pleasant bottle of Burgundy to be drunk relatively young. There is some white wine too, but much of that would go into straight Bourgogne in the shippers' cellars.

Savigny-Lès-Beaune: The *appellation* Savigny covers red and white wine, with the emphasis very much on reds. The best can be really attractive wines, with great charm, delicacy of flavour and persistence. In style, they are perhaps between Pernand-Vergelesses and Beaune, which is in fact where the small town is situated physically. The greatest bottles of Savigny that I have tasted have been from the Premiers Crus of La Dominode and Les Lavières. The 1976 Dominode from Clair-Daü is excellent, rich and long, as fat as the 1964. The 1978 is also juicy and fat, but not big or tannic. Fine wines are also made by Chanson Père et Fils, Joseph Drouhin, and Champy Père et Fils. The Lavières of Bouchard Père et Fils has enormous charm and seduction, as does the same *climat* from Robert Ampeau, although it is perhaps lighter; however, that could not be said about the 1978. The shippers Henri de Villamont are a strong force in this *appellation*, owned as they are by the large and well-run Swiss firm of Schenk. The wines of M. Pierre Petitjean are also good and a Premier Cru Aux Guettes 1980 from Simon Bize was delicious. The red wines of Savigny can also be Côte de Beaune Villages.

Beaune: Beaune is a beautiful old walled town with wine in its stones. Many of the most important shippers of Burgundy have their headquarters here, and vineyard ownership in the *appellation* is dominated by these *négociants*. Over twenty times as much red wine is made as white, and there are no Grands Crus. This is an indication of the nature of the wines, which are straightforward and frank but do not have great hidden depths or complexity. Red Beaune has a full-bodied approach, uncomplicated and fruity. The fascination lies in comparing the top Premiers Crus, which show consistent and marked differences. I have often had the opportunity to do this at Bouchard Père, and the vineyards keep their individuality while holding the respective vintage characters. One leads in with a restrained Clos de la Mousse, then goes into a more robust Teurons, followed by a fuller, fatter Marconnets, almost Côte de Nuits in its assertiveness (Marconnets is the Premier Cru that lost so much land to the autoroute coming down the Côte), finishing with the beautiful elegance, scent and finesse of the Grèves Vigne de l'Enfant Jésus. The Clos de la Mousse, on a rocky base, will always be the first to develop, some would call it feminine, while the other, better, Premiers Crus will need time to show their nuances of flavour. In 1977, I enjoyed the 1962 l'Enfant Jésus and 1947 Marconnets, both in perfect condition. In 1979, the 1961 l'Enfant Jésus was rich and concentrated. At Bouchard Père, their Cent Vignes often goes into their splendid non-vintage Premier Cru blend, Beaune du Château, one of the most reliable and best value bottles of Burgundy you can buy – the white blend is equally good, rustic rather than complex. Clos du Roi is usually bigger in character than Cent Vignes. The other top Premiers Crus are les Fèves, much of which belongs to the shippers Chanson, who sell it under the name of Beaune Clos des Fèves. Les Vignes Franches from Louis Latour is always splendid, with the 1976, 1978 and 1979 wines showing great promise. Louis Jadot's Clos-des-Ursules is an enclave within Vignes-Franches. Les Bressandes is another top Premier Cru, usually very good from Chanson, and red and white Clos des Mouches from Joseph Drouhin are recommended; the 1976 white, seen in 1979, was delicious. Other noted Premiers Crus are Champimonts, Cras and Toussaints. The Domaines of Jacques Germains and Besancenot-Mathouillet produce lovely wines.

The Hospices de Beaune is a very important owner in the Beaune Premiers Crus. The top vineyards donated to this charity, devoted to looking after the sick and old, supported the good works, and still play a significant role in the welfare of Beaune's citizens. The lots of wine sold at the famous Hospices de Beaune auction on the third Sunday of every November are named after vineyard workers connected with the wines or the benefactors of the Hospices. When buying, check with *négociant*. With one exception, all the wines sold at the auction come from the Côte de Beaune, and they bring a prestige value which is not a weather-vane for the prices in the ordinary market-place, although it can indicate a trend.

Côte de Beaune and Côte de Beaune Villages: The Côte de Beaune *appellation* is both red and white, but is rarely seen. It only applies to wine from the Beaune vineyard area. However, Côte de Beaune Villages is for red wines only, and very much in evidence. The villages that have the right to the *appellation* are: Auxey-Duresses; Blagny; Chassagne-Montrachet; Cheilly-les-Maranges; Chore-lès-Beaune; Dézize-les-Maranges; Ladoix; Meursault; Monthelie; Pernand-Vergelesses; Puligny-Montrachet; St-Aubin; St-Romain; Sampigny-les-Maranges; Santenay and Savigny.

Pommard: If Gevrey-Chambertin is where the side is let down in the Côte de Nuits, Pommard is the Achilles heel of the Côte de Beaune. Somehow the name is a password to success, especially in the United States, and there has been much abuse. However, now that is less possible and the risk is more of paying a great deal of money for mediocrity. Pommard should have a fine, sturdy character, firm and rich, but the best of the Premiers Crus go way beyond that into finesse and delicacy, with underlying backbone. Top wines from Les Epenots and Les Rugiens exemplify this, perhaps none more so than Les Epenots from the Domaine de Courcel – the 1976 is set for a very long life indeed. Other top domains are Comte Armand (with superb Clos des Epeneaux), Michel Gaunoux, Parent (with both Epenots and their Clos Micault) and the Domaine de la Pousse d'Or. Jaboulet-Vercherre, the shippers, own the Château de la Commaraine and its Clos, and the Château de Pommard is commercial without being sought-after for its quality. The Premier Cru Clos Blanc of Domaine Machard de Gramont and the Domaine Billard-Gonnet are highly recommended. A Premier Cru Les Pézerolles 1979 from de Montille was superb at five years old, with great keeping potential.

Volnay: Volnay at its most distinguished presents a different picture of charm, scent and delicacy, not highly-coloured, but lingering and flowery. Working upwards, and using the marvellous range of Bouchard Père wines as a yardstick, one can begin with a delicate Volnay Taille-Pieds, go on to a flowery Frémiets, and then to a more complete, powerful, rich Caillerets. This combines the seductive charm of the *appellation* with something much more lasting – the superb domain of the Marquis d'Angerville also makes wines that show these qualities. Another owner in Caillerets is Jean Clerget. Champans and Chevret are the other top Premiers Crus of Volnay – there is also the splendid Santenots, which is in Meursault but which is allowed to use the Volnay *appellation* for the red wines. Robert Ampeau makes excellent Volnay-Santenots, even in the less impressive years – the wines have real grace. The Domaine des Comtes Lafon produces magnificent Santenots-du-Milieu. The Domaine de la Pousse d'Or make really distinguished wines, even in only moderate years; the Volnay Clos de la Bousse d'Or 1970 was very good as were the Volnay les Caillerets, Clos des Soixante Ouvrées 1972 and 1980. Bernard Delagrange, Henri Boillot and Louis Glantenay are other owners, and the Volnay Clos des Chênes of the Domaine du Château de Meursault must be mentioned. Mâitre Hubert de Montille makes spectacular wines.

Monthelie: This is a lesser-known name of Burgundy, but the best wines speak for themselves. They tend to mature somewhat faster than the best Volnays. De Suremain makes some of the finest wines and owns the Château de Monthelie, and the Domaine A. Ropiteau-Mignon makes excellent wine from the Clos des Champs-Fulliot, one of the Premiers Crus. The Domaine Parent and the Deschamps family are also owners in Monthelie.

Auxey-Duresses: This is an *appellation* of both red and white wines (considerably less), and some of the whites are quite remarkable especially in youth, when they have a charming, biscuity quality. I particularly admire those of Bouchard Père, which show great character when drunk comparatively young. Domains of great note are the Duc de Magenta and Roland Thévenin's Domaine du Moulin aux Moines. There are worthy wines to be found amongst growers here, treading, as always, with care. The shipper Leroy is based in Auxey.

St-Romain: There are more white wines than red here, due to the higher location, and careful choice can produce some fine examples. Roland Thévinin is well-known here, under the Domaine du Château de Puligny-Montrachet label.

St-Aubin: Red wines, and about half as much white are produced here. Unlike St-Romain, there are some Premiers Crus. The *négociant* Raoul Clerget has his headquarters in St-Aubin, and the best-known growth is Frionnes. Bernard Morey and Hubert Lamy are recommended.

Meursault: To many, Meursault is archetypal Côte de Beaune white wine, rich, fat and with a glorious, full-blown Chardonnay nose and generous colour. The top Premiers Crus are Les Perrières, Les Charmes and Genevrières, followed by Poruzot and La Goutte-d'Or. There are some big owners in Meursault, as well as the multitude of small growers evident in every Burgundian commune – beware those with land down in the plain near the N74 road. This will either be marketed by the grower himself or sold to a shipper as straight village Meursault, and it will be a disappointment. The firm of Ropiteau have important holdings in Meursault, as do Patriarche, who now own the Château de Meursault. They produce wines of high repute. The Domaine des Comtes Lafon makes remarkable Meursault-Perrières and the less expensive Clos de la Barre – the 1969 of the latter was wonderful in 1980. Other top producers are the Domaine Jacques Prieur, Bernard Michelot, Domaine Joseph Matrot, Darnat, Guy Roulot and Raymond Javillier. J.P. Gauffroy has excellent Les Poruzots under the Selection Jean Germain label, and one of the greatest Meursaults I have drunk for sheer balance and finesse (rather than obvious lushness) was the Genevrières 1973 from Jean Monnier, drunk in 1979. Naturally enough, Louis

Latour and Bouchard Père both produce classic Meursaults, wines with a long finish and almost a lanolin texture. There are also the Meursault-Blagny vineyards, the best being La Pièce-sous-le-Bois and Sous le Dos d'Ane. These whites are very like Meursault, sometimes a bit firmer. Ampeau is a good grower.

Puligny-Montrachet: The greatest vineyards and *appellations* of this commune are on the border with Puligny-Montrachet and Chassagne-Montrachet. The great Le Montrachet itself has its seven and a half hectares divided between the two communes, and although the direction of the slope changes slightly, one tends to believe that the differences in Le Montrachet are more due to the different owners. The main owners are the Marquis de Laguiche (the shipper Joseph Drouhin distributes this), the Domaine Baron Thénard (distributed by the shippers Remoissenet), and Bouchard Père et Fils. Other owners are the Domaine Jacques Prieur, the Domaine de la Romanée-Conti (their 1971 is magnificent), the Domaine René Fleurot and Comte Lafon. Montrachet should never be drunk too young – it cannot begin to show its incredible breed and layers of taste until eight to ten years of age.

Bâtard-Montrachet is also divided between the two communes, and it can rival Le Montrachet for sheer splendour, in the right hands. These can be the hands working at. the Domaine Leflaive, or Delagrange-Bachelet (Blain-Gagnard), Albert Morey or the Domaine Ramonet-Prudhon. I remember some magnificent wines from Jean-Nöel Gagnard in the 1960s, wines that were so full of body and flavours that they replaced a meal. The 1976 Bâtard from Jadot is good. Chevalier-Montrachet, which lies completely in Puligny, is about the same size as Le Montrachet, and again can rival it for quality at its peak. It might not have quite the same power as Le Montrachet. Bouchard Père own the greater part here, but there is also Leflaive, Louis Jadot, Louis Latour. A Domaine Jacques Prieur Chevalier 1970, drunk in 1980, was superb. There is also Criots-Bâtard-Montrachet and Bienvenues-Bâtard-Montrachet, with similar owners. As one is paying so much for these wines, it is best to go for the owners with the very best credentials.

The commune of Puligny-Montrachet has some excellent Premiers Crus, amongst which Le Cailleret, Les Combettes, Les Pucelles and Les Folatières. Logically enough, those vineyards near the Montrachet family have some of their characteristics (Le Cailleret, Les Pucelles, Folatières and Clavoillons), while Champ Canet, Les Combettes and Les Referts are nearer Meursault, and are perhaps more mellow – commune Puligny wines in youth often have more 'attack' than young Meursaults, which are soft sooner. The top Premiers Crus can, and should, be slightly austere in extreme youth, and as they become less 'green', they develop richness and complexity. Names to trust are Leflaive, Etienne Sauzet, Domaine du Duc de Magenta, Roland Thévenin's Domaine du Château de Puligny-Montrachet, Joseph Drouhin, Bouchard Père, Louis Latour, Pierre Matrot and Domaine J. Pascal.

Chassagne-Montrachet: Producing both red and white wines, at *village* level, they often reach readiness for drinking quicker than the next-door commune. However, the red wines from the Premiers Crus of Clos-St-Jean, Morgeot, Abbaye-de-Morgeot and La Boudriotte need some years in bottle to show their full interest. The top white wines come from Cailleret and Les Ruchottes, but some of the red wine Premiers Crus make fine white too. The Beaune shippers, the de Marcilly family, make excellent red Clos-St-Jean, of the traditional, full, rich kind much loved in the United Kingdom. Indeed, many of their wines have this quality, with rich Pinot Noir nose and influence of oak. They have small holdings also in Beaune and Gevrey Chambertin, and use these wines as a base for excellent *appellation* Bourgogne blends going under the names of Marcilly Première and Marcilly Réservé which always give very good value. Albert Morey, Delagrange-Bachelet, André Ramonet, Domaine du Duc de Magenta and the Château de la Maltroye (Marcel Picard) are names to trust. Bachelet-Ramonet's Caillerets is excellent.

Santenay: Virtually all the wines produced are red, and they can have a nice, fruity, earthy character about them. This is less attractive when the wines are thin but the best keep and have great flavour. The top Premiers Crus are Les Gravières, Clos-de-Tavannes and La Comme, followed by Maladière. The domain that stands out is that of La Pousse d'Or and the manager, Gérard Potel, must be congratulated on the consistent fine quality of his wines. The Clos Tavannes 1976 has a deep, soft Côte de Beaune nose (and even the Côtes can be difficult to tell apart in the hands of some houses!), velvet fruit, youthful attack and a lovely earthy finish. Another 1976, Château de la Charrière, Gravières, from the Domaine Jean Girardin, greatly impressed for its balance and taste of violets. There are also the domains of Hervé Olivier Mestre, Lequin-Roussot, Roux and Prieur-Brunet, and the wines of the *négociant* Prosper Maufoux.

Bourgogne Hautes-Côtes de Beaune: The *appellation* of Bourgogne Hautes-Côtes de Beaune can be used by twenty villages in the Arrière-Côtes. In an effort to revive the area, Pinot Noir and Chardonnay have been planted to augment the Aligoté and Gamay, and the wine is often made at the Cave Coopérative des Hautes-Côtes at Beaune. The quality has reached a most acceptable standard. There are individual domains where the owners sell their own wine, such as Jean Joliot at Nantoux and the Domaine Louis Jacob of Echevronne. The Château Mandelot wines are vinified and distributed by Bouchard Père. These areas tucked away in the hills do need sun to produce wines of charm and interest, but under the best circumstances, it is one of the best value bottles of Bourgogne one can buy.

COTE CHALONNAISE

The 1970s saw a great revival of interest in the wines of the Côte Chalonnaise, an interest which is solidly based and sure to continue and grow. It is unlikely that the region will ever regain the size of pre-phylloxera days, but replanting has been steady and well thought out. In general, the red wines can have quite an earthy flavour, strongly marked by the region (the locals often say of a wine, *il terroite*), with the weight varying with the actual *appellation*. The whites can be light and delicate, elegant rather than full and fat in the Côte de Beaune sense. On the whole, one would not keep Côte Chalonnaise wines as long as their counterparts on the Côte d'Or. The vineyards are not all along a clear slope, or Côte, but they tend to cluster round the four *appellation* villages of Rully, Mercurey, Givry and Montagny, and break out in patches where the site is particularly advantageous. There has been considerable new planting in the area during the 1970s, which shows the confidence that both big shippers and small growers have in the region. Apart from the four main *appellations* of the Côte Chalonnaise, the area is a good source of supply for Bourgogne Rouge and Bourgogne Blanc. The former is often relatively light in colour but full of flavour, and in this area will come from the Pinot Noir. Bourgogne Blanc will come from the Chardonnay.

Bourgogne Passetoutgrain: A deal of Bourgogne Passetoutgrain also comes from the Côte Chalonnaise. When made carefully by people who understand the different nature of the grape varieties (Passetoutgrain is a blend of Gamay and Pinot Noir, never less than a third of the latter), it can be very good, but too young, or badly blended, the marriage can be unhappy, with dominating acidity.

Rully: This first *appellation* of the Chalonnais region produces predominantly white wines of great finesse. They have delicacy and interest, and a clean, incisive taste. The oenologist and vineyard-owner, Jean-François Delorme, has done a great deal for the reputation of Rully wines, both white and red, and his modern cellars and equipment have kept pace with the growing new vineyards. His Rully-Varot and Rully La Chaume have great complexity and nutty finesse, and all wines from the Delorme Domaine de la Renarde inspire confidence. The wine-making emphasis is always on bringing out the fruit character of the grape and achieving balance, and bottling is done early. Jean-François Delorme owns about forty-two hectares at Rully (twenty hectares in Rully Blanc and twenty-two in Rully Rouge), including all Varot (eighteen hectares in one parcel), and parts of Monthelon, Les Cloux, La Fosse and Grésigny.

Rully is a great centre of Bourgogne Mousseux wines, and Crémant de Bourgogne, both of which must be made by the Champagne method. The crisp acidity of the Aligoté grape is needed with Pinot Noir, Chardonnay and Gamay. Some of the red wine is also turned into sparkling Burgundy by the Champagne method and, although decried by wine 'purists', can be extremely pleasant drinking. Delorme is a top name for 'sparklers'. The still wines from the Domaine de la Folie are admirable, and I have been impressed by their red Rully Clos de Bellecroix 1976 and 1978. Jean Coulon makes excellent Rully Blanc Grésigny and Pierre Cogny has very good red and white Rully.

Mercurey: Mercurey makes almost entirely red wine, and it is the most solid, definite of the reds of the Chalonnais. Those vineyards facing southeast and well-exposed can give wines of good colour, body and concentration. The production is large enough to have attracted Côte d'Or shippers, amongst them Faiveley, who has the Clos de Myglands, and Bouchard Aîné. The Protheau family own the Clos des Corvées, la Fauconnière, les Vellées and Clos l'Evêque, and also run a *négociant* business from the Château d'Etroyes. Another leading shipper, Antonin Rodet, owns the Château de Chamirey, and there is also the superb Mercurey les Crêts from de Suremain. The Mercurey Clos des Barraults of Michel Juillot maintains an excellent standard, and Voarick is a strong name in Mercurey. The other *climats* to look out for are Clos du Roi, Clos Voyen, Clos Marcilly, Clos des Fourneaux and Clos des Montaigus. Mercurey can keep well, but has a tendency to dry out if this is exaggerated, especially if the cask ageing was too long.

Givry: The wines from Givry are nearly all red, and can have a fruity delicacy, if not the body of Mercurey. I have admired the Givry Cellier aux Moines from the domain of Baron Thénard, as well as the almost floral, fruity Clos du Cellier aux Moines from Delorme. There is also Givry Clos St-Pierre from the Domaine Baron Thénard, distributed by Remoissenet, Clos Salomon and Clos St-Paul.

Montagny: The white wine from Montagny tends to be fuller than that from Rully, sometimes with more fat, but with less finesse and elegance. The shipper Louis Latour always chooses excellent *cuvées* in the region. The Cave Coopérative de Buxy, one of the communes within the *appellation*, has a wide range of wines, with varying qualities, as befits an establishment whose sales grew enormously in the 1970s. But good Bourgogne Rouge and Blanc, as well as Aligoté, can be found there together with the Montagny – the name can also be the Cave des Vignerons de Buxy.

The village of Bouzeron is renowned for its Aligoté and also for two excellent domains, Chanzy Frères and A. and P. de Villaine.

COTE MACONNAISE

The Mâconnais is a prolific wine region, dominated by the power of the cooperatives, and specializing in white wines on chalky soil from the Chardonnay grape. Some of this is pretty basic stuff, and some is quite delicious, but none is great. The red wine from the Gamay grape is more everyday, but well made it can produce very useful and reasonable drinking, and there has been a considerable improvement in the quality of Mâcon Rouge in recent years. The Cave Coopérative 'Les Vignerons de Mancey', for example, make their wines with great care. The Gamay grapes for the red are not crushed, and a semi-*macération carbonique* fermentation takes place. They also make a good Bourgogne Rouge from Pinot Noir which has some wood age. The area of the Mâconnais is very beautiful, with rolling hills, white cattle and Romanesque churches. In spite of the huge production of the Mâconnais, vineyards are often not very visible – but they are to be found between the lovely town of Tournus, what remains of the historic Cluny, and the riverside town of Mâcon. There are also areas of vines round Mancey and Chapaize. The cooperatives of the Mâconnais have strong links with *négociants* for white wines, selling a large part of their production to them. Louis Latour always offers superb Mâcon-Lugny les Genièvres, and Piat has very reliable Mâcon-Viré. Georges Duboeuf's Mâcon-Prissé is always full and interesting. Duboeuf makes excellent selections of white wine in the Mâconnais, including St-Véran and Pouilly-Fuissé.

Pouilly-Fuissé: The *appellation* of Pouilly-Fuissé reigns supreme in the area, and popularity has sometimes helped sell wine that was no more than ordinary. The villages of Pouilly, Fuissé (where you can find the superb Château Fuissé of Marcel Vincent and the more moderately priced wines of Joseph Corsin), Solutré, Vergisson and Chaintré are included in the *appellation*, and the weight of the wine depends on the exposition of the slopes (some really catch the sun, by now becoming more southerly than on the Côte d'Or) and the style of wine-making. Small growers still have a good deal of wood and oxidation can be the result of careless handling, while the top cooperatives are equipped to modern standards.

Pouilly-Loché and Pouilly-Vinzelles: Pouilly-Loché and Pouilly-Vinzelles are neighbouring *appellations* for which one does not have to pay so much – they can lack the finesse of the very best Pouilly-Fuissés, and have a slightly more earthy character about them, but in the right hands, they can be excellent wines. These *appellations* are not for keeping, but, as with all Chardonnay, drunk *en primeur* the wines lack any dimension to them. A few years of bottle age for this top category of Mâconnais wine can sometimes produce wines of more depth of flavour than would first appear.

St-Véran: The *appellation* of St-Véran was created in 1971 and, confusingly, some of the communes entitled to the name also make red Beaujolais, notably St-Amour, and I drink regularly good Beaujolais-Villages Domaine de la Citadelle from the village of Leynes, which is also entitled to call its white wines St-Véran. The village of St-Vérand is also within the *appellation* St-Véran. St-Véran wines usually mature slightly faster than Pouilly-Fuissé, but nevertheless, often show more complexity after two years than after one. The St-Véran Cuvée les Crais from M. Roger Tissier gives an indication of the chalky soil.

Mâcon Villages, Mâcon Supérieur, Mâcon and Pinot-Chardonnay-Mâcon: The *appellation* of Mâcon Villages, or Mâcon followed by the name of a village, is for white wines. Good examples are Mâcon-Clessé from the Domaine of Jean Thévenet, the Mâcon-Viré Clos du Chapitre of Dépagneux, and Joseph Drouhin's Mâcon-Villages Laforêt. Adrien Guichard's Mâcon-Villages is always good. The use of the words Mâcon followed by the village name and then Villages is for red wine, which is somewhat more earthy than Beaujolais, with less zingy Gamay fruit and almost a nuttier taste. Mâcon Supérieur is for red or white wines, and Mâcon for red, white and rosé. There is also the rather strange Pinot-Chardonnay-Mâcon which can be made of Pinot Blanc or Chardonnay, as can Mâcon itself, but it is nearly always Chardonnay, the rather sweet-soft tasting clone of the area.

BEAUJOLAIS

If there is one instantly recognized wine word in the world's vocabulary, this is it. It encompasses the good, the bad and the beautiful, and the wine-growers are some of the luckiest of the *métier*. They live in delightful, hilly countryside, they usually sell their wine within the year after it is made and usually there is plenty of it. There are some growers who do honour to their *métier*, others who are careless and greedy, and large establishments who take the product of these lax growers and 'arrange' it in their fashion. If you have once had 'good' Beaujolais, it is easy to know when you are not getting it.

The nine Beaujolais *crus*, or top growths, are all in the north of the area, in very hilly country of granitic origin. The Gamay Noir *à jus blanc* grape shows *race* or breed when planted on a granitic base, and this is not repeated when the soil becomes more chalky, for instance. Gamay grown on granite with clay topsoil also changes character with age, and can take on Pinot Noir characteristics that are quite astonishing. The nine Beaujolais *crus* can be declassified into Beaujolais Villages. It is less widely known that they can also be labelled Bourgogne Rouge, so not all the wines of this *appellation* will be made from Pinot Noir.

Moulin-à-Vent: Old Moulin-à-Vent can taste surprisingly like Côte d'Or wine. The soil has volcanic origins here, and a good deal of manganese has been traced in it. These mineral trace elements add to the complexity of the wine and its indubitable longevity. Moulin-à-Vent should have a deep colour, good backbone and a velvety texture if it is to last any time successfully. Wines to look out for are the Château du Moulin-à-Vent owned by the Bloud family, Château Portier, Les Carquelins and Château des Jacques.

Morgon: Morgon produces the most robust of the nine Beaujolais *crus*, often showing the most closed at the outset, big and beefy, and opening out with some years in bottle and showing individuality and strength. The soil is almost schistous here, *roche pourrie* as it is known locally. The distinctive bouquet has created a verb in the area – *morgonner*. Apart from Brouilly, more wine is made in this *cru* than in any other. Jean Descombes, who has his vineyards on the Mont de Py, is a reputed grower, and the Château de Bellevue produces excellent wine.

St-Amour: St-Amour is a small *appellation*, right on the border in the north with the Mâconnais region. The wines are sprightly, fruity and delicate, needing sunny years, and at their best when two to three years old. The Château de St-Amour, which is commercialized through Piat, is worth looking for, as is the Domaine des Billards from Jean Loron. St-Amour can be the epitome of Beaujolais.

Juliénas: Nearby there is Juliénas, with its wonderful sturdy, purple fruit. This crushed-grapes character makes it delicious to drink young, but the fullness behind promises more. Here there is the Château de Juliénas owned by the Héritiers Condemine, les Capitans, the Clos des Poulettes of Paul Loron and the Domaine de Beauvernay sold by Piat.

Chénas: Chénas has an even smaller production than St-Amour and is not as well known as it should be. The wines repay keeping a few years and have a lot of character, though perhaps they lack the silkiness of Moulin-à-Vent. Château Bonnet, Domaine des Journets and Les Rougemonts are worth looking for.

Fleurie: Fleurie's great charm, generous fruit and extreme drinkability, combined with a picturesque name, make this *appellation* much sought-after. It lasts well, and is large enough to have made its mark in many countries. The Château de Fleurie is owned by Jean Loron, and there is also

La Chapelle des Bois and Clos de la Roilette.

Chiroubles: Chiroubles is the highest of the *crus*, perched up on dipping, rolling hills that often become sprinkled with snowflakes in winter. As befits the height, Chiroubles is light, airy, deliciously tempting, graceful wine. At early comparative tastings of all the *crus*, it often looks the prettiest youngest, while some of the bigger wines look more earth-bound and clumsy. The Domaine de Raousset and the Domaine Cheysson-les-Farges are important.

Côte de Brouilly and Brouilly: The wines of the Côte de Brouilly, high up on Mont Brouilly, are considered as slightly better than the far larger Brouilly. However, that is not to denigrate Brouilly, which produces 'textbook' Beaujolais, fruity, giving and mouth-filling. They are delicious from the outset, while some Côte de Brouilly wines will build up a bit more character with a year or two more in bottle. The Château Thivin is well respected in Côte de Brouilly, and the Château de Pierreux and Château de la Chaize in Brouilly. Bouchard Père's Domaine de Saburin is also worth looking for.

Cooperatives play a very important part in the whole of Beaujolais, including the area of the *crus* in the north. One singles out particularly the Cave Coopérative de Fleurie (which makes excellent Morgon, Moulin-à-Vent, and Chiroubles, as well as Fleurie), not only because it is run by a wonderful, old lady, Mlle Chabert, with whom I have had the pleasure of sitting on a tasting panel. The cooperatives of both Chénas (which also has Moulin-à-Vent) and Juliénas (which also has St-Amour) must also be mentioned.

At Corcelles-en-Beaujolais there is an excellent *groupement* of growers called the Eventail de Vignerons Producteurs. The forty members make their wine themselves, and only send it to the Eventail cellars for bottling. Many of the members are in the *crus*, others make Beaujolais Villages, and there is also Pouilly Fuissé, St-Véran and Mâcon. Each grower's wine is kept apart and labelled differently and, together with the wines of Duboeuf, they tend to sweep the board at the Concours of Paris and Mâcon. The Brouilly, and Côte de Brouilly of Lucien and Robert Verger, the Morgon le Clachet of M. Brun, the Juliénas of M. Monnet and M. Pelletier, the Chiroubles of M. Passot and M. Savoye, the St-Amour of M. Patissier, the Chénas Château de Chénas, the Fleurie Domaine Montgenas, and the Moulin à Vent of the Héretiers Finaz-Devillaine are just the flagships of a group of growers who really bring out the particular characteristics of each Beaujolais *cru*. The Eventail also has a range of individual Beaujolais Villages, such as the Vignoble de Chêne.

Beaujolais: Beaujolais as an *appellation*, or what is sometimes called Beaujolais *tout court*, can be red, white or rosé; a tiny amount of white Beaujolais is produced in the north, on the borders of the Mâconnais. The Beaujolais Blanc of Louis Jadot is well-known, as is the Château de Loyse of Thorin. The red is mostly produced in the south of the region, above Lyon and south of Villefranche and is for drinking quickly and young; it is in this category that one can find some horrid, thin, acid examples, or some equally noxious, over-chaptalized (in spite of the controls that grow stricter), heavy brew. If the wine is very young, in a good café or bar in Lyon or Paris, the chances are that youthful charm will disguise faults, but in the year following the vintage, if you want to drink straight Beaujolais, it is better to go for a reputable and well-tried shipper's wine. The lightest wines are those suitable for making Beaujolais Nouveau, the fly-by-night wine released normally on November 15 after the vintage. Obviously, very careful vinification must take place if the wine is to be palatable, with the most modern techniques of stabilization. Wines from acid years rarely make good Nouveau, and it is equally tragic when the current fashion 'creams off' some would-be fine, more serious wines for instant transformation into Nouveau. There is also Beaujolais Supérieur, which just means 1 per cent more of alcohol – but it is rarely used, and in fact, both *appellations* always sell their wines at more than the minimum level required.

Beaujolais Villages: Beaujolais Villages is an *appellation* made up of over forty communes who have the right to use it, some in the north on the border of the Mâconnais in the *département* of Saône-et-Loire, and the majority in the *département* of the Rhône which is, confusingly, still in the north of the Beaujolais region. Romanèche-Thorins is the most important county town. When buying wine outside the area, and without a clear recommendation, it is always safer to go for Beaujolais Villages rather than just plain Beaujolais.

Côteaux du Lyonnais: The wines from this small area to the south of Villefranche-sur-Saône and around Lyon in the Rhône department were elevated to *appellation contrôlée* status in 1984. Over ninety-five per cent of the wines are red and rosé made from the Gamay, while the whites come from the Chardonnay, Aligoté or Melon de Bourgogne. A mere 10,000 hectolitres are produced each year.

The serried ranks of Beaujolais-Mâconnais *négociants* must be led by Georges Duboeuf, who has done so much for the area as a whole. Loron and Dépagneux are also highly respected, as are Beaudet, Fessy Gobet, Chanet, Piat, Trenel and Louis Tête. Mommessin, Pasquier-Des-vignes, Ferraud, Sapin, Thorin, Aujoux and David & Foillard are other names. The Côte d'Or *négociants* of Louis Latour, Joseph Drouhin, Bouchard Père and Louis Jadot, among others, also sell honourable Beaujolais. A final plea for Beaujolais – drink it cool, but not too chilled. And if you ever come across an old Moulin-à-Vent or Morgon, treat it as you would a wine from the Côte d'Or.

Burgundy Shippers

The *négociants* form a very important part of the commercial activity of this great wine region. They buy in wine, mature it and prepare it for sale; a few now also buy in grapes, or must, and vinify themselves. Some of them also own vineyards (Bouchard Père is the largest domain of Grand and Premier Cru vineyards on the Côte d'Or). Undoubtedly, in the current climate of many growers bottling their own wines, those *négociants* with a solid proportion of their own vineyards are better placed. At the head of a list of important, highly reputable *négociants* would be Louis Latour, Bouchard Père et Fils, Joseph Drouhin and Louis Jadot, the latter now American-owned, although the vineyards remain the property of the Jadot family. Many good wines can be found amongst the following:

Bouchard Ainé   Leroy
Champy   Marcilly
Chanson   Remoissenet
Clerget   Ropiteau
Delaunay   Thévenin
Faiveley

Others include:
Belin   Labouré-Roi
Bichot   La Reine Pédauque
Boisseaux-Estivant   Les Fils de Marcel
Boisset   Quancard
Bruck   Lupé-Cholet
Chauvenet   Maufoux/Marcel Amance
Cruse Hasenklever   Moillard
Doudet-Naudin   Morey
Dufouleur   Morin
Geisweiler   Morot
Henri de Villamont   Naigeon-Chauveau
Héritier-Guyot   Patriarche
Jaboulet-Vercherre   Ponnelle
Jaffelin   Poulet
Labouré-Gontard (sparkling wines)   Viénot

On the Côte Chalonnaise, the *négociant* that stands out is André Delorme (or Delorme-Meulien). There are also Antonin Rodet, Chandesais, Picard, and Protheau.

Burgundy Vintages
Vintages really matter in Burgundy, logically enough for a wine-producing area not so far from the northern limit for growing vines successfully. Burgundians have to cope fairly regularly with both rain and hail, and often have to play a 'dicing with death' game with those last few days before the

151

vintage in order to gain maximum ripeness. A general rule is that poor red wine vintages can make better white wines – warmth at the last moment is not quite so vital for white grapes as for red. As far as older vintages are concerned, only top wines (Grand and perhaps Premier Cru standard) from impeccable growers are relevant.

1945: Very good, small vintage. They still look big.

1947: The extreme heat made the fermentations difficult to handle, and some wines inevitably 'went over the top'. The best have lasted beautifully.

1948: Some great wines have lasted well to start the 1980s.

1949: Some excellent 'finds' still with this vintage.

1950: Whites very good, reds not.

1952: Good wines, but they cannot last much longer. Excellent whites.

1953: These wines had the balance to last, and many have. Very good whites.

1955: Wines with style and character. Some are still showing well – excellent whites.

1957: Wines with good body and flavour which have generally lasted well.

1959: Generous, popular wines. The heat made the acidities low, so they will not go on improving. Can be lush. Whites mostly too old now.

1961: Very good wines indeed, and still tasting marvellous. Small crop.

1962: Again, very good wines, sometimes with less concentration, but more acidity balance, than the 1961s. Still excellent. Wonderful whites.

1963: Poor – it is rare to find something drinkable now.

1964: Some very good sturdy bottles, most of them at their prime. This applies to white and red.

1965: Best forgotten.

1966: A generous vintage, from all points of view. Lovely fruit and delicious drinking. Elegant, stylish whites.

1967: Very mixed vintage – the best have elegance, but many reds were over-chaptalized and now look totally out of balance and brown. Whites often have a good deal of breed.

1968: The reds were a write-off, but a few whites were drinkable.

1969: A simply superb vintage – the only complaint is the small size! The reds have great nerve, backbone, and fruit upheld by good acidity. Will last exceptionally well – the vintage to show off wines with *race* and breed. The whites are splendid.

1970: A big vintage of soft, fruity, thoroughly attractive wines. Both reds and whites looked lovely when compartively young, and at ten years old they are mostly at their apogee.

1971: An extremely ripe vintage, producing wines of great concentration and richness. Some were too ripe for balance and lack complete harmony. They are heady wines, intoxicating at their best, sometimes too top-heavy to be 'classic'. The low acidity sometimes causes the reds to brown earlier than would be expected. The whites are very full-blown. There were patches of hail on the Côte d'Or.

1972: The wines have developed beautifully, those rather green and acid reds softening and gaining great character in bottle. One almost never makes a bad buy with a 1972 red now. The whites had unpleasant acidity when young, but the best made now look more in balance, even if they lack luscious fruit.

1973: Very large vintage, producing light wines of charm and fruit. If they were not too chaptalized, they retained that charm. Low natural acidity in the whites, but delicious young drinking.

1974: Good colour reds, often quite straightforward and dependable, but lacking any charm or great individuality. The whites are more interesting.

1975: Rot ruined this vintage, and it is rare to find a red wine free from taint. Some presentable whites, but do not keep them.

1976: An abnormal year producing abnormal wines for Burgundy. The reds are extremely tannic, and this often envelops all the fruit. The top wines need ten years or more to show their paces, but their exact evolution is difficult to predict. There is a thick taste about them which is atypical

Burgundy. The whites were rich and low in acidity, and most are not lasting too well.

1977: A 'miracle' vintage, saved by the fine September weather. The reds are light and are tending to taste a bit dry as they age. The whites are better, and have some have style.

1978: An exceptionally classy vintage, better balanced than either 1971 or 1976. Lovely fruit, with excellent backbone behind. The wines will mature in great style, and both whites and reds need time for their full complexity to emerge. It is rare to get concentration like this in Burgundy.

1979: A large vintage. The wines have charm and fruit and are easily accessible. Their suppleness means that they are suitable for relatively early drinking and these are bottles which give much pleasure. The whites share these qualities and even the top wines are lovely at six years old.

1980: Variable, depending on whether the grower treated against rot. But the best domains have made some remarkably good wines, particularly on the Côte de Nuits. They are also wines which have real concentration, as the crop was not large. The whites do not repay keeping, but there are good bottles.

1981: Hail was a scourge in this vintage, and many wines have this taint. There is a definite taste of dryness on the finish, and there is little evidence that this is a vintage to follow. In any case, the small quantity often precludes this. Some wines may improve with keeping, but choose carefully. Good Beaujolais. A small crop of whites, some of which will mature well.

1982: A record crop, and in many cases, the Pinot Noir overproduced, resulting in weak wines. Where this was avoided, there are some very good wines, but even the best are probably destined for early to mid-term drinking. The style is mostly light and easy, rather than concentrated. Some delicious whites, for early drinking.

1983: An outstanding vintage, easily the best since 1978, in spite of some rot, and hail in parts of the Côte de Nuits. The wines are powerful and concentrated, with a good deal of tannin, although not of the massive sort seen in the 1976s. These are really wines to lay down, and defy those who say that modern Burgundy is 'too light'. Excellent Beaujolais, and the Côte Chalonnaise shines. The whites are also very good indeed, if a trifle over-alcoholic.

1984: Luckily, the cold weather in September prevented the spread of rot, but the grapes did lack sugar, resulting in naturally low degrees. Skilful chaptalization was necessary, but when this is well done, the resulting wines are clean and fruity. In Beaujolais, the Crus are much better than just plain Villages. The whites have a fruity projection and will make really pleasant drinking.

5 *Chablis*

Chablis could be considered as an island, almost equidistant between Paris and Dijon, and is in the *département* of the Yonne. 2,000 hectares of vines produce white wines with a quality spectrum ranging from the banal to the very great. The secret to the greatness is the combination of Kimmeridgian clay soil and Chardonnay, and where this does not exist, the wines are often run-of-the-mill. It is regrettable that in 1976 the area of Chablis was considerably enlarged, with plantings on soil that was not pure Kimmeridgian being accepted as *appellation contrôlée* Chablis. These new plantings should never have been elevated beyond the status of Petit Chablis, which is itself unfortunate as a name (created in 1944, while the Chablis *appellation* area was delimited in 1938) as the wine bears little relation to the aristocratic real thing. Apart from the difference in soil type, planting on the plain cannot rival that on the slopes.

The most marked slopes are those of the seven Grands Crus, over the little Serein river from the sleepy town of Chablis, and regally facing south and southwest. The Premier Cru vineyards are scattered on both sides of the river, in villages such as Fyé, Fleys, Poinchy, Fontenay, Maligny, Milly, Beine and Chichée. At one time, it looked as if Chablis might cease to exist as a vineyard area. The first blow was phylloxera. Then the exposed, northern aspect of the viticultural region attracted remorseless frosts in spring, and time after time whole crops were ruined, with every little valley a prime target area. However, during the 1960s, effective methods of combating frost were developed, starting with smoking pots amongst the vines to raise the air temperature, with gas, oil and irrigation systems following. In the 1970s, with more predictable crops, relatively speaking, and the growing export demand in the United States and in Britain for dry white wine, the region has come into its own. Smaller crops inevitably lead to steep price increases, with market resistance hardening as a result (1978 was an example of this), but Chablis has a much-loved place in the English-speaking world.

The Chardonnay grape is called the Beaunois at Chablis, and it thrives on the sub-soil of Kimmeridgian clay, mixed with chalky and stony matter. The chalk element helps warm up the soil. This combination is ideal for the production of white wine, and it reappears north of Chablis in the valleys of Bar-sur-Seine and Bar-sur-Aube which produce Champagne, and at Pouilly-sur-Loire and Sancerre, here combined with the Sauvignon grape. Kimmeridgian clay is also found in Hampshire, and English vineyards growing white vines have taken advantage of it.

The vines are trained low on wires, so that the grapes can benefit at night from the warmth that the soil can pick up in the day during the ripening period. Traditionally, Chablis growers often left their vineyard land fallow (or planted with a fodder crop like lucerne) for up to fifteen years after pulling out old vines and before replanting, but chemical disinfectants have obviously shortened the time. The greatest change in vinification at Chablis over the last decade is the diminishing use of wood as a material for keeping wine. Small, peasant growers still have the traditional Chablis *feuillettes* which hold 132 litres, but many cellars have gone over to glass-lined vats or stainless steel. Bottling is also now much earlier, with Chablis and Premier Cru Chablis normally being bottled in the early spring after the vintage, and Grand Cru Chablis a few months later. All this has made for wines that are lighter in colour than, say, twenty years ago, and the cold, controlled fermentations have led to delicate bouquet and finesse. Development is now necessary in the bottle for the Grands and Premiers Crus, as they would have had little or no oxidation in the maturing process before bottling.

Grands Crus: The seven Grands Crus, starting upstream and going downstream, are: Blanchot, Les Clos, Valmur,

Grenouille, Vaudésir, Les Preuses, and Bougros. Sometimes you will see Blanchots, Vaudésirs and Grenouilles, but the spellings are interchangeable. The name of Moutonne was given separate identification in 1951, and is made up of parcels in Vaudésir and Preuses. All the Grands Crus are within the commune of Chablis, except for Blanchot which is in that of Fyé. Les Clos is the largest of the Grand Crus, and sometimes the one that requires the most bottle age to open out fully, but, as always, this depends on individual wine-making methods.

Premiers Crus: Originally, there were about twenty-five Premiers Crus, but these have been amalgamated to form a dozen or so that are used regularly. If two Premier Cru wines are blended, only Chablis Premier Cru appears on the label. The main Premiers Crus are: Monts de Milieu; Montée de Tonnerre; Fourchaume (or Fourchaumes); Vaillons; Montmains; Mélinots; Côte de Léchet; Beauroy; Vaucoupin; Vosgros; Les Fourneaux; Vaulorent; Les Forêts; Beugnons; and Les Lys.

In poor vintages, the difference between Grand and Premier Cru is small. However, in good vintages, and unbelievably so in great vintages, there is a large gap between Premier and Grand Cru. Perhaps the most astounding Premiers Crus I have drunk have been from Fourchaume, combining finesse with great flavour, but the *cru* is extensive and there are favoured parts, especially on mid-slope. Vaillons can produce excellent wine (although always it should be remembered that Premier Cru Chablis does not last as long or as superbly as Grand Cru Chablis), and Montée de Tonnerre and Vaulorent are neighbours of the Grands Crus, although the vineyard is not contiguous in either case.

Chablis: This is the wine to drink while biding one's time for the Premiers and Grands Crus! When young, it should have a good acidity (otherwise it will rapidly become 'flabby'), a green-straw colour, and a certain 'flinty' attack. Often it needs a little time in the glass for the nose to come out. Sometimes, Premier Cru wine is declassified into Chablis – if Chablis itself is declassified for some reason, it becomes

Bourgogne (if the wine has a minimum of 10.5 per cent alcohol) and Bourgogne Grand Ordinaire – an *appellation* which is hardly sold on the export markets, but has its place in France. Villages such as Beine, Chemilly and Béru are important.

Petit Chablis: A simple *appellation*, with no pretences – or it should not have. The wine should be drunk within a year or two of being made. Villages such as Maligny, Lignorelles, La Chapelle-Vaupelteigne and Villy are known for their Petit Chablis. However, it is being phased out.

Some Wines and their Wine-makers

TESTUT

Some of my greatest *souvenirs chablisiens* have been wines from the Testut family. The Société Testut Frères now produce wines from fifteen hectares and young Philippe Testut is in charge of vinification. He is a most careful wine-maker, who has become convinced that no wood-ageing at all can lead to wines with a short finish. The 1979 Fourchaumes, under Philippe Testut's own label, was superb and the wines of the 1980s look even better. The family also own a part of Grenouille.

JEAN DURUP

The biggest private domain in Chablis is that of Jean Durup at Maligny. Up to 1973, the wine was sold in bulk to *négociants*, but the bottle sales have greatly increased, as elsewhere in Chablis. Most of the wine is plain Chablis, and the standard is high. Various domain names are used, such as Domaine de l'Eglantière, Domaine de la Paulière and Domaine des Valéry. The Premiers Crus include Montée de Tonnerre, Montmain, Fourchaume and Côte de Léchet.

LOUIS MICHEL

The Chablis of Louis Michel are always excellent. M.

Michel owns eighteen hectares, of which two are Chablis, two and a half are Grand Cru and all the rest is Premier Cru – about thirteen and a half hectares. The 1978 vintage was splendid and in the 1980s the standard remains as high.

ALBERT PIC

The *négociants* Albert Pic (who are also Régnard) vinify extremely well. All the wine sold by Albert Pic is bought as grape juice from growers with whom they have long-standing contracts, and the whole process, from fermentation to bottling, is personally supervised by M. Michel Rémon, the head of the firm. Of the total 60,000 hectolitres produced by the Chablis vineyards in an average year, Albert Pic are responsible for 8,000 hectolitres, or 13 per cent of the total. Of an excellent range of 1976 wines, I particularly liked a Côte de Léchet and a Montée de Tonnerre, and the 1979 Fourchaume showed style. Régnard has produced excellent Beugnons.

RENE DAUVISSAT

A grower who makes superb wine is René Dauvissat, who usually finishes his wines in *feuillettes*, giving them richness and complexity, and bottles some as late as the November after the vintage. Because of the influence of wood, Dauvissat's wines often have more colour than others. The Grand Cru Les Clos 1973 was easily one of the best of this vintage, and the 1973 Premier Cru 'La Forest' was equally fine. Both the 1983s and 1984s show the talent of M. Dauvissat.

Other Producers

The Domaine Laroche wines can be very good, as well as the Domaine la Jouchère, and they are marketed by the *négociants* Bacheroy-Josselin; old labels show the name of Dupressoir. These *négociants* specialize in a variety of Yonne wines. A winemaker whose wines I have often admired is William Fèvre, of the Domaine de la Maladière. He made an excellent 1970 Montée de Tonnerre, and also has Grand Cru

Les Preuses and Premier Cru Vaulorent, amongst other good things. His 1984s are impressive. Moreau is now a huge firm of *négociants*, but with domain wines, which include Les Clos and Vaillons. Forceful marketing in North America also includes the sale of white *vin de table*. Long-Depaquit is a respected name in Chablis – it is now owned by the Beaune *négociants* Albert Bichot. They are the sole proprietors of the 2.35 hectare enclave of Moutonne. Simonnet-Febvre are well-established *négociants* (for all the wines of the Yonne) as are Lamblin, *négociants* at the Château de Milly. The Domaine Robert Vocoret has a totally deserved reputation, producing excellent wines from *crus* such as Les Clos, Blanchot, Valmur and La Forêt. Other growers of note are Louis Pinson, Jacques Philippon, René Rey, Alain Geoffroy, Servin, Raveneau, Rottiers, Defaix and Gérard Tremblay.

The cooperative at Chablis is called La Chablisienne, and its *adhérents*, or members, own in the Grands Crus, Premiers Crus and in the straight Chablis and Petit Chablis area. In the last decade, quality has risen to a good general standard. However, as at all Caves Coopératives, there are *cuvées* and *cuvées*, and the buyer should choose carefully. Much wine is still sold in bulk to *négociants* in Beaune and elsewhere, but a new, greatly improved bottling line has increased the tendency to bottle *sur place*. The cooperative manager is Jean-Michel Tucki, and he has encouraged the extended bottlings of Grands and Premiers Crus – in Grand Cru, the cooperative has members who bought parcels of Grenouille from the Crédit Agricole when the Testut family sold some of their estate to the bank, and there is also a good part of Les Preuses, together with Fourchaume in Premier Cru.

Other Wines of the Yonne

A certain amount of red and white Bourgogne is produced in the Yonne, as well as Bourgogne Grand Ordinaire. Additional grape varieties are allowed in this *département* – the César and the Tressot for red wines, which are on the decline, and the Sacy for the white (but not for Bourgogne Blanc). There is also good Aligoté in the Yonne, often suitable for making sparkling wines, when mixed with the Chardonnay, César or Tressot. I have very much liked still Bourgogne Aligoté de St-Bris from Robert Defrance, a grower in St-Bris-le-Vineux, near Auxerre. There is also a small amount of Bourgogne Passetoutgrain from Pinot Noir and Gamay.

There are two good Bourgogne Rouges in the Yonne, at Irancy and at Coulanges-la-Vineuse. An Irancy would be labelled, Bourgogne-Irancy Appellation Bourgogne Contrôlée. These wines can be a bit acid when young, but soften in bottle. A good Bourgogne-Irancy is made by Cyprien Vincent, a grower at Irancy, and Simonnet-Febvre has Bourgogne-Irancy Côte de Palotte. These villages are really Burgundy, with grey stone and steep roofs and wood-smoke curling along the village street. Tonnerre and Joigny also produce local wines, classic Pinot Noir and Chardonnay near the former, and an unusual *vin gris* from Joigny. The village of Epineuil has both *vin gris* and solid red. Proximity to Paris means that the wine is quickly bought by the buyer at the door. In 1974, a new VDQS was created at St-Bris-le-Vineux – Sauvignon de St-Bris. Obviously, the Sauvignon gives a more Loire-like taste than a Burgundian, but the wine is very quaffable. Jean-Louis Bersan is a reliable grower at St-Bris itself. The other communes making this wine are Chitry, Irancy and Vincelottes.

Chablis Vintages
Vintages in the region of Chablis do not always correspond with those on the Côte de Beaune; the most glaring example being 1975, which was very good indeed in Chablis, and only of medium quality (when rot was avoided) for the white wines of the Côte. Great old vintages of Chablis would include 1947, 1949, 1953, 1955, 1959, 1961, 1962 and 1964, but the oldest here would only represent academic interest, although Grands Crus of the 1960s can sometimes give one a splendid surprise.

1966: Elegant and with a lovely bouquet when at their peak – almost all have passed this stage.

1967: There were some very good wines, but they could be risky now.

1968: Very slight at the time, and now only history.

1969: Big, powerful, ripe wines – some have gone 'over the top'.

1970: Really attractive, but very soft, and most now show age.

1971: A classic vintage, great body and flavour. The greatest live on into beautiful maturity.

1972: Mostly acid and harsh. A few improved in bottle, especially the top *crus*.

1973: A very tempting, delicious vintage, abundant, and with little Chablis acidity, even in youth. Therefore, most should have been drunk relatively young, but a few had more 'bite' to them and are ageing beautifully.

1974: Very inhospitable when young, but took on some character and more fruit when in the bottle.

1975: Really well-balanced wines that had all the ingredients – easily the best vintage since 1971. The great wines have real breed.

1976: Wines that are very 'fat' for the region, but the best have the composition to make mature bottles. Rich and luscious, but not as blowsy as some on the Côte de Beaune. The Grands Crus with bottle age will fool some into thinking of Puligny!

1977: Very honourable wines, with some finesse and length when the initial acidity softened out.

1978: Small vintage, but very good indeed, with wines of great flavour and individuality, depth and harmony. It is a pity to drink the Premiers and Grands Crus in the early 1980s. Splendid wines. Unfortunately, they were scarce and expensive – one producer said he got forty-five hectolitres to the hectare in 1978, and sixty-five hectolitres in 1979.

1979: A very large vintage, giving wines of immense attraction and charm. They have lovely fruit, but are soft and very developed at six years of age. Drink well before the 1978s.

1980: Small quantity. Quality much better than expected, with good acidity which has kept the wines fresh and young.

The top wines will go on developing.

1981: A tragically small vintage, but the wines that survived are full of flavour and character and will keep very well.

1982: A very large vintage, giving ripe grapes, high in sugar but rather low in acidity. The wines are delicious, fruity and attractive, and probably the top wines will have more staying power than the 1979s.

1983: Another large vintage, with some rot in the lesser areas, but superb Grands Crus. The wines all have splendid balance, with fruit, acidity and depth of flavour. No one should be without these.

1984: Here, the problem is more of quantity than quality, with 30 per cent less made than in 1983. There was some rot, but where this was avoided, the results are good and the wines have bouquet and a pleasant 'nervosité' which is very Chablis in style. Only a few have excess alcohol.

Depending on the character of the year, Premiers Crus taste delicious when between three and six years old, the Grands Crus between six and ten, and exceptionally, and when there is body and good acidity, long after that. Essentially, when one thinks of the crisp Chablis taste, the wine to go with oysters, one is imagining a straight Chablis or a Premier Cru – in years of any stature, Grand Cru Chablis is a different wine altogether – rich, complex and mysterious.

6 Champagne

This wonderful description of Champagne was written by André Simon, and we maintained it in the Second Edition of Wines of the World since so much of the material is still applicable today. Where there are changes, they have been described by the author of this book in Part II of the chapter on Champagne.

Champagne is, today, the festive wine *par excellence*, the most lively and one of the most expensive of quality wines, a joy and a luxury. But it was not ever thus. During many centuries the wines of the great Champagne province, stretching from Flanders in the north to Burgundy in the south, and from Lorraine in the east to the Ile de France in the west, were plain, still table wines, mostly red. Whether better or not than the wines of Bordeaux and Burgundy is anybody's guess, but they can certainly claim, without fear of contradiction, to have been French much longer. The wines of Champagne had no other competitors in Paris except those of Orléans and Touraine until the seventeenth century, when both Bordeaux and Burgundy also sent in their wines. The wines of Burgundy were the most dangerous competitors of the two; they were of the same grape, the Pinot, and of the same type as the wines of Champagne made today compared to the still table wines of Burgundy of the same vintages. There is, therefore, every reason to assume that the *vignerons* of Champagne sought to produce a wine that would be, if not better than, at least different from any wine that had ever come out of Burgundy, and eventually sparkling Champagne proved to be the right answer. This is where Dom Pérignon comes in.

Dom Pérignon was born at Sainte-Menehoulde in January, 1639. He renounced the world at the early age of nineteen and never regretted it. In 1668 he was appointed to the post of Cellarer of the Benedictine Abbey of Hautvillers, near Epernay, in the Champagne country. During forty-seven consecutive years, until the day of his death, in September, 1715, Dom Pérignon was in charge of the cellars and of the finances of the Abbey. He had a remarkably keen palate and knew how to use it to good purpose. He had great experience in all matters pertaining to viticulture and wine-making; he was hardworking and shrewd; he made better wines than had ever been made before at Hautvillers; he also made some sparkling wine. He was a good man, he loved the poor. So much, and very little more, is tolerably certain. Dom Pérignon has been hailed as the discoverer, inventor or creator of sparkling Champagne. He has been described as the wizard who first put the bubbles into Champagne. This is mere romance. Dom Pérignon did not discover, invent or create sparkling Champagne. He never claimed to have done so, nor did any of his contemporaries claim any such honour for him. He would certainly have greatly resented being hailed as the first to have put bubbles into Champagne, when neither he nor anybody else ever put bubbles into Champagne. The bubbles of sparkling Champagne are the same as the bubbles of bottled beer; they are tiny drops of liquid disturbed, chased and whipped by escaping carbon dioxide or carbonic acid gas. This carbon dioxide is an inevitable by-product of a most natural phenomenon known as fermentation.

Champagne is a cold-blooded northerner. It begins fermenting cheerfully enough, but thinks better of it and settles down to a long sleep during the winter months. In the following spring or early summer it wakes up and takes up its half-finished job where it had left it. There is still some of the original grape-juice sugar left to be fermented, and after their long winter rest the saccharomycetes will now get busy again and supply the necessary zymase. In fact, to make sure that they will have plenty to do, a little more sugar is added

l'Aisne

Champagne

Vesle Reims Ludes
(MONTAGNE DE REIMS) Chigny-les-Roses
Villedommange• Sacy •Sillery
Rilly-la-Montagne •Beaumont-sur-Vesle
VALLÉE DE Villers Allerand •Verzenay
LA MARNE) Champillon• •Villers-Marmery
Louvois• •Trépail
•Dizy •Mailly-Champagne
Hautvillers• •Ay• •Ambonnay
•Château Cumieres• •Cuis •Bouzy
Thierry Epernay Chouilly
Pierry Cramant Mareuil-sur-Ay
Monthelon• •Avize •Châlons-sur-Marne
Grauves •Oger
CÔTE DE BLANCS Le Mesnil-sur-Oger
Vertus

MARNE

Marne

Bar-sur-Aube
Seine
Bar-sur-Seine
AUBE

0   20 km   0   20 km

☐ ☐ Wine region   ▨▨▨ Main vineyard districts

to the wine, which is then bottled and corked securely
down. Exactly the same thing goes on within the bottle as in
the cask, but with this difference, that the carbonic acid gas
can no longer lose itself in the air; it remains in solution in
the wine, a most amenable prisoner so long as there is no
hope of escape. But once that gate of its prison, the cork, has
gone, it rushes out of the wine with joy, carrying along in its
haste thousands of dewdrops of wine; these are the
Champagne 'bubbles'. Dom Pérignon did not create
sparkling Champagne, but he did a great deal for its fame.
He made better wines than had been made in Champagne
before, both still and sparkling. The excellence of Dom
Pérignon's wines was due to the art with which he blended
the grapes from various vineyards. It was due also to the fact
that the Abbey of Hautvillers owned more vineyards and
received by way of tithes a greater variety of grapes than any
private vineyard owner.

Situated as they are so close to the northern latitude
beyond which grapes will grow but will hardly ever fully

ripen, the vineyards of Champagne are not blessed, nor were they blessed in the seventeenth century, with their full quota of sunshine year after year. They only enjoy a really fine summer now and again, and they produce then, but only then, grapes which give wonderful wine, wine truly deserving to be enjoyed and remembered as a vintage wine. Such years are the exception; other years, poorer years, years of acid, sun-starved wine, are the rule.

Judicious blending has brought fame and riches to the old province of Champagne. By saving wines of the better years and by finding out which blends of various vineyards will harmonize and give the best results, a very much higher level of average excellence has been reached and stocks of wines of fairly uniform quality have been built which have enabled the Champagne shippers to dispense for years and years to a suffering humanity that most exhilarating form of relaxation known throughout the civilized world as sparkling Champagne. Dom Pérignon was the first to show the way; he was not the first to make sparkling wine nor to use corks, but he was the first to show the people of Champagne what was the best use they could make of their wines. It is not only the wine-growers and wine shippers of Champagne who owe Dom Pérignon a deep debt of gratitude but all who appreciate the charm of sparkling Champagne, all those to whom Champagne has brought at some time that which is worth more than gold and silver: health and joy.

The Making of Sparkling Champagne
It is now time to consider in what way the making of sparkling Champagne differs from the methods for making a natural wine. Sparkling Champagne is a white wine made mostly from Pinot grapes that we call black, but they are not black; their juice is white and their skin is blue outside and red inside. To make a white wine from black grapes is not done by magic, but by care and skill. The colouring pigment of so-called black grapes is contained in the lining of their skin, so that grapes must be picked and brought to the press unbruised and without delay if their white juice is not to be dyed pink before they are pressed. In Champagne the grapes

are picked with care as soon as they are ripe, but before being sent to the *pressoir* to be crushed they are first examined at the roadside nearest the vineyard of their birth by a team of women, mostly elderly ones who have had their full share of back-breaking grape-picking when they were younger: they sit in a row with a wide osier tray at knee height before them; the grapes gathered by the pickers are brought to the women at the roadside in baskets, which are tipped over on to the osier tray. The women quickly take up and look over bunch after bunch, removing expertly with a pair of long pointed scissors all defective berries, if and when there happen to be any, either unripe or mildewy, or otherwise undesirable for any cause whatsoever. All such rejects are dropped in a refuse bin, while the bunches with none but sound and ripe grapes go into great osier baskets known as *caques*. These are then loaded on lorries and driven to the nearest *vendangeoir* of the person or firm who owns the vineyard or who has bought the grapes from the *vignerons*. At the *vendangeoir* the grapes are weighted in their *caques* and tipped out into the *pressoir* until there is enough for a pressing or 'charge', usually of 4,000 kilograms. The bunches are kept whole, not *égrappées* nor *foulées* as in Burgundy or the Gironde, and the grapes remain whole when tipped in the *pressoir*. This consists of a square wooden floor with four adjustable open-work wooden rails which make a sort of cage in which the grapes are heaped. The *pressoir* has a heavy lid of oak boards which is lowered and raised at will by a screw, now driven, as a rule, by electricity, but until recently by muscle and sweat. When the lid is clamped on the heaped grapes in the *pressoir*, and slowly but relentlessly driven down, its crushing pressure bursts the grapes, and their sweet juice immediately runs off through the rails into a slightly sloping wide groove that leads it to a collecting 'station' without having been in contact for any time with the skins of the grapes; these are left behind in the cage of the press. The first flow pressed out of the grapes is either led or pumped into a vat which holds 2046 litres of this, the best grape juice or *cuvée*. Greater pressure is then applied and more juice is squeezed out of the wet husks still in the cage of the *pressoir*, but it is neither as white nor as sweet nor as good as the *cuvée*, and it is not mixed with it. Very soon after the *cuvée* has been vatted, it begins to ferment in a rather boisterous manner, throwing off an ugly 'head' or scum, thus getting rid of any dirt or dust or anything else which is not wanted; some of which, the heavier stuff, falls to the bottom of the vat as lees. When the must, as this working grape-juice is called, returns to a more normal temperature, in twenty-four or thirty-six hours as a rule, all that is clear is drawn into ten clean oak casks holding two hundred litres each, and these casks are sent at once by lorry to Reims, Epernay, Ay or wherever the persons or firms who own the wine-to-be have their cellars. All through the vintage, which may be long or short according to the more or less favourable weather conditions from year to year, lorries are busy day and night fetching casks to put the new wine in and delivering full ones at the *celliers* from all parts of the Champagne vineyards. During the next eight to ten weeks the must will be left alone to become new wine, most of the grape-sugar present in the must having become alcohol, which stays put, and carbonic acid gas, which loses itself in the air.

The new wines are then racked, that is transferred into new casks, leaving behind the sediment cast off during the process of fermentation. After being racked the new wines of different pressings or *marcs* of each vineyard are 'assembled' or blended together, in order to obtain one standard wine from each place, irrespective of whether the wine was made at the beginning of the vintage or at the end, from grapes which might have been hardly fully ripe in the first instance and from what may be slightly overripe grapes in the second. The newly racked and 'assembled' wine is given another four or five weeks to rest and to proceed a little further with its slow fermentation, if it has a mind to do so. It is then racked another time, which serves the double purpose of separating it from any lees it may have cast off and to give it plenty of fresh air. Then comes the all-important business of making-up the *cuvées*. The *chef de caves*, whose responsibility it is, must taste with the greatest keenness the wines of all the different vineyards or sets of vineyards, and he has to decide how much or how little of the wines of each different district he ought to blend together to secure the approximately right quantity and quality of each one of the different brands which his firms sells on different markets, in competition with other Champagne shippers. The *chef de caves* may also decide to add to his *cuvées* more or less of older wines which have been kept in cask for that very purpose. When, after many tastings and much hesitation, his choice has been made, the chosen wines are mixed and blended together in great *foudres* or vats with an electrically actioned and mechanical arm churning the wines; after which they are tested for sugar, liqueured and bottled.

The style of each *cuvée* depends entirely upon the skill and taste of the *chef de caves*, but the quality of the wine depends in the first place upon the quality of the grapes which, in Champagne as everywhere else, varies with the soil, sub-soil and aspect of different vineyards. No *chef de caves*, however skilled he may be in the art of blending, can possibly make a first-quality wine out of second-quality grapes. A Champagne *cuvée* made from different wines from none but the very best vineyards would not be an economic or commercial proposition, but the best *cuvées* are always those in which there is a greater proportion of *premiers crus* grapes, a small proportion of *deuxièmes crus* and no *troisièmes crus* at all.

The quantity of *liqueur de tirage* which is added at bottling time to the *cuvées de tirage* is such that the newly bottled wine will have just the right proportion of carbonic acid gas to make it as sparkling as it should be, no less and no more, after fermentation will have intervened. This *liqueur de tirage* is plain sugar candy melted in Champagne wine. When the *cuvée de tirage* is bottled its cork is held by a strong clamp which will keep it safely in the bottle at the *prise de mousse*, that is, when fermentation does its job. As soon as it is bottled, the *cuvée de tirage* is laid to rest in the deep, damp, cold, chalk cellars of Reims, Epernay and Ay, to be left alone for two or three years: long before that, the wine will have

171

fermented out any of the sugar that was in it when it was bottled. It will be sparkling Champagne right enough, but not fit to drink. During its bottle fermentation the wine throws off small but none the less objectionable pieces of tartaric acid, mucilage and other matters of either mineral or vegetable origin. This sediment lies quietly enough in the safely corked bottle, but it would foul the look and taste of the wine the moment glasses were filled. So it must be taken out of the wine somehow, and this is done most skilfully by the *remuage* and *dégorgement*. The *remuage* consists in giving each bottle, day after day, a twist sharp enough to make the sediment slide down towards the neck of the bottle, but not hard enough to make it rise into the wine. The process begins with the bottle in a horizontal position, but when completed the bottle stands vertically, neck downwards, and by that time the whole of the sediment has been gathered upon the inside face of the cork.

The next move is the removing of the cork with its wad of sediment, so that the wine is absolutely 'star bright' and will remain like it to the last drop. This must be done, and it is done, with practically no loss of wine and very little loss of the precious gas in it. The man who does it, *le dégorgeur*, is a skilled and valuable man indeed. He is the first of a team who deal with the bottle of sparkling Champagne when the time has come to make it ready to leave the depths of the cellars and go into the world. Next to the *dégorgeur* comes the *doseur*, the man who adds to the bottle of wine more or less *liqueur d'expédition*, a very sticky mixture of sugar, still Champagne wine and brandy: the wine to melt the sugar, the sugar to sweeten the wine and the brandy to stop the sugar fermenting. The object of this addition of *liqueur d'expédition* is to give to the wine just the degree of sweetness which is to the taste of the customer; it may be as little as half a per cent if the wine is for people who like *brut* Champagne, 1 per cent for those who prefer *extra sec*, 3 per cent for those who prefer *sec* and 5 per cent for the *demi-sec* connoisseurs. All such proportions are only approximate, since each Champagne shipper has his own technique in preparing the *liqueur d'expédition* and using it. When the *doseur* has done his job he passes on the bottle to the *boucheur*, who drives into the neck of the bottle a long and fat branded cork, which has to be forcibly squeezed to half its natural size for half its length to fit in the neck of the bottle. Next to the *boucheur* sits the *ficeleur*, who squashes down the half of the cork jutting out of the neck and makes it fast to the ring of the bottle neck with a three-branch or four-branch wire. The bottle of sparkling Champagne is then ready; when the call comes it is sent up from the cellars to the *cellier*, where it is washed and packed up.

Vintage and Non-vintage Champagne

A vintage Champagne is, or ought to be, the wine made from permitted grapes grown in Champagne vineyards in the same year, the date of which it bears printed on its labels and branded upon its corks. The vineyards of Champagne are very near the northern limit beyond which grapes will not mature in the open, and Champagne grapes do not ripen fully unless there has been a particularly hot summer. There are, unfortunately, a number of years when the weather is not all that it should be, and the wines made in such years are likely to be somewhat tart and thin. Then it is that those wealthy Champagne shippers with immense reserves of wines of past good vintages bring forth the right quantity of soft and fat wine to blend with the others, and they often do produce in this manner very nice wines indeed which cannot be sold under the date of any one particular year, but they are none the less quite good wines, often better value than vintage wines.

Vintage wines possess, naturally, a greater degree of personality, and they age more graciously, especially when they are really self-wines – not assisted or 'bettered' by the addition of older wines. They also invariably cost more than non-vintage Champagne; in the first place because they are, or ought to be, better wines, and in the second because there is a limited quantity of any vintage *cuvée*; sooner or later the time must come when there will be no more; when that time approaches the scarcer and dearer the wines become.

173

The old Champagne province was divided in 1790 into four *départements*, Aisne and Haute-Marne in the north, Marne in the centre and Aube in the south. There are vineyards in all four *départements*, but the fact that the roots of their vines are in Champagne soil is not sufficient to give to the wine made from their grapes the right to the name of Champagne. The soil, sub-soil and aspect of the vineyards must be such that the noble grapes can thrive and produce a wine worthy to bear the honoured name of Champagne. This is why the limits of the *région délimitée*, the only area allowed to call its wines Champagne, have been drawn and fixed by law. This official *région délimitée* covers (in 1981) a total of roughly speaking, 24,200 hectares, of which 18,700 are in the Marne *département*, 3,700 in the Aube and 1,800 in the Aisne. Obviously, although these vineyards are legally entitled to call their wines Champagne, there are very great differences in the quality of their wines. We can, without any hesitation, discard, to begin with, the wines of the Aube and Aisne vineyards. They produce none but the cheaper qualities of Champagne which are drunk either locally or in Paris night-clubs. All the better-quality Champagne comes from the vineyards of the Marne *département*, which does not mean, unfortunately, that all the vineyards of the Marne *département* produce automatically very high quality wines.

There are in the Marne, as in the Côte d'Or and the Gironde, vineyards which are either very much better or just a little better than others. It depends chiefly upon the nature of soil and sub-soil, and also on the altitude and aspect of each vineyard. The climate is the same for all, although some may be more sheltered than others. In Champagne the weather is often bitter in winter, but the vines do not mind hard frost when dormant; spring is the most dangerous time of the year, as late frosts may do and often do do incalculable damage. Summers are often very hot, with occasional thunderstorms and hailstorms; autumn, vintage time, is often warm and sunny, which makes everybody very happy; a wet and cold vintage spells disaster. It was ever thus, or, at any rate, for the past thousand years; we can be fairly certain of the age-long uncertainty of the weather in Champagne, because records still exist of the prices paid at the vintage time from the tenth century to our own day, and they show that prices soared when spring frosts had brought about a shortage of wine, but slumped badly when there was a glut.

All the better vineyards of the Marne have been divided into many classes or categories, according to the quality of the wine which may be expected from their grapes. The best are in what is called the *catégorie grand crus*, and the next three in *première, deuxième* and *troisième catégorie*. When vintage time is at hand the Champagne shippers and the growers, whose grapes the shippers are going to buy, meet and agree upon what shall be the right price to pay for the grapes of the *catégorie grand cru* vineyards, and that settles the price of the grapes of the remaining categories; they are paid for according to an agreed descending scale, from 100 to 90 per cent of the maximum price for *première cru* wines (the wines of this category rated at 100 per cent are the *grand crus*); wines below 90 per cent are of lesser quality. The margin allows for paying more or less according to quality, since all the wines of the same *catégorie* are not likely to be identical. Some *vignerons* may have taken greater care, or they may have had better luck than others.

Nearly all the better growth vineyards are in the *arrondissements* of Reims and Epernay, and a few only in the Canton of Vertus, of the *arrondissement* of Châlons-sur-Marne. They cover the approaches to the Montagne de Reims and its lower slopes facing Reims and Châlons-sur-Marne; the hillside upon the right bank of the River Marne above and below Epernay; and the approaches and lower slopes of a range of gentle hills some distance to the left of the Marne, above Epernay, known as the Montagne d'Avize or Côte des Blancs.

The Montagne de Reims is a cliff of tertiary formation and in the shape of a flat iron with its sharp end pointing eastwards towards Châlons-sur-Marne; it rises sharply from the billowing plain crossed by the little River Vesle, on the north-east, and from the banks of the Marne, on the south-west. A great forest and wild-boar sanctuary covers the broad crest of the Montagne de Reims, but its sides and approaches are covered with closely planted vineyards on all sides. That part of the Montagne de Reims on the Vesle side, and farthest away from Châlons-sur-Marne, is known as La Petite Montagne and its vineyards produce the less distinguished wines entitled to the name of Champagne; the best of them, however, those of Sacy and Villedommange, are in good demand, being cheaper than most and considered to be very good value. Leaving La Petite Montagne and La Montagne and proceeding eastwards, we shall pass through the vineyards of Villers-Allerand, Rilly-la-Montagne, Chigney-les-Roses, Ludes, Mailly-Champagne, Verzenay, Verzy and Villers-Marmery, all of them hillside villages and vineyards, while we shall survey from our vantage point – none of greater beauty than the Moulin de Verzenay – a wonderful panorama of flourishing vineyards, including those of Sillery and Beaumont-sur-Vesle stretching to the main road from Reims to Châlons-sur-Marne.

All these 'Montagne' vineyards are practically back-to-back with the 'Marne' vineyards on the other side, but there are others at the eastern end, or turning-point of the Montagne, forming a sort of connecting link between the two: they are the vineyards of Trépail, Tauxières and Louvois, on the Châlons-sur-Marne side, and Bouzy and Ambonnay on the Marne side. We shall then turn our backs on Châlons-sur-Marne, and, facing Château-Thierry and Paris farther west, we shall pass through the riverside vineyards of Bisseuil, Mareuil-sur-Ay, Avenay and Ay, a little town as quaint as its name and well worth a visit. Beyond Ay, the vineyards of Dizy-Magenta and Cumières, and those of Champillon and Hautvillers much higher up, all produce very fine wines but the same cannot be said of the wines made from grapes grown farther west upon the right bank of the Marne, practically as far as Château-Thierry.

The two great grape varieties of the Champagne district are the red Pinot and the white Chardonnay. The black grape varieties dominate, with about 80 per cent of the vineyard area either under the Pinot Noir grape variety, or the Pinot Meunier, or other clonal variations of Pinot. The Pinot Noir is the nobler of the two main varieties, and predominates in the Montagne de Reims region. The robust Pinot Meunier, which produces wines that are not so suitable for ageing and with less finesse, is much to be found in the Vallée de la Marne. The aristocratic Chardonnay predominates in the Côte des Blancs area, where there is both chalk and marl. The wines are delicate with a light emphasis and an enticing bouquet. But for all the grape varieties, the calcareous soil is an absolutely vital element in the distinctive breed of a Champagne, as against other sparkling wines.

On the left bank of the Marne the better wines are those of Chouilly and Pierry, close to Epernay, to the right and left of the town, but the best wines are those of a range of gentle hills a little farther back from the river; they rise soon after one leaves Pierry and stretch as far as Vertus. This is the part of the Champagne *viticole* known as La Côte des Blancs, or the hill of the white grapes, where the white Chardonnay grapes are grown almost exclusively. The most important township of the Côte des Blancs is Avize, with Cramant on higher ground to its right, or west, Le Mesnil, Oger and Vertus to its left, or east. The other vineyards of La Côte des Blancs, those of Monthelon and Cuis, on the Pierry side of Cramant and Grauves on the other side of the same hill, also produce white wines from white grapes, 'Blanc de Blancs', entitled to the name of Champagne, but they are of plainer quality.

PART II

Clearly, over the past two decades, there have been changes and modifications in the Champagne-making process, gradual developments made necessary by changing socio-economic conditions. Right at the early stages of picking, there is the process of sorting through the grapes for any damaged fruit – *épluchage*. This is much less usual nowadays, largely because greater protection of the vineyards from rot, by means of efficient spraying, has greatly improved the health of the grapes. The traditional wooden presses are still much in evidence, although some very large concerns and cooperatives use the horizontal press with a rubber bag inside which swells up and gradually presses the grapes against the sides of the machine. This is a gentle way of pressing, very necessary in the making of Champagne. The following fermentation is now nearly always carried on in stainless-steel vats, and selected yeasts are the order of the day, thus ensuring a more easily controlled fermentation. The Champagne houses have done much research on the cultivation and selection of strains of yeast, and even export some of the results of their work.

Nothing has diminished the importance of the head blender of a Champagne house, and in a non-vintage wine he will seek to maintain continuity of house style, choose his wines to set aside for a future vintage wine if the year is good enough, and separate the very finest wines, if nature made it possible to produce them, for a top *cuvée*, if this is the policy of his house. Stocks are still the basis of a fine Champagne house, and a minimum of three years of stock is regarded as 'security' level, with top quality houses infinitely preferring to have five years of stock behind them.

The *liqueur de tirage* is still sugar dissolved in the base wine of Champagne, and the sugar is very carefully calculated according to what is already in the wine, and the pressure ultimately wanted in the final Champagne. Six atmospheres is what is required normally, as this goes down a little after disgorging – *crémant* Champagnes are usually about four atmospheres. Extra yeasts are usually also added at this stage, to help complete a satisfactory second fermentation. Nowadays, this fermentation in bottle, the *méthode champenoise*, is nearly always held in its container by means of a crown cork, not a cork held by a clamp or *agrafe*. The crown cork is metal and plastic, with only a strip of cork between that and the wine, and the resultant savings in cost have been marked.

Remuage has obviously become very costly, with its intensive hand-labour and the difficulty of finding young people to take the places of the retiring *remueurs*.

Experiments with rotating metal frames holding quantities of bottles have been successful and inevitably it is the way of the future for much of the production of Champagne. Where it is not used, it is often more due to reluctant trade union agreement than to anything else, and in the 1980s the two methods sometimes co-exist side-by-side. For the future, too, other methods are being devised to force the sediment to precipitate much more quickly, and clearly there will be great financial advantage when these are perfected. *Dégorgement* before consumption, removing the deposit which has gathered on the first cork, is now rarely done completely by hand – *à la volée*. Now, the neck of the upturned bottle is plunged into a freezing solution, and the sediment near the cork solidifies, making it easy to remove in a small block of ice. Before the Champagne receives its second cork, the *liqueur d'expédition* is added, with various degrees of sweetness. The *brut* and *extra sec* might have a little more sugar than indicated, and there is also a *doux* category, a rich Champagne, delicious in the right context. Totally *brut* wines would not appeal to all, but when completely balanced, they can have great finesse. Non-vintage Champagne is the wine on which a house builds its reputation. Vintage Champagne usually has more pronounced character and body, and can be marvellous with some bottle age. Rosé or pink Champagne, made by extra grapeskin contact or by adding red, still wine from Champagne, can be both non-vintage or vintage, and the strengthened influence of the black grapes can give more body. With age a rosé Champagne takes on a beautiful, subtle, tawny colour, and exciting flavours all of its own. Houses that make rosé Champagne include: Taittinger, Perrier-Jouët, Veuve Clicquot, Moët & Chandon (there is also Dom Pérignon Rosé), Heidsieck Monopole, Giesler, Pommery, Laurent Perrier, Piper-Heidsieck, Roederer, Pol Roger, Charles Heidsiec, Mumm and Krug. As with other Champagne, there are different house styles; Roederer, for instance, has depth and great length, while Charles Heidsieck is delicious, light and fragrant, and Dom Ruinart Rosé ethereal. Pale Krug aims for delicacy.

Blanc de Blancs Champagne is simply Champagne made only from the Chardonnay grape, with no red Pinot in it. Consequently, it is usually a lighter, very delicate wine – ideal *apéritif* Champagne. The rarely encountered Blanc de Noirs is logically enough made entirely from black grapes, but is white in colour – a full-bodied wine with marked bouquet. *Crémant* Champagnes can have tremendous finesse, with a real taste of the wine coming through. There are also single vineyard Champagnes, notably from villages in the Montagne de Reims area, but perhaps they lack the balance of the best Champagnes, thereby proving the benefit of astute blending.

Some houses make a 'luxury' *cuvée*, a wine that they consider the very best blend possible, whether vintage or non-vintage. This is usually highlighted by a specially shaped or designed bottle. Some are magnificent, others are disappointing, especially at such a very high price level. It is also rather impudent for such luxury wines to be sold (as some are) when still very young indeed, and very far from their complex best – when asking very high prices, there should be some element of financing by the producer. These de luxe Champagnes include; Dom Ruinart (a wine of great elegance), Dom Pérignon, La Grande Dame from Veuve Clicquot, Roederer's Cristal in the clear glass, Perrier-Jouët's Belle Epoque (with beautiful enamelled flowers fired on to the bottle) and Blason de France, Heidsieck Dry Monopole's excellent and often unsung Diamant Bleu, Taittinger's Comtes de Champagne, Laurent Perrier's Cuvée Grande Siècle, Charles Heidsieck's Cuvée Royale, Mumm's René Lalou, Canard-Duchêne's Charles VII Brut, Piper-Heidsieck's Florens-Louis, Abel Lepitre's Prince A. de Bourbon Parme, De Venoge's Vin des Princes, Mercier's Réserve de l'Empéreur, Irroy's Cuvée Marie Antoinette, and Deutz & Geldermann's Cuvée William Deutz. Bollinger have two unusual Champagnes, the Vieilles Vignes from ungrafted wines, and the Bollinger Tradition RD – the recent disgorging giving the mature vintages a wonderful freshness.

The main Champagne houses are the following: (The non-vintage comments apply to *brut* style)

Ayala: Reliable non-vintage, slightly sweeter style.

Besserat de Bellefon: Much seen in France, classic vintage.

Billecart-Salmon: Elegant champagne, lovely Blanc de Blancs.

Bollinger: Distinguished house and wines, style and black grape character.

Deutz: A big-flavoured non-vintage. Marvellous Blanc de Blancs Vintage.

Canard Duchêne: Light non-vintage, with a good deal of breed, although not great length.

Giesler: Non-vintage on light side, with Chardonnay flavour.

Gosset: Charming non-vintage, and a remarkable 1961 in the past!

George Goulet: Beautifully balanced non-vintage and Crémant Blanc de Blancs.

Alfred Gratien: Flowery, quite full non-vintage. Marvellous old vintages.

Heidsieck Dry Monopole: Marvellous de luxe Cuvé Diamant Bleu – perfect for laying down. Pleasant non-vintage.

Charles Heidsieck: Extremely pleasant non-vintage, and vintage wines that age beautifully. In 1980, the 1966 was still most distinguished, as was the 1966 Cuvée Royale.

Piper-Heidsieck: A light, fresh, apéritif-style non-vintage.

Henriot: Very classic vintage, which ages well.

Jacquesson: Delicious Champagnes, lovely soft vintage.

Krug: This is aristocratic Champagne *par excellence*, always outstanding by its sheer breed. The non-vintage Grande Cuvée is heady, refreshing and distinctive, while the vintage has much more weight and great class. There is now also a single vineyard Blanc de Blancs, Clos du Mesnil. A chance to drink Krug is never to be missed.

Lanson: The non-vintage is pleasant, perfect apéritif Champagne.

Abel Lepitre: Good vintage, non-vintage and a delicious vintage Crémant Blanc de Blancs.

Mercier: Under the same ownership as Moët. The

non-vintage has a soft, full flavour – good, straightforward Champagne, often underrated. Black grape style.

Moët & Chandon: Non-vintage quite concentrated, vintage naturally has more character. Considering amounts sold across the world, standards kept remarkably high, with only occasional lapses. De luxe brand Dom Pérignon combines elegance with body and ages beautifully.

Mumm: The non-vintage is now considerably lighter than it was. Delicious Blanc de Blancs Crémant.

Joseph Perrier: A family firm making really flowery, delicate non-vintage, delicious apéritif wine, and impressive vintage.

Laurent Perrier: A lightish, refreshing non-vintage – all-purpose and ages beautifully.

Perrier-Jouët: A full, really interesting non-vintage. The de luxe blends go under different names for different markets – Belle Epoque, Fleur de Champagne, and Blason de France. Excellent house.

Philipponnat: A light, very *brut* non-vintage, excellent *blanc de blancs* and superb individual vineyard Clos des Goisses.

Pol Roger: Fruitier, beguiling non-vintage, weightier, classic vintage.

Pommery: Rather a one-dimensional non-vintage. Vintage has more class and finish.

Louis Roederer: Outstanding non-vintage, full and with immense class – if you like Champagne with meals, this is it. Also sublime Rosé and really good Rich, which is not cloying but just rounder. Excellent vintage.

A. Rothschild: Very good Champagne. This house also supplies many Buyer's Own Brands (BOBs).

Ruinart: Under the same ownership as Moët. Incredibly elegant and aristocratic non-vintage, lovely vintage, delicious Dom Ruinart Blanc de Blancs and Dom Ruinart Rosé.

Salon: Only vintage wine, and only from Chardonnay grown in the finest vineyards at Le Mesnil. Some wonderful old vintages.

Taittinger: A really good, non-vintage. Comtes de Champagne Vintage Rosé and Vintage Blanc de Blancs are both distinguished wines.

De Venoge: Extremely reliable Champagne – this *marque* is made by the house of Trouillard, which is responsible for many good Buyer's Own Brand (BOB) Champagnes.

Veuve Clicquot: The Widow herself, with quite an assertive non-vintage, and really distinguished vintage wines that age beautifully.

There are also cooperative wines, such as Mailly, and cooperative brands such as St Gall and St Simon, both usually very good. St Marceaux is a noteworthy small house. Of course, it has to be remembered that the dosage in non-vintage Champagnes can vary a little from country to country, but this is hardly detectable. Differences in Champagnes from the same house are far more likely to be caused by different storage conditions and the influence of temperature. No wine suffers more than Champagne from poor storage, and cool conditions away from light are essential. Half-bottles can suffer very quickly from this, in particular, and they should always be drunk as young as possible. If you like Champagne with a little bottle age, magnums are ideal for laying down for some special occasion or party. The very large bottles have delightful names, but take some remembering:

Magnum	2 bottles	Salmanazar	12 bottles
Jeroboam	4 bottles	Balthazar	16 bottles
Rehoboam	6 bottles	Nebuchadnezzar	20 bottles
Methuselah	8 bottles		

Champagne, being a very northerly vineyard area, has enormous fluctuations in the size of the annual crop. The following table showing the harvest yield over a period of fifteen years proves this point. The two huge vintages of 1982 and 1983 did much to restore the critical stock situation which arose as a result of the preceding two lean years. The backing of a full cellar is essential in the making of good quality Champagne.

Year	Bottles	Year	Bottles
1969	91,264,000	1977	186,660,533
1970	219,017,200	1978	79,297,600
1971	84,945,467	1979	228,581,961
1972	154,896,267	1980	113,179,850
1973	210,189,067	1981	92,246,666
1974	169,751,467	1982	295,199,926
1975	175,324,000	1983	302,033,326
1976	211,675,667		

Champagne will never be cheap. Firstly there is the cost of the grapes themselves, which tends to spiral ever upwards, although large crops can help mitigate this. Then there is the long, complicated process that is the *méthode champenoise*. That is why standards in Champagne must be kept high – and in the main, they are. Good Champagne has a taste and complexity that cannot be achieved elsewhere, due particularly to the difference in the base wine, and above all it has a bouquet that is quite inimitable to the area. It probably gives more pleasure per drop than any other wine.

Good vintages in Champagne have included:
1952, '53, '55, '59   1961, '62, '64, '66, '69
1970, '71, '73, '75, '76, '79   1982

Still Wine from Champagne
These non-sparkling wines used to be called Champagne Nature, but this was naturally very confusing and even open to abuse, so in 1974 a new *appellation* was created for them, Coteaux Champenois. The amount made is strictly controlled, and although the *appellation* covers white, red and rosé wines, white still wines made from the Chardonnay grape are the most common. Some well-known Coteaux Champenois names are Ruinart Chardonnay, Moët's Saran still wine and that of Laurent Perrier. These white wines are never as great as white Burgundy, but can provide simple enjoyment and the added tinge of excitement when drinking something of a curiosity – albeit at far from simple prices.

The same could be said of the red still wines from black Pinot grapes, mostly in the villages of the Montagne de Reims – the wine suffers if compared with red Burgundy. However, if staying in Champagne for a length of time, an occasional change of colour is welcome. These Coteaux Champenois red wines come from vineyards round Bouzy, Ay, Ambonnay, Dizy and Cumières, Verzenay and Rilly, between Reims and Epernay.

7 Alsace

The chequered history of Alsace has forged an individuality in the people and the wines that is good enough reason for getting to know the region through the glass. From the reign of Louis XIV to 1870 Alsace was French, from 1870 to 1918 it was German, the Riesling and the Traminer (as it then was) were forbidden, and the Alsations were forced to make cheap wines, from 1918 to 1940 Alsace was French again and the region once again opted for quality, always a long, slow business of replanting, from 1940 to 1944 Alsace was again German and greatly devastated as well, and from 1944, happily, to this day Alsace is French again. Since the end of the Second World War, when Alsace once more became French, her entire policy has been to maintain quality standards, and it is no accident that Alsace has the most stringent anti-fraud squad operating in France. The, at the time, startling decision in 1972 to bottle all Alsatian wines in the area of production was also taken with quality standards and respect for professional integrity in mind, and although its reversal has been discussed, the reasons for keeping this decision still hold good.

There are 11,500 hectares of *appellation contrôlée* vineyards in production, from which, there are 800,000 hectolitres average annual production of *appellation contrôlée* wines – or 115 million bottles. Wine is very important to the whole region of Alsace, as it represents 25 per cent of the total agricultural production – and here it should be remembered that we are in a very fertile area, particularly renowned for its fruits. Alsace has 20 per cent of the total French production of *appellation contrôlée* white wines, and the very high figure of 45 per cent of the French market of white *appellation* wines drunk at home. Exports are very important to Alsace, and in 1979, 20 million bottles were exported, or 21 per cent of the total sales of Alsatian wine in bottles. The large houses of *producteurs-négociants*, in particular, are heavily dependent on export sales – Hugel export 80 per cent of its wines, Trimbach 65 per cent. The home market tends to be more supplied by *propriétaires-viticulteurs* and cooperatives, although the latter are now well represented on export markets to.

The whole pattern of Alsace wine production is one of small units, 9,200 separate producers declare *appellation contrôlée* Alsace wine, of which only 2,900 have more than one hectare – 1,000 have between one and two hectares, 1,450 between two and five hectares, 450 have more than five hectares with only the tiny number of forty-five having more than ten hectares. So, the highly individual character of the Alsatians is reflected in the manner in which they divide their vineyard area. Obviously, very small owners have other jobs – three hectares is probably the minimum viable size. There is one *appellation* Alsace, which went on the statute books in 1945, about a decade later than most of the other *appellations* in France, but it only became a decree in 1962. This governed such things as the area of cultivation, the species of grape, the processes involving the improvement and preparation of wine and the date on which the grapes are gathered. The bottle used is the traditional green *flûte*. There is also the *appellation* Alsace Grand Cru, which must be completed by the name of the grape variety used. The grape varieties grown are the Gewürz-traminer (21%), Muscat (3.7%), Riesling (17.9%), Pinot Noir (4.5%), Pinot Gris or Tokay d'Alsace (4.6%), Pinot Blanc, sometimes called Clevner (16.8%) and Sylvaner (22.4%) – the *cépages nobles*. The *cépages courants* are the Knipperlé, the Chasselas (ennobled in the early 1970s), the Goldriesling and the Müller-Thurgau, all of which are gradually being phased out. So, *appellation contrôlée* Alsace Grand Cru or Grands Vins will be of superior quality, and must also have a higher degree of natural sugar (when converted into alcohol) before any chaptalization – for instance, a minimum of 11 per cent for the Gewürztraminer and 10 per cent for the Riesling.

The main points to note in the choice of grape variety today is the growth of the Riesling (which the Alsatians consider their top grape) and the Pinot Blanc, and the drop in quantity of the Sylvaner and the lesser Chasselas, or Gutedel. To the Alsatians, the essential part of their duty as wine-makers is to bring out the individual characteristics of each grape variety. They lay particular emphasis on the nose of a wine, saying it should project the essence of the grape used, and look for harmony, freshness and clean fruitiness on the palate. Except in rare years, when the weather conditions are particularly favourable, the wines are always fermented out to dryness.

Riesling: The epitome of delicacy and finesse, elegant rather than big or overblown, although in years like 1971 and 1976 it can be rich. Riesling should have marvellous, full fruit, and length of finish. It is less steely-fruity than German Riesling from, say, the Saar, and more aromatic, earthy and heady.

Gewürztraminer: This is perhaps the grape variety that beginners in wine like best, because of its wonderful 'come and get me' nose of spiciness and fruit, with a strong positive taste. It makes immensely attractive wine, although occasionally, in the hands of vulgarians, it can be a bit blowsy, and one would perhaps tire of the taste faster than one would of Riesling. The grape has a reddish hue when ripe. The Gewürztraminer can be rather fragile to grow, with berries falling off in poor weather conditions.

Tokay d'Alsace or Pinot Gris: Rather the dark horse among the Alsatian varieties, as people first get seduced by the more widely planted, better-known grapes. With Tokay, one gets rather an earthy taste, which has real *typicité* as the Alsatians say – the taste is one of *terroir* and richness, rather than straightforward fruit. Ideally, it should have over 88° Oechslé to be good – the great ones are over 100°. (In Alsace, sugar is measured in Oechslé degrees, as in Germany.)

Muscat: Muscat has a lovely, unmistakable 'catty' nose when young, followed by a pronounced, pungent taste. Unlike the wines of the south of France from this grape variety, in Alsace Muscat is vinified completely dry. The main clone in Alsace is the Muscat Ottonel, perhaps the most delicate, and the Muscat Blanc d'Alsace which is very grapy. Unfortunately, the Muscat is very susceptible to flowering problems (*coulure* and then *millerandage*) and very small yields can follow.

Pinot Blanc: Clearly growing in popularity, as it is more reasonable in price than the foregoing varieties, Pinot Blanc has a fresh fruit taste in abundance and is delicious drinking, but lacks a long, complex finish.

Sylvaner: A pleasant grape variety, without 'breed' (except when grown very high in the Alto Adige, right on the Italian-Austrian border), but in Alsace, nice young drinking. It can go a bit flattish and 'fat' if left too long in the bottle.

Chasselas: A grape variety without much character – the best one can hope for is a round fruitiness, without distinction. Usually goes into wines for quick, local consumption, or in the blends of *Edelzwicker*, which has to contain noble varieties. *Zwicker* ended its life as a wine term in 1972.

Pinot Noir: Some would say that it is hardly worth trying to make red wine in Alsace, as the northerly climatic zone does not favour extraction of any colour or depth. Occasionally, cleverly vinified and with a good year to back it, the wines can have a fruity charm and taste somewhat like a Sancerre Rouge. The words *rouge* and *rosé* are often interchangeable.

At vintage time, the Chasselas and the Sylvaner are picked first, with the Riesling and the Gewürztraminer coming in last. Picking usually starts at the beginning of October and lasts about a month, with rare exceptions when there is a real *Vendange Tardive* very late in the season. When a wine is labelled with a grape variety, it is 100 per cent that variety. The same principle applies to the use of the vintage year. The climate of Alsace is a very continental, as opposed to a temperate, one, befitting a region far away from the sea. The area is protected by the Vosges mountains, and the rain falls on the western side of the range, causing Alsace to be one of the driest regions of France. The summers tend to be hot and

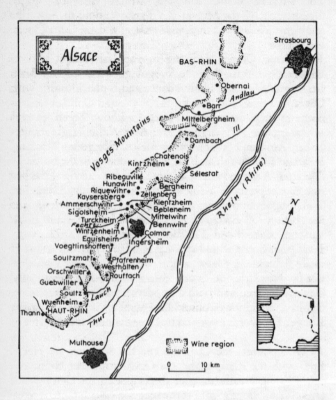

sunny, and the winters can be bitter, sometimes with snow, and there is always the danger of frost until late spring. There is the plain of Alsace, and the vine-covered sub-Vosges hills running east to west – the best vine-bearing slopes face south and southeast, to gain the best possible micro-climate. The finest sites are usually mid-slope, and do not go too far up the Vosges. There is such multiplicity of soil that it allows for the ideal sites for each grape variety to be chosen – this also applies to site and position on the slope, especially with regard to the shy, late-ripening Riesling, which must have a particularly favoured slice of the land. Tokay and Pinot Blanc are hardier, but obviously the Pinot Noir must have shelter from cold and winds. The very best soil is *argilocalcaire* or calcareous clay, but there is also sandy soil, loamy soil, and combinations of all. The two *départements* where vines are grown in Alsace are the Bas-Rhin, the northern part towards the border with Germany, and the Haut-Rhin, the southern part, with Colmar as its centre. In fact, the area round Colmar perhaps marks the high point of quality in Alsace, with villages such as Ribeauvillé, Hunawihr, Riquewihr, Kientzheim, Bennwihr, Kaysersberg, Ammerschwihr, Turckheim, Wintzenheim and Eguisheim. In the Bas-Rhin above Sélestat there is Dambach, Barr and Obernai, but Sylvaner and Chasselas are grown more in this area, and the wines generally do not have the same breed. Way south of Colmar, there are Rouffach and Guebwiller, which should not be forgotten.

Alsace combines modern with traditional, using up-to-date presses and methods of vinification, but still keeping wood in the cellar, especially in the smaller establishments, where it is a delight to come upon large carved casks, German-fashion, with painted quotations from Goethe on the walls! But large houses like Hugel also have old, often historical wooden casks, usually encrusted with tartrates inside so wood/wine contact is minimal. The great wines are sometimes vinified in wood, others in stainless steel, and temperatures at fermentation are usually around 20°C. It is desirable to have casks of all sizes as, with a wide range of grape varieties, some of them producing very small amounts, it is necessary to have adaptability – a wide selection of cask sizes is also vital where racking is concerned. So you can see huge casks holding seventy hectolitres, or small ones with anything between 250 and 650 litres of wine in them. Some houses have centrifuges to clarify the must, and bentonite fining to remove excess proteins is usually done at must, rather than at wine state. The malolactic fermentation is usually encouraged in lesser years, although it is not needed in great, ripe years, and bottling takes place from April to September, with the great Gewürztraminers and Tokays being bottled last.

After the vintage, the vines are usually cut back to two sprigs and the earth mounded up round the base. Vines can be led up to the height required on wires, to about 1.8 metres high, with frost being taken into account and when maximum sun is desired. Training is lower in the Bas-Rhin. A very top vineyard, aiming for the greatest quality, might have 5,000 vines per hectare and the pruning might limit production to twenty-four buds per square metre. There are quite high yields in Alsace by comparison, say, with Burgundy – 100 hectolitres per hectare for *appellation* Alsace (plus sometimes the *plafond limite de classement* of 20 per cent), and seventy hectolitres per hectare for Alsace Grand Cru. The top grape varieties tend to produce less than the maximum allowed, and it must be remembered that quantity affects white wines less than red.

There are a number of historical site names in Alsace, that have always been used locally, but which have rarely been used on labels. It was felt that this might muddle the customer, especially on the domestic French market, as the site names are more Alsatian than French. However, now it is felt that the consumer is more sophisticated, and would like to know when his wine comes from a special, usually very favoured, site. So, a top echelon of Grands Crus is proposed, and these would be true Grands Crus (or *climats*) based on certain proven vineyards, not only on a superior natural sugar strength, as at present. Some of the best-known sites, many of which could be in line for Grand Cru status, should the project ever come to fruition, are:

Haut-Rhin
Ammerschwihr 'Kaefferkopf'; Beblenheim 'Sonnenglanz'; Bergheim 'Kanzlerberg'; Colmar 'Hardt'; Eguisheim 'Pfirsigberg' and 'Eichberg'; Guebwiller 'Kitterlé' and 'Wanne'; Hunawihr 'Muhlforst'; Ingersheim 'Florimont'; Kaysersberg 'Schlossberg'; Kientzheim 'Schlossberg' and 'Clos des Capucins'; Mittelwihr 'Mandelberg'; Ribeauvillé

'Osterberg'; Riquewihr 'Sporen' and 'Schoenenberg'; Rouffach 'Langenzug' and 'Bollenberg'; Sigolsheim 'Mamburg'; Soultzmatt 'Zinnkoepfle'; Thann 'Le Rangen'; Turckheim 'Brand'; Voegtlinshoffen 'Hatschburg' and 'Grosskohlausen'; Westhalten 'Clos St Landelin'; Wettolsheim 'Steingrubler'; Wintzenheim 'Hengst'; Wuenheim 'Ollwiller'; Zellenberg 'Buergen'.

Bas-Rhin
Andlau 'Kastelberg' and 'Moenchberg'; Barr 'Kirchberg', 'Zisser' and 'Rotluf'; Chatenois 'Hahnenberg'; Mittelbergheim 'Zotzenberg' and 'Brandluft'.

Some of these sites, according to their soils and expositions, are particularly suitable for certain grape varieties; for example, the Schoenenberg at Riquewihr specializes in Riesling and Muscat (both are late-ripening), the Sporen, also at Riquewihr, in Tokay and Gewürztraminer, and the Eichberg at Eguisheim produces excellent Gewürztraminer.

The Wines and Who Makes Them
The large houses of Alsace, many of which concentrate on exporting, usually own a proportion of their vineyard needs, and buy in other grapes. This gives them total control over the wine-making process and ensures quality. Some of the larger houses will charge higher prices than the cooperatives, but their reputation is high and you buy with complete security. They are also, with financial and technical power, able to take full advantage of great years, when they make exceptional wines.

HUGEL (Riquewihr)

A house that must come first for many Britons and Americans, as they form the main export market for Hugel. The family tradition of this firm is typical of Alsace, where ties are strong and people faithful to their land and customs. With the death in 1980 of the great Monsieur Jean Hugel, his three sons, Jean, Georges and André carry on the fine aims of the firm, which is to make wines as naturally and as well as possible. In Alsace as a whole, wine-makers like to treat wine as little as possible, letting the true identity of the fruit speak for itself. Hugel own twenty-five hectares, composed of 48 per cent Riesling, 47 per cent Gewürztraminer, 3 per cent Pinot Gris and 2 per cent Muscat, including a good part of the Sporen and the Schoenenberg. They own no Pinot Blanc, Sylvaner or Chasselas, and only buy in grapes, not wine. In common with most growers and wine-makers in Alsace, they use Vaslin horizontal presses, but with special non-standard stainless-steel parts to the machines. Since the 1979 harvest, Hugel have the newest version of the Vaslin press, which has not only a rotating outside cylinder, but also a counter-rotating central screw to avoid pressure problems with easily crushed grapes like Sylvaner. It is this kind of detail which tells.

Hugel's basic wine is Couronne d'Alsace, or Flambeau d'Alsace, which is fruity and frank and for young drinking. Les Vignards is a delicious Pinot Blanc. With Riesling, there is the straight wine with a vintage year, then the Riesling Cuvée Tradition from a better exposed slope, more smoky and with a fantastic fullness, and finally the Riesling Réserve Exceptionnelle or Réserve Personnelle from the very best slopes. The same graduation can apply to Gewürztraminer and Tokay and Muscat, and most other houses have similar names to show differences in quality – the choice of names is personal and not enshrined in law. The Pinot Noir of Hugel is one of Alsace's best red wines. Some of the truly grand wines of recent years have been the marvellous ripe ones of the 1976 vintage, when the weather was so clement.

TRIMBACH (Ribeauvillé)

Hubert Trimbach is as astonishing an ambassador for Alsatian wines as Johnny Hugel, both of them travelling indefatigably, but still very much in touch with the vine-roots. Hubert's brother, Bernard, controls vineyard and cellar. The family has owned vines since 1626, and you do not trifle with traditions as strong as these. Trimbach produce one of the most stately wines to come out of Alsace, perhaps the most subtle and complex I have ever tasted – the Riesling Clos Ste Hune, a small, sheltered vineyard above Hunawihr. This should be kept in bottle for as long as you can resist it for the full dimension of the wine to come out – from six to ten years would bring its rewards. Their Gewürztraminer Cuvée des Seigneurs de Ribeaupierre, and Riesling Cuvée Frédéric Emile are other top wines. As the Trimbach wines do not go through malolactic fermentation, they are often restrained, even austere, when young, but with a year or two in bottle all the flavours open out.

LEON BEYER (Eguisheim)

Like all the big houses, there are a great many *cuvées* of different qualities to choose from, but the top wines of Léon Beyer rank with the finest. In 1980, their Gewürztraminer 1978 was impressive, as was the Gewürztraminer Cuvée des Comtes d'Eguisheim 1975, while the 1971 Gewürztraminer Vendange Tardive was superb.

DOPFF & IRION (Riquewihr)

An extremely large firm, where perhaps commerce sometimes reigns over real individuality. But I usually like their Gewürztraminer Les Sorcières and their Muscat Les Amandiers, and in 1980 I saw an astoundingly beautiful Gewürztraminer 1976 Domaine du Château de Riquewihr, unfortunately, like all these special wines, in very limited supply. A 1975 Tokay Sélection also tasted well. Their Les Murailles Riesling comes from the Schoenenberg. The future of the firm seemed uncertain in 1985.

DOPFF AU MOULIN (Riquewihr)

Usually very pleasant wines. In 1980, I particularly liked their 1976 Gewürztraminer Eichberg, Propre Récolte Tardive, Réserve Spéciale.

LOUIS GISSELBRECHT (Dambach-La-Ville)

This part of the Gisselbrecht family own some vineyards, but also buy in grapes. Riesling wines are often excellent.

WILLY GISSELBRECHT (Dambach-La-Ville)

This branch of the family both owns more vineyards and buys in more grapes. They frequently win medals for their wines, and the Gewürztraminer seems particularly popular.

ZIND-HUMBRECHT (Wintzenheim)

A small, family enterprise, owned and run personally by M. and Mme Léonard Humbrecht. Their wines are made to a very high quality, and what makes them especially interesting is the fact that most come from definite sites with well-defined tastes of their own. They make superb Tokay du Rangen, Clos St Urbain, which usually needs time in bottle to come out. The Riesling du Rangen (the famous site at Thann) is impressive – here the soil is schistous, the same as in the Moselle, but rare in Alsace. The Rangen faces south, and M. Humbrecht owns five of the total six hectares. Some of the Humbrecht wines have considerable natural carbon dioxide when young, as well as some acidity, as there is no malolactic fermentation here. Humbrecht also have vineyards at Hengst (Wintzenheim), Brand (Turckheim) and at Gueberschwihr, where the deep clay makes for wines with less finesse than the granite at Brand or the quite heavy *argilo-calcaire* at Hengst.

SCHLUMBERGER (Guebwiller)

Schlumberger at Guebwiller make rather different wine, exclusively from their own vineyards (140 hectares, making them the largest owners in Alsace) on steep slopes with rather red sandy soil. The wines have a special flavour, rather earthy and highly individual. The vines are on narrow terraces here, difficult to work, and producing less yield than normal in Alsace, giving Schlumberger wines a certain body and concentration. The steeply sloping Kitterlé vineyard produces Gewürztraminer and Riesling of great interest, and the Gewürztraminer Cuvée Christine Schlumberger is justly renowned for its grand *pourriture noble* character. Fermentation is in wood, and there is a wide variety of casks of different sizes from 17,000 to 7,000 litres for different qualities. Top quality wines are stored in 7,000-litre barrels, and these wines tend to be stored for a year or two in bottle before sale.

Faller Frères of the Domaine Weinbach at Kaysersberg make really interesting wines, including the Riesling Schlossberg Grand Cru and the Riesling Cuvée de la Ste Cathérine. Kuentz-Bas, Laugel and Muré are also recommended. Willm's Grande Réserve Exceptionnelle Clos Gaensbroennel Gewürztraminer 1976 is a fine wine, as is Boeckel's straight Gewürztraminer 1979. Marcel Blanck at Kientzheim makes delicious wines, including a Riesling from the Schlossberg. Other houses that export, and which produce reliable wines, are: Bott, Ribeauvillé; Heim, Westhalten; Charles Jux, Colmar; Klipfel, Barr; Kuehn, Ammerschwihr; Lorentz, Bergheim (both Gustave and Jérome); Muller, Bergheim; Preiss-Henny, Mittelwihr; Preiss-Zimmer, Riquewihr; Louis Sipp, Ribeauvillé; Sparr, Sigolsheim; Jacques Baumann, Riquewihr and Rolly Gassmann, Rohrschwihr.

Small growers in Alsace abound, and I know of none better than M. Wiederhirn of Riquewihr. He sells mostly direct to the customer in France, but exports a little, including to England. The SYNVA is a Syndicat of Négociants/Viticulteurs that works from the Chamber of Commerce in Colmar. Their 1976 Gewürztraminer Réserve Exceptionnelle certainly lived up to the name. The Gewürztraminer from Pierre Ritzenthaler, Cellier du Muhlbach at Guémar is also good. The cooperatives, on the whole, hold up the reputation for quality that Alsace guards with so much care and they are very important because of the mass of small growers. The main ones are:

Haut-Rhin

Cave Coopérative de Ribeauvillé; Cave Coopérative Vinicole de Gueberschwihr et environs Gueberschwihr; Cave Coopérative Vinicole de Bennwihr à Bennwihr; Cave Coopérative Vinicole d'Eguisheim (one of the most reputed); Cave Coopérative Vinicole de Hunawihr; Cave Coopérative Vinicole de Kientzheim-Kayserberg à Kientzheim; Cave Coopérative Vinicole de Pfaffenheim; Cave Coopérative Vinicole du Vieil Armand; Cave Coopérative Vinicole de Turckheim; Cave Coopérative Vinicole de Westhalten; Cave Coopérative des Viticulteurs d'Ingersheim et des environs dans la région des Trois-Epis à Ingersheim; Coopérative Vinicole d'Alsace Réunies Codival' à Beblenheim; Société Coopérative Vinicole de Beblenheim; and Société Coopérative Vinicole de Sigolsheim.

Bas-Rhin

Cave Coopérative Vinicole d'Andlau; Société Coopérative Vinicole d'Orschwiller; and Union Vinicole pour la Diffusion des Vins d'Alsace, Obernai.

Crémant d'Alsace

A relatively new *appellation* for sparkling wines made by the Champagne method from grapes grown in Alsace. Dopff au Moulin in Riquewihr and the cooperative in Eguisheim are well-known for their *Crémant*. The quality is always good, and it should be remembered that the price can never be cheap for wines such as these from expensive base material and where the method requires financing. Like Crémant de Bourgogne, this is a really good alternative to Champagne.

Vintages in Alsace

The vital things to remember about Alsace vintages are that the great years keep well, the lesser ones should be drunk young, and certain years favour certain grape varieties. As examples of longevity, in 1978 a Gewürztraminer Hugel Sélection de Grains Nobles 1945 (an exceptionally good year) was still rich and interesting, while a magnum of Gewürztraminer Vendange Tardive Hugel 1945 was superb in 1975. At the 1978 tasting, a 1947 Riesling Hugel Réserve

Exceptionnelle (in magnum, which helps) was in good form. In 1975, a magnum of 1953 Tokay Hugel was still young with great finesse, and three years later a magnum of 1953 Tokay Hugel Vendange Tardive elicited perfect marks for its wonderful smoky taste, typical of the Tokay, its breed and its young elegance. Vendange Tardive averages 100° Oechslé and Sélection de Grains Nobles 115°.

1959: A very great year, and in 1979, a 1959 Gewürztraminer Hugel Sélection de Grains Nobles combined delicate fruit, with elegance and fullness, with the great richness not yet fully out.

1961: A very great year, as shown by a magnum of 1961 Tokay Vendange Tardive Hugel, which got near perfect marks in 1976 for its characteristic smoky taste, its balance and its richness.

1964: A very fine year.

1966: This year produced some remarkable wines, especially Riesling and Gewürztraminer, as evidenced in a memorable 1966 Riesling Vendange Tardive from Hugel tasted in 1976.

1967: Excellent, especially for the Gewürztraminer and the Tokay – in 1979, a 1967 Hugel Tokay Vendange Tardive was very rich and ripe and *grand vin*.

1968: A poor year, and not worth considering after a few years.

1969: A very good vintage indeed, combining richness with marked acidity.

1970: Good, plentiful year, with some wines having *pourriture noble*.

1971: A great year, the best since 1961. At this time, record Oechslé readings, especially in the Gewürztraminers. The wines are lasting beautifully, if chosen with care – some are at their apogee.

1972: Mediocre – tended to be harsh and green. Muscats were the best.

1973: Pleasant, fruity wines, excellent for drinking relatively young.

1974: Reliable and good, without having great charm – some very nice Gewürztraminers, the low yield giving some concentration.

1975: Very good vintage, with wines showing breed and elegance. They have very good balance.

1976: This is a really exciting year, a great rarity. Exceptionally high Oeschslé degrees giving wines of real berryish character. In other years (1934, 1945, 1959, 1961 and 1967) there was a small amount of wines of comparable quality, but 1976 had them in abundance. *Enfin,* a vintage of the century! The late-harvested wines literally reek of noble rot, and these are the ones to treasure for the future.

1977: Good, average quality, with the Gewürztraminers and Tokays particularly attractive – Rieslings and Muscats are lighter.

1978: Very small harvest, very nice wines made which show well their grape character. Rich and fruity Gewürztraminers.

1979: Very good quantity and quality. Some wines will even attain quality of 1976 (the wines from the Sporen look that way), even if they do not quite reach the same Oechslé readings.

1980: Quality good, especially for Pinot Gris (Tokay), Pinot Blanc and Riesling, but Gewürztraminer and Muscat were virtually wiped out through *coulure.*

1981: A very good vintage, which is coming into its own. The Gewürztraminer did particularly well and the style is quite luscious.

1982: An abundant vintage, with well-balanced wines. There are some late-harvest wines, and the Gewürztraminer and Pinot Gris are particularly fine.

1983: This is an astonishingly good vintage, which has caused much excitement. There will be great *vendange tardive* wines.

1984: Initial pessimism disappeared with a dry and sunny October and there will be some most agreeable wines. Unfortunately, the size of the crop is about 25 per cent less than in 1983, with Muscat, Gewürztraminer and Tokay Pinot Gris particularly badly hit.

8 *Loire*

While the Loire is hardly of Amazon length, it certainly dominates a good deal of France and offers a challenging diversity of scenery, history and, happily, of wines. Kings and monks have enjoyed and fostered the produce of the vine from the Atlantic to the Massif Central, and a goodly number of saints have passed into Loire wine lore. But although great monasteries have played their vital part in the unbroken tradition of wine-making along this great river and its tributaries, this is not a progress of aristocratic domains – it is rather a paean of praise for the small peasant grower. In a few instances the ancestral château has been turned into a fine wine property, or sometimes a dynamic marketing enterprise, but it is an army of *petits vignerons* who make the wines of the Loire. There are important cooperatives, some of which sell to the Loire *négociants*, a powerful group, while a few operate their own efficient direct selling business, especially to Paris restaurants. In 1983, the Loire valley produced 882,807 hectolitres of red and rosé *appellation contrôlée* wine, and 1,340,904 hectolitres of white *appellation contrôlée* wine, making a total of 2,223, 711 hectolitres. This compares with 2,314,915 hectolitres of *appellation contrôlée* wine in the Rhône Valley and 2,199, 268 hectolitres of *appellation contrôlée* wine in Burgundy, while similar figures for Champagne in 1983 were 2,241,391 hectolitres and for Bordeaux, 4,127,058 hectolitres.

MUSCADET

Muscadet is mostly drunk within the year, it is perfect bistro and café wine, and there is lots of it. The international demand for light, dry white wine has boosted exports to a high level. The generally large yields have led to certain

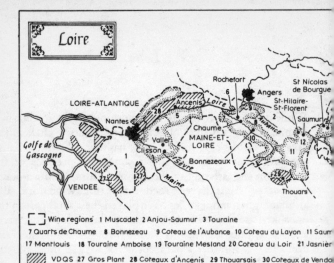

Loire

Rochefort

LOIRE-ATLANTIQUE   Ancenis   Loire   Angers   St Nicolas de Bourgue
                                                   St-Hilaire-St-Florent
Nantes   Chaume   MAINE-ET-   Saumur
Golfe de   Vallet   LOIRE
Gascogne   Clisson   Bonnezeaux

Maine
VENDEE   Thouars

[ ] Wine regions 1 Muscadet 2 Anjou-Saumur 3 Touraine
7 Quarts de Chaume 8 Bonnezeau 9 Coteau de l'Aubance 10 Coteau du Layon 11 Saum
17 Montlouis 18 Touraine Amboise 19 Touraine Mesland 20 Coteau du Loir 21 Jasnièr
VDQS 27 Gros Plant 28 Coteaux d'Ancenis 29 Thouarsais 30 Coteaux de Vendo

rather supple interpretations of the *appellation contrôlée* law in
the area with regard to wines to be released and wines to be
'blocked' – only to be deblocked some time later – it was
amazing how long the 1976 vintage lasted in Muscadet, and
how rarely one saw the 1977; small as the latter was, it did
exist! There was also a good deal of recent concern over the
misuse of the term *Mis en bouteille sur lie* – which is bottling
the wine directly off its lees, thereby imparting a particularly
fruity flavour and sometimes a touch of carbon dioxide gas.
When correctly fulfilling the proper procedures for a
bottling off the lees, now much better controlled, only
Muscadet and the VDQS of the region, Gros Plant du Pays
Nantais, can benefit from the extra descriptive qualification
of *sur lie* – *vins de pays* are excluded.

The Muscadet grape variety itself bears a mysterious name.
People used to speak of the Melon *musqué* de Bourgogne,
and it is certain that the grape did come west from
Burgundy. The roots are strong and the vine stock thick, the
branches are short, the leaves are big and the bunches are

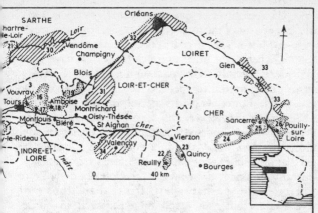

Appellations 4 Muscadet de Sèvres-et-Maine 5 Coteaux de la Loire 6 Savennières
...umur-Champigny 13 Bourgueil 14 Chinon 15 Touraine Azay-le-Rideau 16 Vouvray
...uilly 23 Quincy 24 Menetou-sur-Loire 25 Sancerre 26 Pouilly-sur-Loire
...everny 32 Vins de l'Orléannais 33 Coteaux du Giennois 34 Valençay

small and dumpily shaped. The juice is a greeny white with
quite a pungent taste. The Muscadet should be harvested
early to preserve its acidity and give the wine finesse, but it is
naturally early ripening, with the vintage usually in the
second half of September, which is just as well since October
is the wettest month in the area. Although the Muscadet area
can be very sunny, especially in winter, the influence of the
Atlantic can bring down the temperature at the same time.
There are, in fact, three *appellations* for Muscadet, of which
by far the most important from a quantity point of view is
Muscadet de Sèvre-et-Maine. This *appellation* covers
communes in the cantons of Clisson, Loroux-Bottereau,
Vallet, Vertou and Aigrefeuille-sur-Maine. The *appellation* of
Muscadet des Coteaux de la Loire covers communes on both
sides of the river in Loire-Atlantique, and some communes in
Maine-et-Loire. The straight *appellation* of Muscadet covers
the wine produced from the area of production not
mentioned in the two other categories. The total surface of
all the Muscadet *appellations* covers 9,400 hectares, with an

average production of 350,000 hectolitres although the figure was 595,683 hectolitres of *appellation contrôlée* wine in 1983. Nearly 85 per cent of the total volume comes from the area of Sèvre-et-Maine. The latter area is very intensively planted with vines, whereas the other two *appellation* areas have vines planted more patchily. The maximum yield for Sèvre-et-Maine is forty hectolitres per hectare, the same for the Coteaux de la Loire, with fifty hectolitres per hectare for Muscadet *simple*. However, this is often increased on an annual review basis, and sixty hectolitres per hectare would be allowed in Sèvre-et-Maine in a good year. It cannot be denied that sometimes very high yields indeed are attained.

Generally speaking, the wines of the Coteaux de la Loire are drier with perhaps less fruit than those of Sèvre-et-Maine, but they stand up quite well in bottle. Muscadet de Sèvre-et-Maine has charm and fruit, and is extremely attractive young drinking – obviously, those producers making wines with more flavour and body find that their wines last better in bottle than those which have a flowery, attractive nose, but not much behind that. In Sèvre-et-Maine, the triangle between Vallet, Mouzillon and La Chapelle-Heulin is supposed to produce the best wine – it is certainly the heart of the region. The wines coming from Le Landreau are also highly prized. There are different characteristics between communes – the excellent wines from Mouzillon stand up well in bottle, while those from La Chapelle-Heulin are supple and delicious young. When the wine does not come from a single domain, a blend of the two can produce a very complete wine.

Methods of vinification vary according to the size of the enterprise and the capital available. The governmental body of the SAFER tends to prevent too large holdings, preferring that the land should be held by a larger number of small growers. The installations of a domain such as Pierre Lusseaud's Château de la Galissonnière at Le Pallet near Vallet (the vineyards of Château de la Jannière and Château de la Maisdonnière are also within the estate) are of the most modern, with fermentations of three to four weeks at 18 to 22°C giving wines of enormous character and flavour for the region. At La Chapelle-Heulin, the Fleurance family at the Domaine des Gautronnières relies much more heavily on wood throughout the whole wine-making and keeping process, and the result shows in the wine, full-bodied and concentrated. Casks can be large, many of 600 litres.

The soil of the Sèvre-et-Maine region has a great deal of sand, from 60 to 80 per cent, with clay making up from 10 to 30 per cent. At Galissonnière, the soil is siliceous clay, on a base of granite – there is no calcareous soil in Sèvre-et-Maine. Malolactic fermentations are usually prevented in Muscadet, as the acidity is necessary to give some backbone to the wine. On the other hand, chaptalization is needed, but Muscadet must never be more than 12 per cent, the only *appellation contrôlée* to have an upper alcohol limit. The wines must all pass tasting and analysis, and there is no doubt that in the 1970s the amount of badly produced wines, be they oxidized or suffering from excessive sulphur dioxide, diminished dramatically. Machine picking is becoming more usual in the Muscadet, especially on the large domains such as Galissonnière. The vines have traditionally been trained very low on one wire, but probably for the future a compromise between high and low training is best, as always walking the tightrope between too much vegetation, or leaves, leading to *pourriture* when it is humid, but with enough to nourish the ripening grapes.

Estates such as Galissonnière/Jannière/Maisdonnière, and Henri Poiron's Les Quatre Routes are of the very top quality, and completely bely the view that Muscadet is pleasant, but neutral. The Fleurance Domaine des Gautronnières and La Berrière at Barbechat, La Chapelle-Basse-Mer, belonging to the de Bascher family, are examples of two very good domain wines. M. Gabriel Thébaud at Saint-Fiacre is also a most careful wine-maker and *négociant*, with his Domaine de la Hautière usually very good, and M. Léon Boullault at his own Château la Touche near Vallet has a justifiably high reputation. The very erudite Comte de Malestroit has the Château la Noë, which perhaps needs a little more technical expertise to fulfil its true potential. The *négociant* Drouet at Vallet produces wines to a very high standard, as does the family firm of Guilband Frères at Mouzillon, whose great experience at choosing wines both for straight Muscadet de Sèvre-et-Maine and specific domains (such as the much acclaimed Domaine de la Roche and the Domaine des Pierres Blanches) is now well known. Martin at Mouzillon is well distributed, as is Sautejeau (M. Jean Beauquin) at La Chapelle-Heulin; both make wines that are good value but need to be drunk when very young. Donatien Bahuaud is a very large concern indeed, and their wines include their own Château de la Cassemichère. They have also planted a little Chardonnay, which they sell as Vin de Table, Le Chouan. The Marquis de Goulaine has made a great success of his Muscadet business round the world. Sauvion, Louis Métaineau and Chérau-Carré are also recommended.

Muscadet should always be drunk young. 1975 and 1976 were both good, but should have disappeared down thirsty throats long ago. 1978 and 1979 were both fruity and good, with 1978 perhaps firmer and 1979 fruiter. 1982 was very ripe, 1983 splendid, and 1984 shows good fruity projection.

Gros-Plant du Pays Nantais: This VDQS wine is often, justifiably, criticized for its high acidity, and it is only in ripe years, such as 1976, 1982 and 1983, that it attains really pleasurable proportions. In other years, it is necessary to pick as late as possible to give the acidity a chance to fall. Known as the Folle Blanche in the Charente, the wine produced from the Gros Plant grape variety has a rustic freshness and a low alcohol reading. It is grown on poor, acid soil, often with schist as a base. The area covered by the VDQS includes a great many communes in the Loire-Atlantique, the Vendée and in Maine-et-Loire. The total surface area is 2,400 hectares, and the average production 80,000 hectolitres. Some of the best Muscadet producers also have a Gros Plant on their list, and the wine is well-known for its diuretic qualities.

Coteaux d'Ancenis: The right bank of the Loire round Ancenis produces some light but pleasant Gamay wines, rather acid in poor years, but benefiting from those with more sun. There is also a little Cabernet, and some rather surprising patches of less usual grape varieties. Jacques

Guindon at St-Géréon makes some excellent, full Malvoisie (which is really the Pinot Gris). In the same village Joseph Toublanc is even making some dry white Verdelho. Auguste Athimon is another good *vigneron*, with Gamay and Cabernet. The VDQS Coteaux d'Ancenis covers red, rosé and white wines, but the name must be followed by the grape variety.

ANJOU-SAUMUR

This large area, on either side of the Loire, produces a wide variety of wines for all tastes. In 1983, 293,632 hectolitres of *appellation contrôlée* white wine and 549,975 hectolitres of red and rosé were produced in the region. The Chenin (Pineau de la Loire) is responsible for the white wines (occasionally, now, mixed with a small proportion of Sauvignon or Chardonnay when dry), be they sweet or dry or hovering in between, and the reds are made predominantly from the Cabernet Franc, occasionally mixed with a little Cabernet Sauvignon. The Cabernet Franc is also the grape behind the rosés of superior quality The Groslot, the Gamay and the Côt (or Malbec) are also used for lesser rosé wine, the rockbed of Rosé d'Anjou. The Chenin Noir, or Pineau d'Aunis, is less seen.

Savennières: Going upstream, the first important Angevin *appellation* is Savennières, an enclave on the right bank of the Loire, within the Anjou Coteaux de la Loire *appellation*. Savennières, like Quarts de Chaume, Bonnezeaux and Vouvray, is a wine that makes history; people talk tantalizingly about bottles of up to fifty years old with rare richness and complexity. Unfortunately, when Savennières is young, it gives little indication of its greatness – the Chenin grape is rather crude when young, the wines often have a whiff of sulphur and seem rather acid, and one wonders what all the fuss is about. Savennières is usually dry, attaining some richness in very ripe years, but often with that Chenin characteristic of appearing very full, but ending dry in the mouth – bottle age always makes the wine more ample. These slopes of Savennières are really rocky spurs advancing towards the Loire, beautifully exposed to the south, giving the late-ripening Chenin the sun it so much needs. The yield is usually small, the soil on the slopes thin and with fragmented blue volcanic rock, together with some pebbles.

Within Savennières, there are two Grands Crus: La Roche aux Moines (about twenty planted hectares), and La Coulée de Serrant (less than five hectares). The Vignoble de la Bizolière is now part of Yves Soulez's estate with eighteen hectares of vineyard, mostly in small parcels. The estate includes vineyards in La Roche aux Moines which is more fertile than Savennières Clos du Papillon, another site along this slope, but can become very dry in summer. These wines really need time to 'marry' and become harmonious – the 1947s are still fresh here. In 1980, the 1976s were still too young, the 1971s only just coming into their own. Frost can be a problem on these slopes, and 1945 and 1977 bear witness to that. There is a second white wine of the property, Clos des Fougeraies, with *appellation* Anjou. A dry white Savennières has to have 12.5 per cent minimum alcohol, and 5 grams acidity would give good balance for this type of wine, suitable for ageing. Savennières is limited to a yield of twenty-five hectolitres per hectare, but is often less.

Yves Soulez also owns the Château de Chamboureau and the vinification techniques are of the most modern. Another Savennières for long ageing is made at the Château d'Epiré, the property of M. Armand Bizard, with cellars in the church behind the château. The Domaine du Closel is also a most worthy property. The Château de la Roche aux Moines and vineyard of Coulée de Serrant belong to Madame Joly, who has made a very prestigious niche for her wines. She also owns part of La Roche aux Moines, and has a red Cabernet, Château de la Roche. Coulée de Serrant is somewhat lean and austere in youth, but can develop honey-like tones with bottle age. 1983, 1981 and 1978 are most promising, with the 1970 a perfectly balanced wine at fifteen years old. Monsieur Jean Baumard from across the river also produces Savennières and Savennières Clos du Papillon. The Baumard domain own nearly half of the four hectares which make up the vineyard of Clos du Papillon.

Coteaux-du-Layon (Bonnezeaux and Quarts de Chaume): Across
the river, and this can be difficult when it floods in winter,
one arrives at Rochefort-sur-Loire. Somehow the wines
from around Rochefort itself are between Savennières and
Layon in character. Here, along the Layon river, the overall
appellation is Coteaux-du-Layon, and within it two distinct
appellations, Bonnezeaux (approximately 100 hectares) and
Quarts de Chaume, about half that size. The Layon river,
running from the south-east towards the Loire, has made a
sheltered valley for itself and the surrounding vineyards,
protecting them from the north and the east. It is a real
micro-climate, and six communes were recognized in a
decree of 1955 as Coteaux-du-Layon-Villages – Beaulieu,
Faye-d'Anjou, Rablay-sur-Layon, Rochefort-sur-Loire, St-
Aubin-de-Luigné, St-Lambert-du-Lattay, together with the
hamlet of Chaume. Bonnezeaux, near Thouarcé, and Quarts
de Chaume are *grands crus,* classified in 1951 and 1954
respectively. At their greatest, these wines are a subtle and
magic blend of scents and fruits, with an uncloying
complexity that makes one almost question whether the
grape alone has gone into their making. People talk of
quince and peach and honey, but underlying all there is the
lively spirit of the Chenin grape itself. However, this is
Layon wine at its pinnacle. When the fermentations are
stopped with sulphur, racking and sometimes refrigeration,
the wines can be merely common.

   The vintage can be very protracted, usually beginning
during the first days of October and sometimes lasting until
about 10 November. Occasionally, when the autumn is hot
but dry, the *Botrytis cinerea* cannot develop; here, the must
becomes rich by a simple concentration of all the
ingredients. This concentration of sugar, whether it be due
to the influence of *pourriture noble* or a simple evaporation of
the water in the grapes, obviously makes for a reduced yield.
Fermentations can last from four to six weeks, sometimes
requiring the cellars to be warmed so that they proceed
continuously. The alcohol in these wines can reach 14 or 15
per cent or more, contributing to their longevity. The wines
do not need ageing in cask, many of which are the large

600-litre type, and benefit from being bottled in the spring after the vintage.

Quarts de Chaume can produce the most concentrated and rich wines of all. The soil is hard schist, and the situation particularly protected from the winds from the north, the east and the west, helping the grapes ripen more quickly than elsewhere. The maximum yield is 22 hectolitres per hectare, but is often less. It must have 13 per cent alcohol minimum. I have tasted excellent Quarts de Chaume from the Domaine Baumard (the 1959 was remarkable) – the Baumard domain has one of the three main holdings in the *grand cru*, although there are five proprietors in all. Monsieur Lalanne at the Château de Bellerive produces excellent wine, as does the Laffourcade family with their two properties, Suronde and Echarderie.

The Bonnezeaux vineyard is within the commune of Thouarcé on the right bank of the Layon. The wines are perhaps softer and gentler than Quarts de Chaume, but still golden and unctuous. No one makes better Bonnezeaux than M. Jean Boivin at the Château de Fesles – he also makes the wine of Madame Fourlinnie, his sister. The Raimbault family at Thouarcé also makes very good Bonnezeaux. M. Jean-Paul Tijou, with his cellars right on the quayside at Rochefort always at the mercy of the rising waters, makes the very fine Château de Bellevue and excellent Coteaux-du-Layon Chaume, as does M. Jaudeau at the Château de la Roulerie. Two Chaumes from the higher part of the slope, and easily the equal of Quarts-de-Chaume, are the Château de Plaisance of M. Henri Rochais, and La Guimonière of M. Doucet. M. Jacques Lecointre at the Caves de la Pierre Blanche has very good Coteaux-du-Layon Rablay, and M. Jean Petiteau at St Lambert-du-Lattay is worth visiting. The Clos de Ste Catherine, Coteaux-du-Layon Rochefort of Jean Baumard is also recommended – it is a very well-placed site. At Beaulieu, there is the Domaine de la Soucherie.

Other Anjou appellations: The *appellation* Cabernet d'Anjou is only for rosé wine made from Cabernet Franc with or without Cabernet Sauvignon (a grape which is more fragile here) – the same applies to the *appellation* Cabernet de Saumur. The skins are left in contact with the juice from anything between a few hours to a day, according to the depth of colour preferred. Rosé d'Anjou is of inferior quality, and usually rather sweet, giving a wine much appreciated in the United Kingdom and in Germany and Scandinavia; it can also be *pétillant*. Rosé d'Anjou is commercially very important to the region – production was 219,309 hectolitres in 1978, and 317,491 in 1979. It is interesting to note that the wines of Anjou and Saumur, after Bordeaux, Burgundy and the Côtes du Rhône, take fourth place in the list of *appellation contrôlée* wines exported from France. Three-quarters of this amount is rosé. A little more than half is exported in bottle. Rosé de la Loire is a recent (1974) *appellation* producing dry wines, but it has been slow to make its mark. It is a blend of Cabernet (30 per cent), Groslot, Côt, Gamay and Pineau d'Aunis. There are also the *appellations* of Anjou (Blanc et Rouge), Anjou-Gamay, Saumur (Blanc et Rouge), Anjou (Blanc) *pétillant*, and Saumur (Blanc) *pétillant*. Brissac is regarded as a very good area for the Cabernet, with good finds amongst small growers and the large cooperative. Good red Cabernet, sappy and fruity, will be found under the *appellation* Anjou. The Saumur whites are usually nervier, more acid and perhaps drier than the Anjou whites. Anjou certainly has a soft and gentle climate for much of the year. From April to September, the average temperature at Angers is a degree higher than that in Paris. However, Anjou and the Saumurois have many differences, although they both come under the Anjou 'umbrella'. The Saumur area is predominantly calcareous, while to the west and at Layon the soil is predominantly hard schist, with occasional sandstone. Saumur produces *vin de tuffeau*, Anjou *vin d'ardoise*. The soil has a direct influence on the types of wine produced – lighter on chalky soil, heavier on the schist where the blackish soil stores the heat better. Calcareous and siliceous soils give good red wine; on schist, red and rosé wines are thicker, with less breed. Apart from the rosé Cabernet de Saumur, the Saumur growers can choose between the Anjou

211

or Saumur *appellation* when they declare their harvest.

Coteaux de l'Aubance: Coteaux de l'Aubance wines are white from the Chenin, and most successful when *demi-sec*. Running parallel to the Layon *appellations*, they can be very good value. Biotteau at St-Jean-des-Mauvrets is highly recommended, as is M. Papin at St-Melaine-sur-Aubance and Didier Richou.

Anjou Coteaux de la Loire: Anjou Coteaux de la Loire is an *appellation* that includes villages on both sides of the river, nearly all to the west of Angers. The vineyards cling to the slopes near the river, as the plateaux behind them are mostly clayey, with the soil too humid for good ripening of vines. As with all Chenin white wines, poor years can give rather mean, acid wines, but kinder vintages can give a nervy lusciousness that is most tempting. Villages that produce a good deal of wine are Bouchemaine, St Georges-sur-Loire, Champtocé and Ingrandes – and on the left bank, Montjean, La Pommeraye and a part of Chalonnes, where there is a wine fair towards the end of February.

Saumur Appellations: The best rosé wines originate from around Saumur, Tigné and Brissac. The wonderful *craie tuffeau* soil gives seemingly endless underground cellars, which serve the large *négociants* and cooperatives well. After the devastation of phylloxera in the Saumurois region, the reconstitution of the vineyard, always difficult in calcareous soil, was not always helped by the choice of root stocks which would favour maturation of the grapes. Saumur concentrated too much on its sparkling wines, and neglected its still wines, particularly in the case of white wines, where Bas Anjou gave formidable competition – at that time, the area around Saumur was 'Haut Anjou'. In many ways, the Saumur region is more akin to Touraine, with its *tuffeau* and Vouvray-like caves. The *appellation* Coteaux-de-Saumur is for white wines only, made from the Chenin, and includes villages like Montsoreau, Bizay, Brézé, Parnay, St-Cyr-en-Bourg, Turquant and Dampierre, but now the Saumur *appellation* is normally used. The wines are nearly always dry or *demi-sec*, with a great deal of youthful vivacity. In poor years, they can be 'green'. Locally, they say that they have a

212

goût de tuf, which is picturesque, if difficult to identify.

Occasionally, when the year permits, there are rich wines from these communes, and these are the bottles that last. In days past, they were often labelled with the name of the village and the *lieu dit* or site, with no mention of the word 'Saumur' – I remember one such marvellous bottle, which simply announced itself as Brézé 1959, Baron Brancard. I admire the wines of M. Chauvat at the Château Fouquet at Brézé, and have seen good wine from Le Floch-Ernoult at Turquant. At Parnay, the Château de Parnay wines of M. Jacques Collé are excellent, with the reputed Clos des Murs, and in the same commune M. Bertholet also has a fine reputation. At Bizay, there is the estimable Domaine Bougoin, and at Souzay-Champigny, M. Chevallier at the Château de Villeneuve produces very well-made wine. Two Saumur Blanc wines to look out for are those of M. Pichot at the Clos de Boismenard at Tourtenay, Thouars, and M. Claude Daheuiller at Les Varinelles, Varrains. Of course, many of these producers also make excellent red Saumur-Champigny, which became very popular indeed in France during the 1970s. The wines are made almost entirely from the Cabernet Franc, which gives a sappy, somewhat 'grassy' nose, and a lot of life and fruit on the palate. Many of the wines are nice drunk comparatively young, within a few years of their birth, but there are exceptions. One is M. Paul Filliatreau at Chaintres, in the Dampierre area, who makes wines with more body, colour and depth than is usual for the region, with more tannin; his wines need more time to smooth out – it is worth waiting. He also has a plot of very old vines, which he keeps separate. There is also the Château de Chaintres at Dampierre, belonging to the de Tigny family, making consistently good wine. Apart from many of the producers mentioned above for white wine, one can add the wine of M. Maurice Rebeilleau and the Domaine des Roches Neuves of Denis Duveau at Varrains, where there is more gravel and less tufa, the Château de Targé of M. Pisani-Ferry at Parnay, and M. André Sanzay in the same commune. This part of the Loire is lucky to have two excellent cooperatives. The Vignerons de Saumur at St

Cyr-en-Bourg work with great seriousness, and all their wines can be relied upon – Saumur Blanc et Rouge, Saumur-Champigny, Crémant de Loire and Mousseux made by the Champagne method. The underground cellars cover three hectares, and can be visited by car! The other large cooperative, Les Caves de la Loire at Brissac, is nearer Angers, to the west – it also is most reliable. There is also the INRA at Montreuil-Bellay, which has helped raise the standard of the red wines of the area and does not neglect to make a good one itself.

Sparkling Wine

The Saumur area is also famous for its Champagne-method Mousseux, or sparkling wine – 80 per cent of the total is made by the Champagne method, the rest is non-*appellation contrôlée*. Saumur Mousseux is white, Anjou Mousseux can be white or rosé. The acidity of the Chenin lends itself to *champenisation*, and the wines are very carefully made, often by firms with connections in Champagne. They lack the breed on the nose that the grape varieties of Champagne impart (occasionally at Saumur there is a bit of Chardonnay in the blend), but they are good alternatives when the occasion calls for something light-hearted. Up to 60 per cent *blanc de noirs* can be added, essentially from the Cabernet. The *appellation* wines must always be made using the method of a second fermentation in bottle, not in vat. The house of Gratien-Meyer (the same family ownership as Alfred Gratien Champagne) has a justifiably high reputation, only buying in grapes not wine, and Ackerman-Laurance, Bouvet-Ladubay (belonging to Taittinger), and Veuve Amiot are also most reliable. These firms tend to give their wines a couple of years of rest before disgorging. The houses at St Hilaire-St Florent benefit from marvellous natural cellars in the tufa. The laws for the production of Crémant de Loire, an *appellation* dating from 1975, are stricter than for Mousseux, with regard to grape varieties permitted. *Pétillant* wines also have a second fermentation in bottle, but the pressure in the bottle is two times less and the cork can be held in place by a simple *agrafe*.

214

Vins du Thouarsais: Right to the south of Anjou-Saumur, round the town of Thouars, there is the VDQS called Vins du Thouarsais. The whites are Chenin and sweetish and there are light, fruity reds, and some rosé. Michel Gigon at Oiron is a good producer.

Vins du Haut-Poitou: South-east of here, towards Poitiers, there is another VDQS of great note, the Vins du Haut-Poitou. The production is virtually entirely in the hands of the Cave Coopérative du Haut-Poitou at Neuville-de-Poitou, which now has about 300 grower members. This cooperative is surely one of the best run in the whole of France, and has a formidable history of enterprise behind it. The area, which looks more suitable for cereals than for the vine, used to supply a large amount of low-alcohol white wine, mostly from hybrids, to the Cognac producers. After the Second World War, the remarkable director of the cooperative, M. Gavid, began a policy of persuading the growers to plant good grape varieties, and gradually he built up the quality to a standard today that is more worthy of many *appellations*. M. Gavid also developed a clever selling plan which reduced the sale of wine *en vrac*, in bulk, and bottled his wines young and well for direct sale to the best restaurants in France. His successor, M. Raffarin, has continued all these ideas and the Cave has gone from strength to strength, with excellent modern installations. The wines made are dry, crisp Sauvignon, Chardonnay, a red Gamay and an excellent Méthode Champenoise Chardonnay Blanc de Blancs.

TOURAINE

Touraine shares the soft light and gentler climate of Anjou with that region, and a good deal of the *tuffeau* soil of Saumur. It shares with both a preponderance of Chenin and Cabernet Franc, but also makes a speciality of Sauvignon and Gamay in certain areas of the region. Touraine itself is not very large, with the total vineyard surface area about 9,950 hectares. In 1983 the region produced 272,173 hectolitres of *appellation contrôlée* white wine and 302,059 hectolitres of red. The most famous *appellations*, Chinon,

Bourgueil, Vouvray, and Montlouis, are in the *département* of the Indre-et-Loire, less famous wines, such as Touraine Mesland, are in the Loir-et-Cher (it is a muddling fact that a tributary of the Loire is called the Loir), and the vineyard even stretches into the Sarthe with the Coteaux du Loir and Jasnières. It is the sides of the valleys that give the best vineyard sites in Touraine, and Touraine is rich in rivers – the Loir, the Loire, the Cher, the Indre, the Vienne and the Creuse, to name the most important.

Chinon and Bourgueil: Going upstream the first vineyards of Touraine that one encounters are those red *appellations* of Chinon and Bourgeuil. Both are predominantly produced from the Cabernet Franc grape, that zingy, sappy, fruity varietal that gives a tempting, almost 'grassy' or 'herby' nose and a definite and generous taste. It has neither the astringence nor the tannin of the Cabernet Sauvignon, nor its long life. The two *appellations* of Bourgueil and St-Nicolas-de-Bourgueil are only for red and the rarely met rosé wine, made almost entirely from the Cabernet Franc (or the Breton, as it is often known in the region), although the Cabernet Sauvignon is allowed. The same applies to Chinon, although the *appellation* exists for white wine as well, made from the Chenin. However, the wines that count are red.

Bourgueil, and St-Nicolas-de-Bourgueil, north of the Loire, are on banks or terraces of ancient alluvia, giving very well-drained gravelly soil. Wines from this alluvial mixture of sand and large gravel are very scented and refined and develop quite early. But above these pebbly gravel soils, higher up, the soil is more clayey-calcareous on a sub-soil of *craie tuffeau*. Here the wines are slightly harder, take time to show their fruit, and keep better. The vine covers 870 hectares in *appellation* Bourgueil and 470 hectares in *appellation* St-Nicolas-de-Bourgueil. The communes of the Bourgueil *appellation* are Benais, Bourgueil, La Chapelle-sur-Loire, Chouzé-sur-Loire, Ingrandes, Restigné and St-Patrice. St-Nicolas-de-Bourgueil is only produced in the commune of the same name. In both Bourgueil and Chinon, the grapes are de-stalked, often on the vine, vatting is long, and the cellars in the rock are cold. Cutting the grape from the stalk in the vineyard leaves the grape intact, while mechanical *égrappage* is more brutal – thus, *égrappage manuel* helps give supple wines, without astringence, in spite of the long vattings. Obviously, the process can only be followed in relatively small holdings. Fermentation can be for twenty to twenty-eight days in Bourgueil and Chinon, without making the wines tough, but giving them bouquet and character. Clearly, the temperature must be watched carefully, and in 1976 there were some 'accidents' in the region at this stage. But normally, the cold cellars give long, cool fermentations, and morning and evening the growers push down the *chapeau* or hat that has formed on top of the fermenting vat. This 'floating hat' method, often dangerous in hotter climes, suits the wines of Chinon and Bourgueil, and helps in the extraction process. These red wines usually have good tannin balance and alcohol levels of between 11 and 12 per cent. Their bouquet seems to draw out an imaginative vocabulary, with that of Chinon likened to violets or wild strawberries, and Bourgueil to raspberries.

Some remarkable St-Nicolas-de-Bourgueil is made by M. Claude Ammeux at the Clos de la Contrie. Perhaps it is not altogether typical, because there is an *égrappoir* here, the soil is stony and flinty and, very unusually, they use a yeast from the Côte d'Or, which, whether real or imagined, for me seems to have an influence on the nose and taste. There is no fining or filtering, just racking, and bottling is at about eight months – many growers bottle a bit later. The result is big wines with depth and body. The Amirault family also makes excellent St-Nicolas, as does M. Pierre Boireau, a small, welcoming grower. Other really good Bourgueils are made by Paul Maître at Benais, Lamé-Delille-Boucard at Ingrandes-de-Touraine, La Hurolaie by Caslot-Galbrun, and the Clos de l'Abbaye of the GAEC de la Dime.

Chinon scatters her vineyards over a wider area, between the Loire and the Vienne and all along the valley of the Vienne. The most densely planted communes are on the best exposed sites of the right bank of the Vienne. The soil is more diverse than in Bourgueil, mixing sand, gravel and pebbly slopes. The vineyard covers 1,060 hectares and includes eighteen communes. Cravant-les-Coteaux is often regarded as the best, and has some good gentle slopes. The Loire *négociant* of Aimé Boucher makes some excellent selections in Cravant, and also chooses robust Bourgueil. Couly-Dutheil and his domain of Clos de l'Echo are well known, if expensive (as are Audebert in Bourgueil). The Angelliaume family at Cravant has very good value wines as does M. René Gouron, and M. Paul Zéja at Ligré has Chinon of character. Different members of the Raffault family at Savigny-en-Véron are recommended. The wine of M. Raymond Desbourdes at Panzoult is very carefully made, and the *négociant* Langlois-Château always has very good Chinon. M. Jean Baudry of the Domaine de la Perrière at Cravant has a good reputation. Good years for Bourgueil-Chinon are: 1983, 1982, 1979, 1978, 1976, 1975, 1971, 1970, 1969, 1964 1959, 1955, 1953, 1949, 1948 and the great 1947s.

Vouvray: Great Vouvray is a remarkable experience of long-lasting flavour in the mouth, and a wonderful contrast of honey and fruit flavours, backed with Chenin firmness. But the wines made in this *appellation* are also very pleasurable when they cannot be rich and luscious, just smooth and slightly sweet. The vineyard area is to the north of the Loire. river, very near Tours, and produces *tuffeau* wine *par excellence*, with its chalky soil and incredible natural cellars. Well away from the river the soil becomes more clay/flint. Here the Pineau Blanc de la Loire, or Chenin, reigns supreme, and the wines can be still, *pétillant*, or *mousseux*. These latter are made by the Champagne method and the whole process is frequently looked after by *champenisateurs*, specialists who visit the growers' cellars at the propitious moments to carry out the various manoeuvres necessary for the *appellation* Vouvray-Mousseux. On the whole, the less well-placed sites provide wines that are dry or that are suitable for base wine for Mousseux (low alcohol), and the best sites give *demi-sec* or *moelleux* Vouvray. Mousseux wines throughout Touraine are sold at 4.5 kilograms of pressure, Crémant de Loire 3.5 kilograms, and *pétillant* 2.5 kilograms. The vineyard area covers 1,550 hectares, and includes the communes of Chançay, Noizay, Parçay-Meslay, Reugny, Rochecorbon, Tours-Ste-Radegonde, Vernou-sur-Brenne and Vouvray itself. The area is criss-crossed by little valleys, such as the Vallée Coquette, the Vallée Chartier, the Vallées de Cousse, de Vaux and de la Brenne. The best sites are still referred to locally and much recorded in old volumes, but unfortunately, very few wines are now sold under their site names.

The art of making good Vouvray is careful selection – choosing the best grapes for the great sweet wines, and then going down the scale to the totally dry wines and the sparkling wines. The wines always have a good balance of malic acidity, with no malolactic fermentation taking place, to give freshness, and are not too vulnerable to oxidation – a great advantage. Some years give conditions for *pourriture noble*, which always requires a certain amount of humidity with the sun, and others, such as 1947, were rich through great ripeness, *surmaturité*, with no *pourriture noble*. Obviously, quality differs according to the communes and sites, and there are wines of the Côtes (nearly all in the case of Rochecorbon) and those of the Arrières Côtes.

A Vouvray house that has a justifiably very high reputation for blending marvellous wines is that of Marc Brédif, at Rochecorbon. The large Pouilly-Fumé firm of Ladoucette bought Marc Brédif in 1980. The late Marc Brédif's son-in-law, M. Jacques Cartier, has great experience of the wines of Vouvray, and makes wines to last when vintage conditions permit. The wines are blended in glass-lined vats (Brédif buys wine, not grapes), and only receive about a month in wood. I have had generous tasting with M. Cartier, seeing satiny *moelleux* 1971 wines, a *moelleux* 1953 with *pourriture noble* character but not really *liquoreux*, and a magnificent 1928 Rochecorbon, rich, old and venerable, with that noble rot taste, silky texture and a lightness of touch that was sheer joy. M. Gaston Huet at the Haut-Lieu in Vouvray is a renowned producer of fine Vouvray. Amongst many wines, I particularly recall a *demi-sec* of great breed from the small yielding 1969 vintage, and a wonderful *moelleux* wine from the 1973 vintage, giving the impression of a bouquet of flowers in the mouth. The sites are often kept separate here, Clos du Bourg, Le Haut-Lieu, Le Mont. Other top producers are M. Foreau at the Clos Naudin, M. Allias at the Petit Mont, M. Delaleu who has the Clos Dubois, M. Raoul Diard, M. Maurice Audebert with his Coteau Chatrie. M. Jean Bertrand at Rochecorbon, and Prince Poniatowski at Le Clos Baudoin, with his wine, L'Aigle Blanc. And I have a particular affection for the Huguet family at Le Grand Ormeau, who makes all types of Vouvray, still, sparkling, sweet and dry, with honesty and warmth. The Château Moncontour makes quite stylish wines with very modern methods of vinification. Vouvray of great years is almost indestructible. 1979 and 1978 were good, 1976 was great, 1975 good, 1973 good with some really ripe wines, excellent *moelleux* wines in 1971, good in 1970, great 1969s, wonderful 1964, 1961, 1959, 1955, 1953, 1949, 1947, 1945, 1943, 1937, 1934, 1933 (rather curiously, but some great surprises), 1928, 1924, and the fabled 1921. The 1947 and 1921 years are the great rivals – both were high in alcohol. The years with marked *pourriture noble* character are 1933, 1934, 1937 and 1949. It might seem esoteric to cite these old vintages, but great old Vouvray has a habit of turning up occasionally in a wine-lover's life.

Montlouis: Just across the river from Vouvray is Montlouis, a slightly lighter wine, sometimes with marked acidity when dryish and young, and never attaining the great lusciousness of the very best Vouvray. The climate and soil are the same, but the sites less well exposed in the main. Only the very best have the definition and 'edge' of good Vouvray, but they can be really pleasant, soft, and very good value. I have admired the wines of MM. René-Pierre Dardeau, Moyer, Berger, Denis, Leblois, Tessier and Lavasseur. As at Vouvray, the site names have all but disappeared, although I still have a very old label from the Clos de Cangé at St-Martin-le-Beau. The vineyard is about 260 hectares and covers the communes of Lussault, Montlouis-sur-Loire, and St-Martin-le-Beau.

Touraine Azay-le-Rideau: Touraine Azay-le-Rideau is rather an outpost of vines – the wines of the commune of Saché used to be famous, even rivalling Vouvray in great years. It is rare that these white products of the Chenin become rich and complex, but they can. Otherwise, they are fresh and crisp. M. Gaston Pavy makes the very best of the *appellation* at Saché itself, as does M. Francis Paget at Rivarennes. There are also rosé wines made from the Grolleau, and some red wines from Gamay, *appellation* Touraine.

Touraine Amboise: Touraine Amboise gives white wines from a sub-soil of *craie tuffeau*, but also red and rosé wine from the Côt (or Malbec), Gamay and Cabernet. M. Yves Moreau at Cangey and M. Jacques Bonnigal of Limeray both have a range of Touraine-Amboise, as well as M. Hubert Dennay at Le Breuil and M. Dutertre at Limeray. These wines are always reasonable and so, if well made, good bargains.

Touraine Mesland: Touraine Mesland is for white, red and rosé wines grown in the Mesland area on the right bank of the Loire in the Loir-et-Cher. Much bigger than the previous two *appellations*, it concentrates on red and rosé. The Domaine Girault-Artois and the Domaine Lusqueneau of M. Brossillon are worthy producers.

Gamay de Touraine: Gamay de Touraine (the *appellation* is Touraine with the grape variety name) is a very good buy in sunny years. The Gamay flourishes along the valley of the river Cher, and the left bank, around St Aignan, is particularly noted. In years with high acidity, some Gamays are made by the *macération carbonique* method, and bottling is in the January or February after the vintage, with some people even doing a November bottling to catch the Primeur market. There are good cooperatives at Francueil and Civray, and the area as a whole is cooperative orientated.

Sauvignon de Touraine: The Sauvignon de Touraine of the cooperative at Oisly-Thésée had made its mark; all the whites here have quite a firm acidity, as there is no malolactic fermentation. The most 'aristocratic' Sauvignon de Touraine wines I have seen in the Oisly area (if that is a term that can be applied to this grape variety) belong to M. Maurice Barboux, whose grandfather introduced the grape variety to the region from Pouilly-Sancerre. His Vignoble des Corbillières is quite excellent, and all his wine-making is of the most intelligent. He also has some Chardonnay and Pinot Noir (experimentally), Gamay, and Cabernet. There is flint in this area, which is ideal for the Sauvignon. The Janvier family at Thésée is also known for quality. The much-respected *négociant* Aimé Boucher makes a specialty of these wines, working from his cellars near Chambord at Huisseau-sur-Cosson. At Montrichard, the *négociant* Monmousseau specializes in *mousseux*.

Coteaux du Loir: The area of the Coteaux du Loir (white, red and rosé) is due north of Tours, round La Chartre-sur-le-Loir.

Jasnières: The white wines of Jasnières can become quite rich with age in bottle – this can be proved with the good wines of MM. Legreau, Gigou or Pinon – but when young they are more often hard and austere.

There are a few VDQS wines in Touraine, some of more than passing interest, particularly Valençay. All the grape varieties are found here, as well as the local Arbois (nothing to do with the Jura) which is related to the Chenin. M. Paquier at Chabris and M. Berthonnet are both honourable producers, and the prices are good. I have my doubts about Cheverny, as I find the local white grape variety, the Romorantin, acid in all but the ripest years. Two other VDQS are the Coteaux du Vendômois and the greatly diminished Vins de l'Orléannais.

POUILLY FUME AND SANCERRE

These are very important *appellations* for lovers of French dry white wine, although in years when quantity is affected, their prices tend to go higher than their intrinsic worth. But their teasing, smoky flavour and glancing elegance will always attract those who dislike neutral wines – these make a statement. Happily, their great popularity has helped encourage the *vigneron* to stay and cultivate his vines because many became disenchanted with spring frosts and other bad weather, particularly hail at Pouilly, giving very irregular harvests.

Pouilly: In fact, there are three *appellations* at Pouilly: Blanc Fumé de Pouilly, Pouilly Fumé (which are none other than the crisp Sauvignon wine we know and love), and Pouilly-Sur-Loire, a wine lower in alcohol made from the Chasselas grape, with or without an admixture of Blanc Fumé (Sauvignon); it should be consumed young. The communes included are Pouilly-sur-Loire, St-Andelain, Tracy-sur-Loire, St-Laurent, St-Martin-sur-Nohain, Garchy and Mesves-sur-Loire. Here, as at Sancerre, the small *vigneron* is 'roi', producing about 200,000 cases of the two Fumé wines a year, whereas at Sancerre the quantity is nearer 500,000 cases. Pouilly Fumé wines are very similar to Sancerre, although the former can be fuller and more complex, and tend to improve still further with a year or two in bottle, whereas Sancerre is delicious and fragrant when really young. Both are on chalky, flinty soil – the vineyards of Pouilly rise from the river Loire and go into rolling hills and plateaux.

I have always enjoyed the attack and sheer definition of M. Maurice Bailly's Fumé wines, and M. Serge Dagueneau at Les Berthiers is a master at his craft. Also recommended are M. Michel Redde, M. Georges Guyot, M. Robert Penard at Les Loges, M. Blanchet of Les Berthiers, M. Paul Mollet of Tracy-sur-Loire, MM. Robert Minet and Seguin of Le Bouchot, M. Marcel Laugoux of Le Soumard, M. Paul Figeat of Les Loges and M. Jacques Foucher of Pouilly. I have drunk older wines of the Château de Tracy which were really complex. The very dynamic Baron Patrick Ladoucette has enlarged and expanded his business in an enviable way. The Château du Nozet now has one single holding of fifty hectares, but of course a very large part of the production is bought in. Vinification is of the most modern, enabling encouragement of the malolactic fermentation in acid years, such as 1977, and inhibition of it in ripe, full years such as 1976. In the 1970s, a *tête de cuvée* Pouilly Blanc Fumé was also launched, the Baron de 'L'. Comte Lafond Sancerre, also from the Ladoucette enterprise, is entirely bought in, but the same attention to detail goes into the *élevage*. Ladoucette is also behind the Baron Briare *appellation* Touraine wines.

Sancerre: Sancerre is all hills and dipping valleys, with fine, chalky well-exposed slopes. Limestone and the Sauvignon grape give great finesse and a lingering flavour. The communes in the *appellation* are Bannay, Bué, Crézancy, Menetou-Râtel, Ménétréol, Montigny, St-Satur, Ste-Gemme, Sancerre, Sury-en-Vaux, Thauvenay, Veaugues, Verdigny and Vinon. A big name at Sancerre is the Clos de la Poussie of Cordier, but the quality does not always match the price. Two growers make very fine wine from the famous Clos du Chêne Marchand, Lucien Crochet and Lucien Picard; the latter also has the Clos du Roy. High quality Sancerres come from MM. Marcel Gitton, Prieur, Vacheron, Vatan, Carobolante, Marcel Boin, Bernard and René Laporte, Reverdy, Henri at Chavignol, and the Cotats, who have Les Monts Damnés at Chavignol. Les Montachins of the Domaine Henri Brochard is always good, as is M. Gustave Fouassier's Les Groux. The cooperative has a serious reputation at Sancerre. Pouilly Blanc Fumé and Sancerre should always be drunk young; 1983 and 1982 were very ripe years, 1979 and 1978 were very good and 1977 too acid. Other good years were 1976, 1975, 1974, 1973 and 1971. There is also some red and rosé Sancerre made from Pinot Noir.

Menetou-Salon: Just to the south-west of Sancerre there is the small *appellation contrôlée* area of Menetou-Salon, where there is more white wine from the Sauvignon than red from the Pinot Noir. As throughout this region, Kimmeridge clay adds character and 'zip' to the wines. Good growers are Jean Teiller, Bernard Clément at the Domaine de Châtenoy, and the delightful small growers' cooperative of Les Vignerons Jacques-Coeur; the area is certainly 'on a revival'.

Quincy and Reuilly: Further away to the west, around Vierzon, there is Quincy and Reuilly, the former only producing crisp Sauvignon wines, but the latter also branches out into red and rosé. The wines can have great mouth-watering charm given favourable weather conditions. In Quincy, I have enjoyed the wines of M. Raymond

Pipet, Pierre and Jean Mardon, M. Maurice Rapin and M. Marcel Fragnier. The Domaine de Maison Blanche is by far the largest property in the area; the 1983 was exceptionally ripe. In Reuilly, M. Robert Cordier makes white wine from Sauvignon, red from Gamay and a delicate rosé from the Pinot Gris. The Renaudat family, M. Pierre Beaujard and the delightfully named M. Olivier Cromwell are other reliable growers.

Châteaumeillant: Way to the south of Bourges, there is the VDQS of Châteaumeillant. Here the wines are red or *gris* – the grapes are Pinot Noir, Pinot Gris and Gamay. The cooperative is good, and M. Maurice Lanoix is a very conscientious producer.

Coteaux du Giennois: The Coteaux du Giennois VDQS, along the Loire between Pouilly and Gien, has all the colours, and Gamay, Pinot Noir, Sauvignon and Chenin. The area does not produce much, but at St-Père, MM. Carroué, Jarreau and Nérot make honourable wines.

St-Pourçain-sur-Sioule: In the Bourbonnais and Auvergne, there are a clutch of VDQS wines that are eminently quaffable. Pride of place must go to St-Pourçain-sur-Sioule, residing on a tributary of the Loire, and greatly appreciated by those taking the cure at Vichy. The red and rosé wines are predominantly Gamay, but the dry white has up to 50 per cent Tressaller, a very local grape variety, mixed with Sauvignon, Chardonnay and even Aligoté. The result is an interesting, fresh taste. The cooperative is most reliable, as are MM. Maurice Faure, Joseph Laurent, Jean Cherillat and Jean Ray.

Côtes d'Auvergne, du Forez and Roannaises: In the Massif Central, the Côtes d'Auvergne are white (Chardonnay), red and rosé (Gamay and Pinot Noir), round the town of Châteaugay. The Côtes du Forez make red and rosé wine from the Gamay – the cooperative and M. Paul Gaumon at Chozieux, Leigneux are good producers here. The Côtes Roannaises are very similar – MM. Chargros and Servajean at Changy, M. Désormières at Renaison and M. Villeneuve at Champagny, St-Haon-le-Vieux make delicious wines for young drinking.

9 *Rhone*

The Rhône is one of France's main arteries, dividing *départements*, fostering trade and commerce, and nurturing agriculture. The Romans used it on their way north, and holidaymakers in the 1980s use it on their way south. It rises in Switzerland and meets the sea at Marseille, and has forged for itself in parts a deep ravine to challenge the Massif Central. The vine follows the river spasmodically, sometimes clinging to steep sides, as in the northern Rhône immediately below Lyon, or spreading out over flat, stony terrain, as around Avignon in the south. This difference between the Rhône Septentrional and the Rhône Méridional should be emphasized. The climate is often dissimilar, the land is different, and the grape varieties, although largely the same, vary greatly in proportion between the two areas. One can separate the vinous north and south Rhône very clearly, because although there are about 200 kilometres between Lyon and Avignon, the grape is not planted without a break down the river. At Valence, the vineyards virtually stop, apart from an outpost at Die about sixty-four kilometres south-east of Valence, and the river continues vineless past Montélimar. The vineyards begin in earnest again round Bollène, and from thence one can hardly ignore them. The Rhône and south-east France produce about 3 million hectolitres of *appellation* wine each year. Of this, about 1½ million hectolitres is Côtes du Rhône, and about 90,000 hectolitres Châteauneuf-du-Pape. The area entitled to the Côtes du Rhône *appellation* falls into six *départements*, which are, in order of volume: Vaucluse, Gard, Drôme, Ardèche, Rhône and Loire. The Vaucluse is particularly known for its red wines, the Gard for fine rosés and good

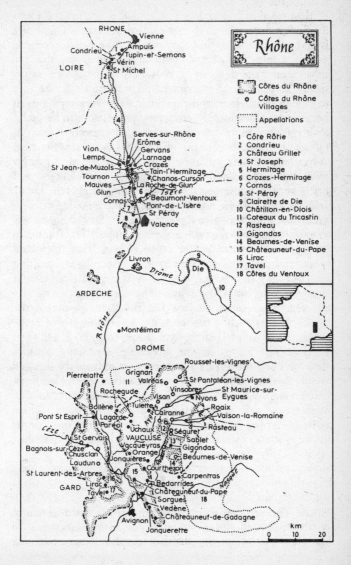

RHÔNE

Vienne
Ampuis
Condrieu
Tupin-et-Semons
LOIRE
3 Vérin
2 St Michel

Rhône

Côtes du Rhône
○ Côtes du Rhône
Villages
Appellations

1 Côte Rôtie
2 Condrieu
3 Château Grillet
4 St Joseph
5 Hermitage
6 Crozes-Hermitage
7 Cornas
8 St-Péray
9 Clairette de Die
10 Châtillon-en-Diois
11 Coteaux du Tricastin
12 Rasteau
13 Gigondas
14 Beaumes-de-Venise
15 Châteauneuf-du-Pape
16 Lirac
17 Tavel
18 Côtes du Ventoux

Serves-sur-Rhône
Érôme
Gervans
Vion
Larnage
Lemps
Crozes
St Jean-de-Muzols
Tain-l'Hermitage
5 Chanos-Curson
Tournon
La Roche-de-Glun
Mauves
6 Isère
Glun
Beaumont-Ventoux
Cornas
7 Pont-de-L'Isère
8 A St Péray
Valence

Livron
9
Drôme
Die
10
ARDÈCHE

Rhône
• Montélimar

DROME

Rousset-les-Vignes
Grignan
Pierrelatte
11 Valréas
St Pantaléon-les-Vignes
Rochegude
Vinsobres
St Maurice-sur-
Visan
Nyons
Eygues
Bollène
Tulette
Caîranne
Roaix
Pont St Esprit
Lagarde
Vaison-la-Romaine
Paréol
Uchaux
12 Rasteau
Cèze
13
Séguret
St Gervais
VAUCLUSE
Sablet
Bagnols-sur-Cèze
Vacqueyras
Gigondas
Chusclan
Orange
Beaumes-de-Venise
Laudun
14
Jonquières
Courthezon
Carpentras
St Laurent-des-Arbres
15
Lirac
16
Bédarrides
GARD
17
Châteauneuf-du-Pape
18
Tavel
Sorgues
Vedène
Châteauneuf-de-Gadagne
Avignon
Jonquerette

km
0 10 20

whites, with the others mostly pleasant red wines, including some of the great ones.

Most classical historians consider that it was on the Côtes du Rhône that vines were first planted in France. One thing is certain and that is that they would have had to contend with the relentless Mistral wind in the same way that the inhabitants have to today. It blows down the Rhône valley from the north, icy in winter and sometimes drying and scorching in summer, and psychologically very trying in its persistence. Occasionally, its drying properties can be useful after rain, but more often the vines need protecting from its influence, either by pruning low or by having rows of trees as barriers. The climate, as befits an area for the most part far from the sea, is continental, with dry, cold winters, and often very hot summers. The rain mostly comes in spring and autumn, and is not very equally distributed. Different grape varieties are given predominance according to the prevailing soil and the type of wine required. The Rhône, in fact, provides virtually every type of wine that one could want, from deep, long-lived reds, to more light, quaffing versions, dry rosé wines, dry white wines, luscious dessert wines and dry sparkling wines. The north is dominated by the red Syrah grape variety and the hard granite of the Massif Central, while the south has a veritable fan of grape varieties and soils to match, from stony, to alluvial, and even chalky. The art is in the matching. Pruning, equally, depends upon the terrain and its protection from the dreaded wind. In the south, there are a great deal of 'bush' vines, often round one stake – *taille gobelet*. The vine can often do without the stake when it is older and more resistant. There is also Guyot pruning along wires. On the very steep slopes of Côte Rôtie, special measures have to be taken, described on page 230.

GRAPE VARIETIES

Syrah: This red grape variety, often known as the Sérine in the Rhône, produces deep, long-lived aristocratic wines on the granite of Hermitage, Côte-Rôtie and Cornas, but used on its own in the south, it would be much too tannic. It gives wines of deep, intense scent, great colour, structure and body, eminently suitable for ageing.

Grenache (Noir): The great grape variety of the southern Rhône, and indeed, of the south of France (the Midi). The main type of this red grape is the same as the Spanish Garnacha. The grape produces wines with good colour, high alcohol levels and all-round strength. But for real longevity, it should be blended with the Syrah. There is also Grenache Rouge, Grenache Gris and Grenache Blanc.

Mourvèdre: An excellent red variety, which blends well – it contributes very good colour, generosity, and has ageing properties.

Cinsault: The Cinsault has a good deal of fruit and, when grown on stony soil, is ideal in red blends of class.

Viognier: A great, aristocratic white grape variety, unique of bouquet and flavour – the former is sometimes likened to mayblossom. Grown only in the northern Rhône of France, it is full but vinified dry. It is shy yielding and can oxidize if not handled with care. A great experience at its best.

Marsanne and Roussanne: These white grape varieties of the northern Rhône are related, but the Marsanne is the better and more widely planted. There is also an improved version of the Roussanne called the Roussette, which appears to be a cross between the Clairette and the Roussanne. They tend to make white wines of high alcohol which are full and assertive, but can have a classy austerity when older, if made in the traditional way. Vinified fresher, they are for younger drinking.

Bourboulenc, Clairette, Picpoul (Folle Blanche), Grenache Blanc, and Ugni Blanc are grape varieties used for white wines in the southern Rhône; the first three also go into red Châteauneuf-du-Pape. The red Carignan is good when blended with Grenache, but common on its own. The Muscat à petits grains is responsible for some of the best dessert wines.

In the north, starting at Vienne, the first vineyard reached is on the right bank of the *Rhône*.

Côte-Rôtie: This is one of those rare red wines which contain a proportion of white grapes – in this case, the predominant red grape variety is the Syrah (minimum 80 per cent), and this is softened by a small proportion of the fragrant Viognier. The result is intriguing, combining the power of the Syrah with the tempting scent of the Viognier, often now added in rather small proportion. The south-east facing 'Roasted Slope' certainly attracts all the sun-rays it can, from its terraces and supporting walls. The steepness of the terrain necessitates special pruning and training, with the Syrah vines trained together in groups up sticks, in a pyramid-like form, stretching the vines out in order to gain maximum exposure. Explosives are sometimes used to make an impression on the granite. Work in the vineyards is often done by cable and winch, and at harvest time, when the grapes are gathered in *bennes* (large baskets), they are winched up to the tracks at the summit for transport to the press house. Mules are sometimes still used where even this is not possible.

Above Ampuis, there are two individual slopes within the *appellation*, the Côte Brune, and the Côte Blonde, just to the south. The feudal Seigneur of Ampuis apparently once had two daughters, a blonde and a brunette, who were each given a vineyard as a dowry. The Côte Brune is, in fact, a dark brownish clay, while the Côte Blonde is of a silico-calcareous nature and lighter, more suitable for the Viognier grape. Nowadays, the two slopes are nearly always blended, giving a harmonious whole. Vinification tends to be traditional, although stainless-steel vats are to be seen now. Time in cask varies, but is usually two years or more. The wines thereafter need time in bottle to attain the great complexity of which they are capable, becoming the most subtle red wines of the northern Rhône.

Some of the greatest wines are made by the Guigal family, who blend Côte Blonde and Côte Brune, but also produce La Mouline, which only comes from the Côte Blonde. Guigal both own, and buy in grapes from small growers. Robert Jasmin makes magnificent Côte Rôtie La Chevalière d'Ampuis. More tannic, the Côte Rôtie of Emile Champet is also of majestic character. M. Albert Dervieux is also a highly recommended grower. The great house of Ampuis is that of Vidal-Fleury, which makes an excellent blended Côte Rôtie of the two main Côtes, which they call La Rolande. In 1985, Videl-Fleury was for sale. The Côte Rôtie Les Jumelles from Paul Jaboulet Ainé is always of depth and class, with the 1979 quite magnificent, and the houses of Chapoutier and Delas also own at Côte Rôtie. The wines of M. Alfred Gérin, the mayor of Ampuis, are also recommended.

Condrieu: Just south of Côte Rôtie, these could be called the strangest white wines of France, springing from the rare Viognier grape, and grown on steep slopes with a topsoil of soft, powdery *arzelle*, which is decomposed rock. This meagre soil can easily be washed down the slopes after rain, and has to be laboriously replaced. The vines are again trained up poles, usually two. The Viognier is one of those rare grapes that actually has a pungent smell at must stage, most varieties only attaining their particular character when made into wine. The attractive mayblossom flavour is most evident when young, but if the wine is very carefully treated and there is no oxidation, you can find really complex old wines. The area is very small, fourteen hectares, and the Viognier yields shyly, rarely going over 25 hectolitres per hectare and often well below. Unfortunately, this has led to many of the terraces being abandoned, even with the high price that Condrieu can command. Condrieu used to be bottled when there was still unfermented sugar in the wine, thereby producing a second fermentaion in bottle and a wine that was just slightly sparkling, or *perlé*. Nowadays, nearly all the wine is vinified dry, so the real essence of the Viognier can be seen more clearly, uncluttered by sugar. The undoubted *roi* of Condrieu is M. Georges Vernay, who makes wine under modern methods with great style. There is also the Château du Rozay belonging to the Multier family. Other owners are Delas Frères, now linked with Champagne Deutz, and M. André Dézormeaux, one of the last exponents of sweet Condrieu. Two delicious wines are made on the Coteau de Chéry, the Domaine Pierre Perret version being elegant with great finesse, and that of Jean Pinchon flowery and round. Domaine Guigal buy in grapes and make an excellent example. Robert Jurie-Descamier has a good reputation.

Château Grillet: This *appellation* consists of only 2½ hectares of vines, an enclave within Condrieu and, like it, made entirely from the Viognier grape. There is only one owner, M. Neyret-Gachet, and he has gradually reclaimed terraces, which often carry only one row of vines. South-facing, the grapes can attain great power and alcohol. Again, the topsoil is decomposed mica. A pneumatic press and stainless-steel vats are concessions to today, but the wine still stays several months on the lees. As at Condrieu, the wine undergoes malolactic fermentation, and the bottling date has been reduced from three years to about half that time or eighteen months, while at Condrieu it is usually in the spring following the vintage. When young, the wine can have great charm and finesse, and honeylike aromas. It darkens considerably with age, and then the alcohol can take over from the youthful fragrance. It is a drinking experience, but is perhaps overpriced.

St-Joseph: Still on the right bank of the river, this scattered vineyard area can produce some of the best value of the northern Rhône. The reds are made from the Syrah, and the whites from the Marsanne and the Roussanne. The *appellation* is compartively modern, having been granted in 1956. The vineyards of St-Joseph lie round the town of Tournon, and they produce mostly red wine, but with a small quantity of white. One of the seven St-Joseph villages forming the *appellation* is Mauves, and since the eighteenth century its wine has been imported into England – Victorian enamel wine labels with the name can still sometimes be found. The red wines have an earthy flavour and pronounced nose, and should be drunk comparatively young. The growers here are carefully replanting some areas, as at one time St-Joseph wines were used for blending and, instead of the Syrah, hybrid vines were grown. Opposite Hermitage, St-Joseph echoes its slopes, hewn out of the Massif Central. Vines are trained up one stake, and there is some clay and sand on the granite. The red wines may not be given the same time in cask as a Hermitage, but they will be robust enough and in good years, startlingly good. The white wines are vinified dry, but yet can be rich and full. The red St-Joseph Le Grand Pompée of Jaboulet is impressive, and the marvellous 1979 was probably the best wine since 1969. Delas own vineyards in St-Joseph and make deep red wines, which can be a bit one-dimensional in youth, but open out with time. M. Gustave Coursodon of Mauves has a justifiably high reputation, as has M. Jean-Louis Grippat at Tournon. Chapoutier also own at St-Joseph, and the Trollat family at St Jean-de-Muzols makes fine wines.

Hermitage: Standing on top of the great hill of Hermitage, by the chapel of St Christopher, one cannot help but be reminded of the Mosel. Far below, the Rhône makes a great turn, and all around are steep terraced slopes. Only here, the terraces are called *chalais*, and the red Syrah grape predominates, wedded to its granite-based soil, covered with a thin, loose, decomposed flinty/chalky topsoil. Legally, the red wine here can have up to 15 per cent white Marsanne and Roussanne added to it, but nearly always does not. The 130-hectare Hermitage slope, in spite of being on the left or eastern bank, of the Rhône, is really part of the Massif Central, and faces full south. The huge, deep red wines of Hermitage have, with top Claret and the Grands Crus of the Côte de Nuits, the longest life of all red wines in France. In the first half of the nineteenth century, Bordeaux used to be sold as 'hermitaged', and this cost more than the non-hermitaged variety! The granite reflects heat and the sun beats down on the slope. Winds are high, however, and the bush *gobelet* vines are tied to one stake. Young Syrah, grown with this intensity and concentration, can carry with it a wonderful peppery flavour. At Hermitage, all the special problems of vine cultivation in the northern Rhône can be easily seen. Since pre-Roman times the ground has been worked here, and the soil on the higher slopes is very thin. When it rains, what soil there is gathers at the foot of the hill and piles up against the iron gates at the entrance to the vineyards – only to be laboriously carried up the slope again. The slopes are often not worked, but anti-weed products are used to avoid disturbing the soil still further. The Syrah is grown on the higher and middle slopes with Les Bessards, Le Méal and Les Greffieux the outstanding vineyards. The plots for the best white wines are Chante Alouette, les Rocoules, les Murets, Maison-Blanche and les Greffieux. The Marsanne is more robust than the Roussanne and therefore usually preferred, but white Hermitage is a mixture of both. Annual production in Hermitage averaged about 3,500 hectolitres over the 1970s, with approximately 80 per cent red, 20 per cent white.

La Chapelle, near the top of the slopes, is probably the most renowned growth, and in the hands of the Jaboulet family, has to be one of the best red wines of the whole Rhône, its long vatting giving great depth and character. Wines of this calibre deserve ageing in bottle if their real nobility is to emerge. Dense, rich and strong, the complexity and style have to come through the tannin. But rarely is the fruit not there to combat the tannin, and it is a strange wine indeed that eventually dries up without first unfolding into great splendour. Wine-making tends to be traditional, often with a minimum of two years in barrel. Although La Chapelle is bottled after a year. Paul Jaboulet Aîné are not only *négociants* of repute, but very big vineyard owners. (They are also known as Jaboulet-Isnard.) They own twenty-four hectares at Hermitage, including the chapel of St Christopher. The Chapoutiers are also *négociants* and owners, with thirty-one hectares at Hermitage. La Sizeranne is their top red wine. The house of Delas has seventeen hectares at Hermitage, and their best red is the Marquise de la Tourette. M. Gérard Chave is another top owner, with highly regarded wines. Léon Revol is also a name in Hermitage.

Great white Hermitages are Jaboulet's Le Chevalier de Stérimberg, now made in a modern way, with no malolactic fermentation or keeping in wood, and bottled early in the spring after the vintage, and Chapoutier's Chante Alouette, more traditional and longer lived, with great fullness. Gérard Chave also makes excellent white Hermitage. When these wines age, they can have a similar *noisette* finish to them as a mature Meursault, but they are more powerful than white Burgundy, with a more austere, alcoholic backbone.

The cooperative at Tain does not always produce wine of character although there are excellent *cuvées*.

Crozes-Hermitage: There are some who think that it is a pity that Crozes ever hyphenated Hermitage to its name, since the vineyards are not in such a good position as Hermitage, being to the north, and there is much more clay in the soil. This can, of course, produce wines of depth and power, but without perhaps the added grace and nobility of more granitic Hermitage. It is, however, bigger than Hermitage, with 600 hectares. The wines tend not to last as long as Hermitage, but have an individual *goût de terroir*. Most of the vines are planted on gentle slopes and mechanization can be used, making this *appellation* less of an endangered species than others in the northern Rhône. The steepest slopes, though, make the best wines. The grape varieties are the same as for Hermitage. Having been rather severe with Crozes-Hermitage, one has to say that the twenty-hectare Domaine de Thalabert of Jaboulet is a magnificent wine, with even the unremarkable vintage of 1977 incredibly good. Chapoutier have Les Meysonniers. One of the villages in the Crozes *appellation* is Gervans, and it is here where the best and steepest sites are to be found – M. Raymond Roure and M. Jules Fayolle (on slightly gentler slopes) both make fine wine in this area. M. Albert Bégot of Serves-sur-Rhône also produces wines with a high reputation, and I have very much admired Crozes-Hermitage from the Domaine Bruno Thierry (Vidal-Fleury). Amongst white Crozes-Hermitage, there is Jaboulet's La Mule Blanche.

Cornas: A little further south, and on the other side of the river, there is the sixty-seven hectare *appellation* of Cornas, on some of the steepest terrain in the northern Rhône. The wine is only red, from the Syrah. It is some of the blackest wine of the area when young, needing time in bottle to throw off its initial coarseness. The best wine comes from the very steepest slopes, not the flatter strip at the foot of the hill. These slopes are away from the river and the Mistral, and the grapes, therefore, can attain great ripeness and are vintaged before the other *appellations*. It must be for this reason that Cornas, a Celtic word, means burnt or scorched earth. Near St-Péray, there is more sand in the granite-based clay soil, and the wines are consequently lighter. But true Cornas is made traditionally, with long vatting and ageing in wood, and the bottles should be kept patiently before drinking. Delas' Chante-Perdrix always repays keeping. M. Auguste Clape makes wine of real depth and power, in the most traditional manner. Other owners are the Lionnet, Michel and Verset families and M. Guy de Barjac.

St-Péray: The last *appellation* of the northern Rhône, just south of Cornas, is made mostly from the white Marsanne, but also from the Roussanne/Roussette. It can be still but is more often made *mousseux* by the Champagne method, even using Champagne years. There the similarity ends, though, as the wine is richer, fuller and heavier than Champagne, and the different grape varieties naturally cannot emulate the ultimate finesse of top Champagne. Ideally, the wine should have a few years of bottle age, and then it can be interesting and most pleasant. The sub-soil is granitic, covered with sand, stones and pebbles, and the vineyard covers about fifty hectares. M. Jean-François Chaboud is a well-known grower, as is M. Milliand. Some good Cornas growers, such as MM. Clape, Juge and Voge, also have holdings in St-Péray, and they must make their sparkling wine here to obtain the *appellation* St-Péray.

Before going into the well-defined southern Rhône, there are two other areas, the Ardèche, that wild country of the Massif Central to the west of the Rhône, and Die, about sixty-four kilometres south-east of Valence.

Côtes du Vivarais and Coteaux de l'Ardèche: The Ardèche is poor, and many of the villages are depopulated, but there is a revival of its wine, which one hopes will encourage those who stayed. The VDQS of the Côtes du Vivarais is made from Grenache, Cinsault and Carignan, with some Syrah and Gamay. The wines are made for young drinking, vinified to bring out youthful fruit. The best sources are the cooperatives at Orgnac and Ruoms, and an extremely conscientious grower is M. André Marron at Vallon Pont d'Arc. M. Léon Brunel at St-Remèze is in the same mould. The *négociant* Amédée, Vin de Pays, officially Coteaux de l'Ardèche, from the cooperative of St Désirat-Champagne, between Condrieu and Tournon, which also makes St-Joseph. The Ardèche, about fifteen kilometres west of Montélimar, is also the place where the renowned Burgundy house of Louis Latour decided to plant Chardonnay in partnership with local cooperatives and the beautifully vinified Chardonnay-Latour, Vin de Pays des Coteaux de l'Ardèche is the result.

Clairette de Die and Châtillon-en-Diois: Before the sparkling wines took over, Clairette de Die was a still white wine from that grape variety. However, now one goes to Die for its traditional sparkling wine made by the *méthode Dioise* – which will be labelled Tradition or Demi-Sec, and made from varying proportions of Clairette and Muscat à petits grains. There is also Clairette de Die Brut, made by the Champagne method, entirely from the Clairette, which does not have the bloomy fruit of the Muscat; it has rapidly gained popularity. The *méthode Dioise* consists of centrifuging the must to clarify after pressing, then lightly filtering the juice to remove some of the yeasts and delay fermentation. Eventually, fermentation starts, and advances slowly – if it speeds up, a light filtering slows things down. Then, when the wine is bottled in the New Year, there is some residual sugar left and this ferments slightly inside the bottle. No yeasts or extra sugar are added. Before sale, the wine is filtered under carbon dioxide pressure and re-bottled. The cooperative at Die is important, as are Buffardel Frères, who sometimes give their wine a vintage when exceptionally good. There are a quantity of growers, with M. Archard-Vincent of Ste-Croix and M. Jean-Claude Vincent of Barsac making attractive wine.

In 1974 the new *appellation* of Châtillon-en-Diois was created, but it should, on intrinsic merit, have remained VDQS. The reds and rosés are predominantly Gamay, with Syrah and Pinot Noir, and the whites are produced from Aligoté and Chardonnay and are marginally better. The sole producer is the cooperative.

Vintages in the Northern Rhône
Really good earlier vintages are, 1929, 1945, 1947, 1949, 1952, 1953, 1955, 1957, 1959, 1961 (superb), 1962, 1964, 1966, 1967,

237

1969, 1970 (particularly good) and 1971. 1972 produced some surprisingly good wines, given the vintage in general in France, especially in Hermitage. There were some good wines in 1973, but 1974 was only moderate. 1975 suffered from rot, as everywhere on this side of France, and the 1976 reds look set for a long life, if the low acidity holds out. 1977 produced light, rather green, wines, but 1978 was magnificent, with exceptional extract and concentration. The abundant 1979s are very good, especially at Hermitage, and 1980 was another successful vintage. In 1981, rain at the harvest caused the reds to be only moderate, but the whites are much better. 1982 was a very good year indeed, and the reds will keep well. The whites are good too, with Condrieu a particular success. Superb wines were made in 1983, of both colours, and the reds are for patient laying down. The 1984 red wines show good balance and medium weight, while the whites will provide very pleasant, probably early drinking.

In the Southern Rhône, the first *appellation* reached is about twenty kilometres north-east of Orange.

Rasteau: Apart from being one of the communes entitled to produce Côtes du Rhône Villages, Rasteau's *appellation* covers Vins Doux Naturels and Vins de Liqueur made from a minimum of 90 per cent Grenache grapes and a maximum of 10 per cent of grape varieties that have the right to the Côtes du Rhône *appellation*. Nearly all this fortified wine is made as white, although the colour is amber or caramel. The Grenache has high natural alcohol and takes on a taste of age comparatively quickly, so it is regarded as ideal fortified wine material, even though it lacks the lusciousness of the Muscat. It can be a little crude when young, and that is why aged Rasteau is prized; some is even kept in cask for anything up to ten years, when it is called Rancio and has a distinctly maderized taste. For the Vins Doux, the Grenache grapes are picked as late as possible, in order that they can attain 15 per cent alcohol naturally. The grapes are pressed, fermented up to 15 per cent or more, away from the skins to avoid colour tinting, and then alcohol is added to arrest the fermentation and retain residual sugar. The resulting Vin Doux has 21.5 per cent alcohol. Vins de Liqueur do not have to start with quite such high natural sugar, and the alcohol can be added before, as well as during, the fermentation – these wines are not as good as the Vins Doux. Both are sold without a vintage, and are mostly appreciated locally as apéritifs, or digestifs at the end of a meal. There is a cooperative, and MM Masson, Charavin and Vache are all important producers.

Beaumes-de-Venise: Also a Côtes du Rhône Villages, the special *appellation* of this commune is Muscat-de-Beaumes-de-Venise, Vins Doux Naturels and Vins de Liqueur, only made from the Muscat à petits grains, also called the Muscat de Frontignan. The Muscat makes particularly tempting fortified wines, delicious drunk slightly chilled both as a pre-and post-prandial glass. Unlike the Grenache-based Rasteau, Muscat-de-Beaumes-de-Venise is at its most delectable when young. The method of vinification is similar to Rasteau. Apart from the cooperative's good example, in screw-topped bottle, the Domaine des Bernardins of Castaud-Maurin and the Domaine de Durban of Bernard Leydier produce lovely Beaumes-de-Venise. M. Guy Rey of Domaine St Sauveur and the Domaine de Coyeux are also recommended. All have good red wine as well. .

Gigondas: Before the days when *appellation* rules were strictly followed, a great deal of Gigondas found its way into the better-known Châteauneuf du-Pape, and those 'in the know' bought Gigondas for themselves at very good value prices. Nowadays, this impish behaviour is no more, and Gigondas itself, granted its *appellation* in 1971, justifiably sells for a fair sum. Nestling in the Dentelles de Montmirail, the foothills of the majestic, often snow-peaked, Mont Ventoux, the dark wine of Gigondas is made principally of Grenache, with some Syrah and Cinsault, Mourvèdre and Clairette. The best vineyards are mid-slope on terrain that is markedly stony; above the soil is clay, and below more sandy. Vinification is traditional, and barrel-ageing varies from under a year to two years, mostly depending on the size of the enterprise. Bottle-ageing is also important, if one is to enjoy these wines fully. When they are young they are often almost purple in colour, have a strong, assertive taste and a good deal of alcohol. The best also add breed to this list. In a good year, it will keep well, with perhaps maximum fruit at about six to eight years, but one should expect flavour, rather than complexity.

The two big grower/*négociants* of the region are Gabriel Meffre (Domaine des Bosquets, Domaine St Jean and Domaine La Chapelle) and, less giant-like, Pierre Amadieu. Top domains are Roger Meffre's Domaine St Gayan, the Archimbauds Château de Montmirail, M. Henri Barruol's Domaine St Cosme, M. François Ay's Château de Raspail, Hilarion Roux's Domaine Les Pallières, Charles Roux's Château du Trignon, Roger Combe's L'Oustaou Fauquet and M. Burle's Les Pallieroudas. The cooperative is highly respected, and Paul Jaboulet Aîné's selections are always first-class.

Châteauneuf-du-Pape: Châteauneuf has a lilting name, a fascinating history and very special soil. Unfortunately, not all the growers of Châteauneuf have always honoured their legacy, and some of the wine is not as good as it should be, failing to bring out the unique character of the *appellation*. This character partly comes from the incredibly stony soil, often formed of enormous *galets*, flattish, smooth stones of a pinkish colour. During the day these stones absorb and reflect a good deal of heat, and continue to radiate heat even at night, ensuring that the grapes ripen almost all round the clock, and even from below. These stones take their toll in machinery and implements, with a high replacement rate. But their presence gives the grapes of Châteauneuf great ripeness and thick skins, so that the result in the wine, if nature takes its course, is a dark colour and great tannin.

Within the *appellation* rules, thirteen varieties of grape are permitted, including some white grapes. Most growers usually settle for about nine varieties, choosing grapes to suit different plots (as estates are often scattered), and those listed first predominate: red– Grenache, Syrah, Mourvèdre, Cinsault, Terret Noir, Muscardin, Vaccarèse, Counoise; white – Clairette, Bourboulenc, Roussanne, Picpoul,

240

Picardan. Each grape adds something to the blend – Grenache ensures good alcohol, Mourvèdre good colour, Cinsault and Syrah give fruity mellowness and backbone, respectively. The addition of white grapes undoubtedly helps the bouquet and provides an intriguing finesse hidden in the structure of the wine which takes it out of the merely robust category. Each variety ripens at a different time, which is an aid to the *vigneron*; the Cinsault is usually picked first, the Grenache last. The vines are in bushes, *gobelet* fashion, except for the Syrah, which is trained on to wires.

The disparity between styles of Châteauneuf and, it must be admitted, the difference in quality between the best and the worst (much of it bottled outside the area, which is unwise in the circumstances), make it essential to have a list of the best domains. This applies to red Châteauneuf – although there is a tiny amount of white wine made as a curiosity – about 3 per cent of under 100,000 hectolitres' average annual yield. The *appellation* area is about 3,000 hectares, completely planted. Château Rayas is often regarded as the king of the area, for its wine of great longevity and depth, partly due to small yields, long wood ageing, and also to the grape variety combination of Grenache, Syrah and Cinsault. The Reynauds also make a very good Côtes du Rhône, Château de Fonsalette. Unfortunately, the estate has become more variable since the late 1970s. The Domaine de Mont Redon is the largest estate at Châteauneuf, run most efficiently by M. Jean Abeille and other descendants of the Plantin family. The wine is not as big and tannic as it used to be, but it is perhaps fruitier. The Domaine de Beaucastel lasts well, as does the excellent Chante Cigale of M. Noël Sabon, the Clos de l'Oratoire des Papes and Château La Nerte. The Château des Fines Roches is one of the best-placed properties in the *appellation*, producing wine of class, and nearby Château Fortia has very good traditional character. Other highly recommended properties are the Domaine du Vieux Télégraphe, Domaine de Marcoux, Clos du Mont-Olivet, Domaine de la Terre Ferme, Clos des Papes, and Les Clefs d'Or, excellent both for red and white. Domaine de Beaurenard, Domaine de la

Solitude and Domaine de Nalys make lighter, 'new style' wines, with the Nalys white perhaps the best in the region. *Négociants* include the Caves St-Pierre, the Caves Eugène Bessac, Louis Mousset and Père Anselme. Paul Jaboulet have their Les Cèdres Châteauneuf and Chapoutier La Bernardine. There are two associations of growers who bottle and store their wines together, Les Reflets, and Prestige et Tradition.

Very good years in Châteauneuf-du-Pape are 1945, 1947, 1949, 1955, 1957, 1959, 1961 (superb), 1962, 1964, 1966, 1967 (tannic and full), 1969, 1970 and 1971. It should be remembered that sometimes these wines of the south do not keep with quite the same consistency as the top reds of the northern Rhône. The 1972s are somewhat 'patchy', but some have improved in bottle to a great extent, the 1973s were too diluted by the quantity produced to hold much interest, and the 1974s are not much better than moderately good. 1975 is to be avoided altogether, 1976 can be good, but depends on whether the property vintaged before the rainstorms, and 1977 is a 'fill-in' vintage while waiting for the 1978s, although some are drying out a bit. The 1978s are quite magnificent, a much-needed classic year for the region. The wines have structure, opulence and fruit, and will make splendid bottles in the future. The 1979s are very good, without the overall *charpente* and body of the 1978s, but immensely attractive. 1980 was successful, with some sturdy wines, while the best selections of 1981 have character and structure. The great heat in 1982 gave some vinification problems, and only the top, well-equipped domains are completely safe buys. The 1983 wines are only medium-term keepers, but the best have balance and substance. 1984, too, has not produced long-term keepers, but the balance, spice and fruit are there. On the whole, these vintage notes can be applied to the southern Rhône appellations, bearing in mind that as the *appellations* get more modest, their keeping time shortens.

Tavel: From a quality point of view, this is the most famous rosé wine in France. Dry, full-bodied and alcoholic, this is not a pretty little holiday wine to toss back, but something more serious to accompany food with a definite taste. On the western side of the river, Tavel has the same large, flat stones as at Châteauneuf-du-Pape, and roughly the same grape varieties, with a preponderance of Grenache and Cinsault. Some of the best soil is chalky on slopes, and the whole terrain is hot and arid. The *appellation* area is about 1,000 hectares, completely planted, and average annual productions is between 35,000 and 40,000 hectolitres. The rosé colour is extracted by a maceration of the grapes in their juice for one or two days, before fermentation starts. Then the grapes are pressed lightly, and fermentation is away from the skins. Bottling is in the New Year after the vintage, and Tavel is best appreciated relatively young, when the colour is pink and not tawny and there is youthful freshness and fruit added to the character of the wine. The cooperative at Tavel has a high reputation and is one of the most conscientiously run in France. Top domains are Château Aquéria, Domaine de la Genestière, Domaine de la Forcadière, Le Vieux Moulin de Tavel, Château de Trinquevedel, Domaine de Tourtouil, the Prieuré de Montézargues, de Lanzac, and the Château de Manissy which is run by the Pères de la Ste-Famille.

Lirac: Just to the north of Tavel, this *appellation* covers red, rosé and white wines, although it is the red that takes pride of place. The rosé is delicious drunk young, often more supple than Tavel. The main grape varieties are the Grenache, followed by the Cinsault, Syrah, Mourvèdre and Clairette. There is also a small amount of the unusual Maccabéo. The soil is mixed, sometimes pebbly, with some clay, and the western part of the plateau of Roquemaure has large stones. The *appellation* area is about 3,500 hectares, of which only 2,000 are planted and only 500 are declared *appellation* Lirac; the rest are Côtes du Rhône. Current annual production is about 20,000 hectolitres, and it is clear that there is room for expansion. These red wines have fruit, charm and body and represent some of the very best value in the southern Rhône. There are some exceptionally well-run domains, some of them bought by ex-settlers in Algeria, and it is well worth finding them. The Pons-Mure family have two separate properties of great note, the Domaine de Castel-Oualou and the Domaine de La Tour-de-Lirac, and a relation has the excellent Domaine Rousseau. The Château de Ségriès has old vines and can be rich and concentrated, and the Domaine du Devoy belonging to the Lombardo family makes delicious wine. A more recent estate is that of Philippe Testut, of the well-known Chablis family, whose wines show immense skill and whose red is a very fine bottle indeed. The Domaine du Château St-Roch has a justifiably high reputation, and Jean-Claude Assémat's Les Garrigues makes delicious, fresh wines. M. Maby's La Fermade is always good, as well as M. Bernard's Domaine de la Genestière and the wine of M. Gabriel Roudil, who actually lives at Tavel. The cooperative at St Laurent-des-Arbres is not recommended.

Côtes du Rhône Villages: Initially, there was just Côtes du Rhône, but in 1953 the INAO decided that four villages could add their name to that simple *appellation*: Gigondas, Cairanne, Chusclan and Laudun. In 1955, Vacqueyras was added to the list, and two years later Vinsobres entered the ranks. In 1967, this group of wines was officially baptized Côtes du Rhône Villages, and now there are seventeen communes which fall into this category, Gigondas now being full *appellation* on its own. If there is inter-communal blending, it is just plain Côtes du Rhône Villages. The Côtes du Rhône Villages are: in the Drôme – St Maurice-sur-Eygues, Rousset-les-Vignes, Rochegude, St Pantaléon-les-Vignes and Vinsobres; in the Vaucluse – Cairanne, Vacqueyras, Rasteau, Valréas, Visan, Roaix, Sablet, Beaumes-de-Venise, and Séguret; in the Gard – Chusclan, Laudun and St Gervais. The alcohol level of Côtes du Rhône Villages must be 12.5 per cent for reds, and 12 per cent for rosé or white, and yield is more limited than plain Côtes du Rhône. The grape varieties are those of the main *appellations* of the southern Rhône, and although red, white and rosé are made, it is the red that is the important wine. This is an area dominated by the cooperatives, most of which are very good, especially when their best wines are chosen. There are a few domains that are becoming known for their quality and, where possible, it is worth finding these two categories, rather than *négociant* wine, which often suffers in less than perfect years. Cooperatives that can be thoroughly recommended are those of Cairanne, La Cave des Vignerons de Chusclan (excellent red, rosé and white and a superb example of what a cooperative can do), Beaumes-de-Venise and Vinsobres.

It is worth noting a few characteristics of the main Villages wines. Cairanne is often grown on clayey slopes, where the wines have body and roundness, combined with the colour and tannin of wine from the *garrigues* area, where it is stony. These are lovely, full wines. L'Oratoire St-Martin and the Domaine des Travers are very good. Laudun makes red, rosé and white wine – the latter is good, from the Clairette and the Roussanne. But the red dominates, usually quite big wine, and the best producers are the Cave des Quatre Chemins, the Domaine Rousseau (the same ownership as at Lirac) and the Domaine Pélaquié, the latter making really powerful, long-vatted wines. Rochegude has a good cooperative making supple wines, and Sablet has the Domaines of Parandou and Trignon. Beaumes-de-Venise has Château Redortier, a beautifully situated property making superb, deep wine. The village of St-Gervais has the Domaine Ste-Anne, where the wines are made by a *semi-macération carbonique* method of eight to twelve days and have great attraction.

Vacqueyras is certainly one of the best Côtes du Rhône Villages, and its red wine has depth of bouquet, fruit and body. The best domains are: La Fourmone of Roger Combe, Domaine des Lambertins, Pascal Frères, the Clos des Cazaux of Archimbaud Frères, Le Vieux Clocher, and the Domaine des Garrigues of Bernard Frères. Valréas has a good cooperative and the Domaine du Val-des-Rois of M. Romain Bouchard, who is Burgundian by origin, as well as the Domaine des Grands Devers of M. Sinard. Vinsobres has good properties, amongst which the Domaine Les Aussellons and the Domaine du Coriançon. Visan is dominated by its cooperative, and the Domaine de la Cantharide Seguret has the Domaine de Cabasse.

Côtes du Rhône: This is the basic generic wine of the Rhône, and its financial rock. About 1½ million hectolitres are made each year of red, white and rosé wine, which must reach 11 per cent alcohol. It can also contain a higher proportion of Carignan than the Villages wines. The red is the most reliable, and the following are domains of note: Domaine de la Chapelle at Châteauneuf-de-Gadagne – M. Marcel Boussier here produces big, long-lasting wine on the same stony soil as at the 'other' Châteauneuf; the very fruity Château du Grand Moulas at Mornas; the deep Domaine des Richards at Violès; Château de l'Estagnol at Suze-la-Rousse; Château St-Estéve at Uchaux near Orange; Château des Roques at Sarrians; Château Malijay at Jonquières, if you like light wines; and Domaine Mitan at Vedène; *Négociants* include the reliable Bellicard at Avignon, Le Cellier des Dauphins at Tulette, which sells wine from ten cooperatives, David et Foillard at Sorgues, and Ogier at Sorgues and Salavert. Paul Jaboulet have the full-bodied Côtes-du-Rhône Parallèle 45.

Coteaux du Tricastin: Elevated to *appellation* status in 1974, this vineyard area expanded with great speed, and now is about 1,500 hectares. As a result, for a time the red wines often showed the influence of young vines, but as we go into the mid-1980s, the quality has improved enormously. Vineyards were planted with difficulty in the stony terrain, and everything is highly mechanized, again with the dynamism behind it of some former settlers in Algeria who returned to France in the 1960s. The grape varieties are Grenache, Cinsault, Syrah and Mourvèdre. Production of Coteaux du Tricastin red and rosé in 1979 was 64,422 hectolires – white wine production is practically non-existent in this area. Some of the best domains in Tricastin are those of the Bour family, with their wonderful Domaine de Grangeneuve and Domaine des Lônes, and M. Pierre Labeye with his Domaine de la Tour d'Elyssas, producing the Cru du Devoy, the Cru de Meynas and the Cru des Echirouses. The Domaine du Vieux Micocoulier has an excellent reputation and the Tricastin cooperative at Richerenches is also recommended.

Côtes du Ventoux: This is another young *appellation* (1974), with predominantly red, but also rosé and a tiny amount of white wine. The dominant grape varieties are Grenache, Syrah, Carignan and Cinsault, but they are mostly vatted for a very short time with resultant light freshness and palish colour. 1979 production was 195,520 hectolitres of red and rosé wine. The two best domains are the Domaine des Anges and the Domaine St Sauveur at Aubignan; otherwise, the cooperatives hold sway. I have liked Côtes du Ventoux from the *négociants* Louis Mousset, Pascal, and Les Caves St Pierre but the branded La Vieille Ferme is probably the wine with the most consistency.

Côtes du Lubéron: This VDQS wine has great charm, not the least of which is the beautiful country from which it comes around the Lubéron hills inland from Marseille. Red and rosé come from Grenache, Carignan and Cinsault, while the white is from the Bourboulenc and Grenache Blanc; red predominates. The Cellier de Marrenon at La Tour d'Aigues makes a good wine, as do the Caves St Pierre.

10 Provence

Provence is a ray of sunlight in a gloomy world, but sometimes sunshine comes expensive. However, this large area provides enough wine to suit all pockets, from really inexpensive rosés and reds, the house wine of local restaurants and some of the most reasonable at the supermarket, to expensive estates. Some of the latter may not be worth it, relying on their *renommée* or, in some cases, small *appellation* area for justification, but some offer real value in the quality/price balancing act. Côtes-de-Provence was elevated to *appellation* status in 1977, continuing a trend to upgrade a number of good VDQS wines that perhaps were more realistically placed in their former category. But once the spiral has started, no one wants to be left behind – or very few. Annual production is approximately 700,000 hectolitres from 17,000 hectares of vines. About a third of the production comes from individual domains, while two-thirds comes from about sixty cooperatives. 60 per cent of the wine is rosé, that delectable holiday wine when it is too hot to appreciate a red (unless chilled), about 35 per cent is red, and rising, and 5 per cent white. Many of the domains doing their own bottling now concentrate mainly on reds, while cooperatives, and the *négociants* buying from them, are the great rosé producers. It must be admitted that much of this rosé could be a deal more interesting, and in some cases, more palatable and *sain*. On the whole, the vintages are the same as the southern Rhône, but with more regularity and fewer failures. The grape varieties are the same: Carignan is preponderant, and must certainly fall in proportion if quality is the aim; Grenache; Cinsault; Mourvèdre; Syrah; Tibouren (Provençal); and, more recently introduced, the Cabernet Sauvignon. The vines are trained on to wire and pruned on the 'Cordon de Royat' system. The best white wines are made from the Rolle, Sémillon, and Clairette in small quantities. There are three main zones: the coastal zone, between the Massif des Maures and the sea (St Tropez, La Londe-les-Maures and up to Pierrefeu); the area inland between Toulon and Fréjus, particularly good for reds, round Pierrefeu, Cuers and Puget-Ville, and also Le Luc, Le Cannet-des-Maures, Vidauban, Les Arcs-sur-Argens and La Motte; and further inland again, round Correns (whites) and Cotignac (reds). There is also the area near Aix, around Puyloubier and Trets, good for reds, the area around Bandol (when the wines are not Bandol), and the area behind Nice.

The following are recommended domains and wines: Château Minuty at Gassin (its Cuvée de l'Orataire is expensive but the tops); the Domaine des Paris from the excellent cooperative Les Maîtres-Vignerons de la Presqu'île de St Tropez; at Cogolin the Domaine des Garcinières and the Domaine de St-Maur; at Bormes-les Mimosasthe Domaine des Campaux; and at La Londe-les-Maures, the Clos Mireille of Domaines Ott, a very expensive white wine, the Domaine du Carrubier, and the Domaine St-André-de-Figuière. At Pierrefeu there is the Domaine de l'Aumérade, at Le Luc the Domaine de la Bernarde, at Le Cannet-des-Maures the Domaine de la Bastide-Neuve, the Domaine des Bertrands, the Château de Roux, and the Domaine de Reillanne. At Vidauban there is the excellent Domaine des Féraud of the Laudon family, with reds and rosés of character, and at les Arcs-sur-Argens, Château Ste Roseline. At Lorgues there is Castel-Roubine and at Trets-en-Provence, Château Grand'Boise. Taradeau has the Château de Selle and the Château de St Martin, the former belonging to Domaines Ott. The Domaine de la Croix also has a considerable reputation. *Négociants* whose Côtes de Provence give confidence are Pradel, now belonging to Cordier of Bordeaux, especially their Impérial Pradel, Bagnis (Rouge Estandon), Cauvières (Mistral) and Bernard Camp-Romain (Bouquet-de-Provence Réserve).

Palette: Palette, on the outskirts of Aix-en-Provence, is a tiny *appellation* with an excellent micro-climate revolving round one property, Château Simone. Fifteen hectares of old vines on calcareous soil here produce red wines aged in wood and capable of lasting for years. They have great complexity and unique flavour. The rosés and white are highly individual, and the quality and originality of all the wines go a long way to justify the high price. The grape varieties are Grenache, Mourvèdre and Cinsault for the reds and rosés, and Clairette for the whites, but there are some old Provençal varieties in smaller quantities.

Cassis: Cassis is another small *appellation*, again making all three 'colours' of wine, but famed for its white. When this is well-made and not oxidized, it has a very interesting taste indeed, influenced by the Marsanne in the blend of more usual varieties of the southern Rhône area. There are four domains of note, all making wines of class that will revive memories of *bouillabaisse* round the port of Cassis: Domaine de la Ferme Blanche; Domaine du Paternel; Clos Ste-Magdeleine; and the Château de Fontblanche.

Bandol: Bandol is a really 'serious' *appellation* – here the red wines are the greatest. The Mourvèdre contributes the greatest part to the blend, when elsewhere it is usually only a small component part of the whole. The Grenache and the Cinsault complete the picture. The vines are grown on terraces, locally called *restanques*. The fault of many Bandol wines in the past was a too-long life in cask, sometimes up to four or five years, which succeeded in drying out the wine before it got to the consumer. Legally, the red wines have to spend eighteen months in cask before being sold (this is an unusual stipulation for an *appellation*), and their main qualities are richness, structure, an array of intoxicating tastes and the capacity to age with interest and grace. About 20,000 hectolitres are produced annually, but there is much room for expansion within the *appellation* area, which can only be a good thing for the consumer, and should help to keep the price within bounds. Recommended properties are: the Domaine Tempier, possibly the best; Château des Vannières; the two domains of the Bunan brothers, the Moulin des Costes and the Mas de la Rouvière; the Domaine du Val d'Arenc; the Domaine de Pibarnon; the Château Pradeaux, perhaps not as consistent as some; La Laidière; and the cooperative, the Moulin de la Roque, which produces excellent wines at a very keen price. Domaines Ott has Château Romassan.

Bellet: Bellet is almost a forgotten *appellation*, forty hectares behind Nice, and sold mainly in the smart hotels and restaurants of Nice and Monte-Carlo. On the whole, the whites are more consistent than the reds and rosés. There are some curious grape varieties in the blends – the Braquet and Folle Noire in the reds and rosés, mixed with Cinsault and Grenache, and the Rolle in the whites, mixed with a very little Roussanne, Chardonnay, Clairette and Bourboulenc. The Château de Bellet and the Château de Crémat are the two best domains.

Coteaux-d'Aix-en-Provence: The Coteaux-d'Aix-en-Provence are VDQS wines from around Aix and made in red, rosé and white. In fact, they are just as good as the wines of Côtes-de-Provence, and should follow their path towards an *appellation*. It is certain that M. Georges Brunet of Château Vignelaure, who planted a high proportion of Cabernet Sauvignon at his domain and eschewed chemical treatments (quite a tendency now in Provence amongst good domains), encouraged others to go for quality. The soils are rather chalky, and the wines often have finesse and can be utterly delicious. There are properties which follow the Cabernet Sauvignon trend (mixed with Syrah and Grenache), and others which prefer to stick to the all-traditional recipe of Grenache, Cinsault, Carignan, Syrah, Mourvèdre, with a touch of Cabernet Sauvignon. The other VDQS of the area, the Coteaux-des-Baux-de-Provence, is now more or less merged with Coteaux-d'Aix.

Good domains are, obviously, Château Vignelaure at Rians, now rather expensive, Château de Fonscolombe at Le Puy-Ste-Réparade of the Marquis de Saporta, which has great charm and quality, together with another good property, the Domaine de la Crémade, Domaine de

Lauzières at Mouriès, the Mas de la Dame at Les Baux-de-Provence, the Château de Calissanne at Lançon-de-Provence, Château La Coste at Le Puy-Ste-Réparade, Château de Beaulie at Rognes, and the Domaine de la Semencière at Les Milles and Château Bas at Vernegues.

11 *Corsica*

Corsican wines are of little interest to those not on the island, for few of them escape in bottle, but it is worth knowing what to hunt down when holidays are taken on this scented isle, where there is mountain and sea, forest and vineyard. A good deal of the two million hectolitres' annual production goes to reinforce weak table wine made elsewhere. But, after the overall Vin de Corse *appellation*, there are seven delimited areas: Patrimonio; Coteaux d'Ajaccio; Sartène; Calvi (Balagne); Coteaux du Cap Corse; Figari; and Porto-Vecchio. These represent only six per cent of the total output of Corsica. Apart from the scent of the herb-filled *maquis*, which seems to impart something to the wine, the distinctive aromas and tastes of Corsican wine are more due to the grape varieties, predominantly indigenous. At Patrimonio, the reds and rosés are largely made from the Nielluccio, a relation of the Sangiovese of Tuscany, with the Sciacarello, which is also found at Sartène, in both cases mixed with the Grenache. White grape varieties are Malvoisie, Ugni Blanc (Trebbiano, again the Italian influence) and Vermentino.

Good domains are: Clos de Bernardi and Clos Marfisi at Patrimonio; the Couvent d'Alzipratu, Clos Landry, Colombu and the Coopérative de Calenzana et de Balagne in the Calvi area; Domaines Péraldi, Martini and Capitoro at Ajaccio; Poggio d'Oro and Domaine de Canella at Figari; and the Domaine de Torraccia and Fior di Lecci at Porto-Vecchio. In the Cap Corse area there is the Clos Nicrosi, with its interesting dry white wine, and the unique Muscatellu, Muscat Doux Naturel. At Ponte-Leccia, there is the Domaine Vico, making *appellation* Vin de Corse wines. The Margnat family (now separate from the table-wine firm) have important holdings on Corsica, amongst which there are the good-value Domaine de Fontanella and the Domaine de Furgoli, *appellation* Vin de Corse, from the Domaines de Tizzano round the Golfe de Tizzano on the south-east of the island. The wines are well made from the Nielluccio, Grenache and Carignan, and sometimes shipped in bulk for bottling in the United Kingdom. The Vin de Pays L'Ile de Beauté is also beginning to be seen in the United Kingdom and the Domaine de Musoleu at Folelli makes excellent examples.

12 *Languedoc-Roussillon*

To a certain extent, these are wines to be drunk (after taking due advice) and not read about and the best, it is to be hoped, will continue to give an example to the worst, of which there is a larger proportion than any government would want. Originally, the vineyards were on the slopes, with cereals on the plains, but in the nineteenth century these flatlands were planted with the Alicante and the Aramon which, on clay and alluvial soils, produced astonishing yields of 200 hectolitres per hectare. The highlands followed suit, and the result was the 'wine-lake'. The situation is hardly helped by the high price paid for poor wine at the distillery. Since 1960, various government bodies and the most far-sighted producers have been searching for ways to improve matters. Obviously, the grape varieties had to improve and they in turn have to be adapted to the multitude of soils, mini-regions and micro-climates that lie in the slopes and valleys of the *coteaux*. There is every type of soil, from terrain of huge stones left by the retreating Rhône, to clay--calcareous slopes, to schist, granite and sandstone. The zones gradually have to be redefined, so that they do not necessarily follow the communes, but the more logical viticultural plots. The cooperatives have to be helped to improve their methods and techniques and to have equipment conducive to the production of healthy wine.

The Carignan grape is still *roi*, with its high alcohol and big yield, but when the vines are old and the vineyard is high, the results can be good. The Grenache and Cinsault are added in varying quantities, followed by the Syrah and Mourvèdre, with some Cabernet Sauvignon. But we are talking about those properties that really care about quality and are prepared to make sacrifices to get it.

255

Costières du Gard: Travelling from the east, the first VDQS of note is Costières du Gard, south of Nîmes. Good red and rosé wines are made, rather similar to Côtes du Rhône, fruity, with some body, but uncomplicated wines. There are cooperatives at Vauvert, Générac and Beauvoisin and, at Gallician, two properties which make worthy wine – the Mas de la Tardine and the Mas Aupellière.

Vins des Sable: Down in the Camargue, there are the Vins des Sables, and at Grau-du-Roi, the Domaine de l'Espiguette, Sicarex-Méditerranée. This is the main centre of practical research of the Institut Technique de la Vigne et du Vin, with regard to clonal selection, viticultural and vinification methods. Some of the wines, naturally, are perfect technically without being exciting, but there are individual lots to be selected of real interest.

Much the same could be said of the Domaines Viticoles des Salins du Midi at Montpellier, whose vast range of wines is made with great technical ability and in the most 'natural' way possible, i.e. no chemical products in the soil, no pasteurization. Nearly all the domains which belong to the Compagnie des Salins du Midi are in the production area of the Vins de Pays des Sables du Golfe du Lion and, as the phylloxera louse does not develop in sand, the vines are largely ungrafted and are on French root stocks. The hot sun of the south is also here tempered by the breezes from the sea and the salt marshes. Listel is a trade mark of the Salins du Midi, and well-known domains are Domaine du Bosquet (red), and Domaine du Château de Villeroy (red and white). For whites, they often judiciously blend the Clairette with the Ugni Blanc and the Sauvignon; for some soft red wines they remove the grapes from the skins, heat the skins to extract colour, which is then added to the juice and fermented – the result is colour and not tannin.

Coteaux du Languedoc: The Coteaux du Languedoc VDQS wines cover a vast area between Nîmes and Béziers – thirteen areas within this region can add their name to the overall title. On the whole, reds and rosés are better than whites, wine-makers often lacking the equipment and technique for the latter. There is quite a bit of *macération carbonique* in the reds, which was often the original way of vinification on the farms, putting the grapes whole into the *cuve* without crushing, as well as some Vin d'Une Nuit, a very light, fruity red achieved by maceration overnight – the rosés take a matter of hours. The most important areas are Faugères and St-Chinian, both awaiting the award of *appellation* status. Faugères red wine can have real richness with good backbone, while St-Chinian, with its two zones of schist and clay-chalk, usually blended together, has style and a scented bouquet. Berlou St-Chinian comes from a high valley and is made from Carignan. St-Saturnin is also important, with a good cooperative and Vin d'Une Nuit. Quatourze is small but with some good properties, while La Clape has an unfortunate name but is producing some remarkably good wines.

Before going further west, there are three *appellation* Vins Doux Naturels made from the Muscat grape, along the lines of Beaumes-de-Venise – Muscat de Lunel, Muscat de Mireval and Muscat de Frontignan. If you like the grapy taste of Muscat and its rich aromas, you will like these. Well-chilled, they can be good apéritifs, but they are also good digestifs, with nuts and fruit. The *appellation* Clairette du Languedoc is dry white wine or Vin de Liqueur, made from the Clairette grape. The VDQS Picpoul de Pinet is small enough to jump over – light dry white wine.

Minervois: Minervois VDQS, between St-Chinian and Carcassonne, encompasses valley and hills, and it is the produce of the latter you want, particularly round St Jean-de-Minervois and Minerve. Another candidate for *appellation* status, the wines from the hills have a full fragrance and body and provide excellent, gulpable bottles.

Corbières and Corbières Supérieures: These cover a huge area of the Aude, VDQS with *appellation* ambitions. There is the coastal zone, where a high alcohol content is obtained, the middle zone round Lézignan, Lagrasse, St Laurent de la Cabrerisse, with supple wines, and the Hautes-Corbières, behind and to the south of the foregoing, with very assertive wines. Corbières can be rounder and more velvety than Minervois, which can have more structure. There is a good deal of *macération carbonique* and Carignan, Cinsault, Grenache, and now some Syrah. The vines are trained *en gobelet*.

Fitou: The *appellation* Fitou falls within this greater area of VDQS of Corbières, and is for red wine only, mostly made of Carignan and Grenache, with other varieties that can be added up to 25 per cent: Cinsault, Terret-Noir, Malvoisie, Maccabéo, Muscat and Picpoul. They have to spend at least nine months in wood before being sold, but that does not improve the mediocre quality of many of them. An exception is the Château de Nouvelles at Tuchan.

Blanquette-de-Limoux: Blanquette-de-Limoux, made both still (unexciting) and *mousseux*, is produced from the Mauzac grape, formerly known as Blanquette (see Gaillac), and the Clairette in very small proportion. Made by the Champagne method, it is a really fine sparkling wine and the local cooperative does it honour, with the most modern techniques and the greatest care. I would rank Blanquette-de-Limoux with the very best Champagne-method wines of the Loire and Burgundy.

The Roussillon appellations: The Roussillon encompasses three *appellations* – Côtes-du-Roussillon, Côtes-du-Roussillon-Villages and Collioure, and the Carignan is perhaps at its best here. There is also Grenache and Cinsault, Syrah and Mourvèdre. The Villages area is around the basin of the Agly, on slaty hills, and the best communes are Estagel, Maury, Cases-de-Pène, Rasiguères, Montner, Caramany, and Latour-de-France. The red wines have great impact on the palate, but are at their most giving when they are young. Amongst the whites, there is Vin Vert, from early picked grapes, and consequently lively with good acidity, but, on the other hand, 'green' and a bit empty. Collioure is mostly made of Grenache Noir.

Banyuls, Rivesaltes and Maury: Banyuls, Rivesaltes and Maury are *appellations* enormously appreciated in France, but hardly known on the export markets. They are Vins Doux Naturels and Vins de Liqueur, red, white, rosé and *rancio* – that peculiar taste that comes with age and maderization. The main grape varieties that make them are the same – Muscat,

Grenache, both Noir and Rouge, Maccabéo and Malvoisie. In Banyuls-Grand-Cru, the Grenache must be 75 per cent. There is also Muscat de Rivesaltes, made only from the Muscat and growing in popularity outside France.

Where to find good wine in such a sea of liquid? Four *départements* – Gard, Hérault, Aude and Pyrénées Orientales – make up the region known as Lauguedoc-Roussillon, where 450,000 hectares are devoted to wine-growing. This represents 35 per cent of the entire wine-growing regions of France and 5 per cent of the total wine-growing area of the whole world. Total annual production in Languedoc-Roussillon (*appellation*, VDQS, Vins de Pays and Vins de Table) is between 25 and 30 million hectolitres, of which Corbières produces about 650,000 hectolitres, Minervois 240,000, and Côtes-du-Roussillon and Côtes-du-Roussillon-Villages about the same on average.

The area is dominated by the cooperatives, which produce and market 55 to 65 per cent of the entire wine output. Cooperatives and smaller producers of the region have also joined together to form about twenty marketing organizations. This cooperation is absolutely necessary in a region where there are as many as 80,000 wine growers – of these, 60 per cent cultivate less than five hectares and 25 per cent over fifty hectares. The cooperatives handle a great range of wines, *appellation*, VDQS and Vins de Pays, with top *cuvées* for those willing to pay a bit more. They, and a few of the top *négociants* of the area, also market some of the best domains, keeping them separate and maintaining their identity. The *négociants*, of course, use the cooperatives as sources of supply.

The huge French firm of Nicolas was one of the first into Languedoc-Roussillon, and worked with oenologists to bring up the quality. Château Les Palais (Corbières) and Faugères are good examples of Nicolas' ability to select. Jean Demolombe is a Narbonne *négociant* with a great deal of talent for searching out the best. He is also responsible for Château Les Palais, Château de Pech-Redon (La Clape), Domaine de Rivière-le-Haut (La Clape), and the Sélections l'Epervier. Chantovent also makes good selections throughout the region – their Minervois is always good value. Paul Rouanet at Béziers makes honourable selections, especially of St-Chinian. Various SICA (or agricultural collectives) do careful work – the SICA du Val d'Orbieu is one. The firm of Jeanjean at St-Félix-de-Lodez makes good selections of Corbières and Coteaux-du-Languedoc, much sold in the better French supermarkets. The Vignerons Catalans at Perpignan have done a very great deal to raise the level of the Roussillon wines, and export with gusto. They also have good *cuvées de propriétaires*. The cooperative at Baixas pursues a policy of quality, as does that of Tautavel, both producing Côtes-du-Roussillon-Villages. In Corbières, the Cave Coopérative Agricole des Viticulteurs at Paziols produces extremely modest-priced wines of good quality. Other reputed domains are Domaine de Fontsainte at Boutenac, Château Le Bouis at Gruissan, the Domaine de Villemajou, St-André-de-Roquelongue, and the Domaine de l'Ancien Prieuré de St-Amans, at Bizanet. Foncalieu at Carcassonne produce very good Corbières from different properties as well as delicious Vins de Pays de l'Aude. At Minervois, there is Château de Villerambert-Julien at Caunes-Minervois, the cooperative at the same place, the Château de Blomac near Capendu, the Domaine Ste-Eulalie at La Livinière, and the cooperative at Trausse-Minervois.

Amongst the mass of producers in the Coteaux-du-Languedoc, time must be spent at Faugères and St-Chinian. At Faugères, the Cave Coopérative Les Vignerons Réunis pursues a path of real quality, and any wine from the Vidal family at La Liquière, Cabrerolles, is worth hunting down. At St-Chinian, the Domaine des Jouglas at Prades-sur-Vernazobres, the Château Coujan at Murviel, and the cooperatives at Roquebrun and Berlou are all excellent producers of wine.

13 *South-West France*

South-west France in the 1980s is one of the best hunting grounds for wines that give interest and pleasure for an acceptable sum. Some of the wines are almost satellites of Bordeaux, using the same grape varieties and following the same styles, but others, further away, have a character and individuality all of their own. The wines must keep standards high because, with Bordeaux and its huge diversity of properties and prices on the doorstep, comparisons are inevitable when looking at value.

Côtes du Marmandais: Coming out of Bordeaux through Sauternes/Barsac and into the Lot-et-Garonne, the first wine area reached is that of the Côtes du Marmandais, right at the top of the VDQS ladder. Production is dominated by two good cooperatives, of which the one at Cocumont is a model of intelligent organization and careful vinification. The *encépagement* is now mostly of Bordeaux varieties, Cabernet, Merlot and a bit of Malbec, with the vestiges of a few, old local varieties. Production is nearly all of red wines, soft and fruity, delicious when two to three years old, but the rosé and tiny amount of white (basically Sauvignon/Sémillon) are now also delicious.

Côtes-de-Buzet: South-east of the Côtes du Marmandais lies the *appellation* area of Côtes-de-Buzet, dominated by the cooperative called Les Vignerons Réunis des Côtes-de-Buzet. The reds, made from Cabernet Sauvignon, Cabernet Franc and Merlot, are aged in oak and can take a few years of age in bottle – but not too much, otherwise they tend to dry out. At two to three years the fruit is delicious, and the top wine of the cooperative is the excellent Cuvée Napoléon. The rosé and the white wines are bottled four to five months after the vintage. Mechanical harvesting is now greatly used in the area. Another excellent source of Côtes-de-Buzet has emerged in the completely replanted Château de Padère at Ambrus and at the Château Sauvagnères.

The Bergerac Appellations: Round the county market town of Bergerac, there are a cluster of *appellations*: Bergerac and Côtes-de-Bergerac (reds, rosés and whites, both dry and sweet); and Côtes de Montravel, Haut-Montravel and Montravel, all white and varying from sweet to dry. Pécharmant (reds); Monbazillac (sweet white wine); Cotes de Saussignac (sweet white). The *appellation* Rosette for sweet white wines has virtually disappeared.

Bergerac Rouge and Côtes-de-Bergerac Rouge are made of a combination of the two Cabernets, Merlot and Malbec, with the latter diminishing in many properties. The wines can be fresh, fruity and 'sappy', often reminiscent of right-bank Bordeaux wines. Côtes-de-Bergerac must have one per cent more minimum alcohol level than Bergerac. As much of the area has been changing from unfashionable sweet whites to red, some of the vines are young, so the wines should not be kept too long. Vintages are much the same as the St Emilion area. Bergerac-Sec is made principally from Sauvignon, Sémillon and Muscadelle with Sauvignon tending to predominate – however, it should not take over, as the mixture gives a more complex wine which, when vinified in a modern way, is quite delicious and good value. Côtes-de-Bergerac *moelleux* is made from the same grape varieties, as are Côtes-de-Saussignac white wines. Monbazillac is made from the same trio of grapes. Unfortunately, the name became tainted with some of the over-sulphured examples sold in bulk to *négociants* for conversion to loftier *appellations*, but those producers who have persevered through the 'bad times' are making a real effort to make their wine correctly, and when this is done, Monbazillac can be a luscious wine of fragrance and peachy charm, drunk relatively young when chilled as an apéritif, or given the years of ageing it deserves and drunk more seriously with fine fruit or Roquefort cheese.

The Cave Coopérative de Monbazillac manages the

Château de Monbazillac; their wines can last beautifully. Other good wines are made at the Château Ladesvignes, the Château Treuil-de-Nailhac, the Château Thieulet and Vieux Vignobles de Repaire. An Englishman, Nick Ryman, at the Château de la Jaubertie at Colombier, has an array of stainless-steel *cuves* and vintages mechanically. His Bergerac *blanc sec* is delicate and classy, with a fine bouquet, and his reds, made predominantly of Merlot and Cabernet Sauvignon, will improve as the age of his vines increases. The Château Court-les-Mûts at Razac-de-Saussignac is owned by oenologist M. Sadoux, who has very good red Côtes-de-Bergerac, Bergerac *blanc sec* and Côtes-de-Saussignac *moelleux*. Further good producers of Bergerac wines are the Château de Fayolle at Saussignac, always impressive, the Domaine Constant at Lamonzie-St-Martin, Maxime Prouillac at St-Laurent-des-Vignes, the Domaine de Bouffevent in Lamonzie-St-Martin, Château le Caillou at Rouffignac, and the Château La Rayre at Colombier. Two châteaux producing Bergerac *blanc sec* are Panisseau and La Reynaudie. Panisseau has great finesse and a long and successful record of exporting. Pécharmant can produce the finest red wines on its chalky plateau to the north-east of Bergerac. The best are made at the Domaine du Haut-Pécharmant, the Château de Tiregand, owned by the Comtesse de St-Exupéry at Creysse, who also has the Clos de la Montalbanie, and the Domaine du Grand-Jaure. I have also had good Pécharmant from Paul Pomar, and from the SICA Producta at St-Laurent-des-Vignes. The Montravel wines (Côtes-de-Montravel and Haut-Montravel just require a higher alcohol level) are made from the Sauvignon, Sémillon and Muscadelle, and the best are crisp and dry and very good value indeed. Good examples come from the cooperative and through the Bordeaux *négociant*, Louis Dubroca.

Côtes de Duras: The Côtes de Duras *appellation* is to the south of Bergerac, making red and white wines which are very similar to their neighbours'. The whites are predominantly Sauvignon, and are at their best when very young. The cooperative is important. The Côtes de Duras Sauvignon from the Cave de Berticot is recommended.

Cahors: Cahors is an important *appellation* (created in 1971), now finding its feet again after a period when it did not quite know where it was going. In the days when it was the real 'black' wine of Cahors (reputedly, due to heating of the must), it went to 'fortify' weaker cousins in Bordeaux. When this ceased, and people were said to appreciate lighter wines, there were many Cahors made that lacked character and regional definition. Now, there are a number of producers who make wines of real interest and, in good years they have the ability to age. The frost of 1956, which so affected St Emilion and Pomerol, did grave damage here too, but it did give the chance to those searching for real quality to rethink the *encépagement* of their vineyards. The ideal is thought to be 70 per cent Auxerrois Rouge (the Malbec, Côt, or Pressac, as it is known in St Emilion), 15 per cent Tannat and 15 per cent Merlot. The Syrah is also allowed in small proportion. The high proportion of Malbec was one of the reasons why the vineyard was so difficult to reconstruct after the devastation of phylloxera – the new root stocks did not suit the grape variety and aggravated its tendency to develop *coulure*, or poor development after flowering. Hybrids were planted in their place, and it took only the most persistent growers to insist on replacement with 'noble' varieties. Now this is established, and the vines are on suitable root stocks, pruned on the Guyot method, whereas it used to be *gobelet*.

About half the *appellation* wine is sold through the cooperative Les Côtes d'Olt at Parnac, which has done so much to revive the region. The Caves, which buy in grapes, are very well equipped, with wooden vats of eighty hectolitres and *barriques* of 600 litres. It is a region of 'polyculture', and the thorough management of the cooperative enables the growers to combine grape growing with tobacco and fruit production. The cooperative's wines are always reliable (much more so than *négoce* wines of the area), and some of its top *cuvées*, such as the non-vintage Vieille Réserve, or the vintage Cahors Comte André de Monpezat, are very good indeed. Les Côtes d'Olt also produce the Vin de Pays, Coteaux du Quercy. Good domains include: the Château du Cayrou of M. Jean Jouffreau at Puy l'Evêque – he also has the excellent Clos de Gamot; the Clos Triguedina of M. Baldès also at Puy-l'Evêque; the wines of the Gayraud family at Soturac and the Burc family at Leygues; Domaine de Paillas; the wines of the Pontié family at Gamot, Prayssac; and Clos La Coutale and Domaine du Cèdre at Vire, Puy-l'Evêque. The Château de Haute-Serre of M. Vigourroux is on the light side, but his vines are ageing and depth will come.

Côtes du Frontonnais: North of Toulouse, there is the relatively unknown (except to the Toulousains) new *appellation*, Côtes du Frontonnais, mostly making red wine, predominantly from the local grape variety Négrette, with some Cabernet and Syrah. The cooperative at Villaudric is very well run, and good domains include the Château Bellevue-La Forêt, which is run with the greatest technical efficiency and which can only improve as the vines age, Château Flotis, the Domaine de la Colombière, the Domaine de Bel-Air and Ferran. The Coopérative de Lavilledieu at La Ville-Dieu-du-Temple makes the very respectable VDQS Vin de Lavilledieu.

Gaillac: Gaillac, almost next door, is proving a source of reasonably-priced wine, perhaps lacking real definition, but very pleasant to drink. The traditional grape variety for white wines is the Mauzac, which has plenty of bouquet and taste but lacks acidity. Blending with Sauvignon also adds acidity, and there is also a local grape variety, L'En de L'El. There is another oddity in the Ondenc, but also the more familiar Sémillon and Muscadelle. The Mauzac is, however, ideally suited to making sweet white wines, whether sparkling or not, but these are more difficult to sell in the decade of the 1980s. The reds are made from the Gamay (used by those who want to make lighter wines) combined in greater or lesser proportions with the Syrah, the Braucol and the Duras, local varieties both, with sometimes some Merlot. The vines are trained *en gobelet*.

There is a good cooperative in the area, which rejoices in one of the longest names yet conceived for one of these worthy institutions: Cave Coopérative de Vinification des

Côteaux de Gaillac et du Pays Cordais – you can find it at Labastide-de-Lévis. They have a good range of wines, including the Sec Perlé, which obtains its slight prickle from being left on the lees after the malolactic fermentation. They also have a Gaillac Crémant which, for the moment, they can sell only in the European markets, not in France until it is passed by the INAO, and a Mousseux. This last can be made by the Champagne method or the *méthode gaillaçoise*, or *méthode rurale*, which is similar to the method employed for Clairette de Die. The Cave also has good Vins de Pays des Côtes du Tarn vinified at the Cave de Cunac – the red is made by the *macération carbonique* method and is quite delicious. The Côtes du Tarn Blanc is very fresh, like spring water. Good domains are: Domaine de Labarthe, Domaine Très-Cantoux, Château de Rhodes, Château Larroze. There is another good cooperative, the Cave Coopérative de Técou.

Madiran: Madiran is a really 'serious' *appellation* for lovers of red wine. The local Tannat grape predominates (usually about 60 per cent), and the name gives the, correct, impression of tannin. This is mixed with Cabernet of both types (the Cabernet Franc is here called the Bouchy), but if it is too pervasive, the wine loses its real Madiran character. There is another local variety called the Pinenc or Couhabort. When the producer adheres to the traditional proportion of Tannat in his wine, Madiran keeps superbly, its deep purple colour of youth and tannin developing richness and great diversity of flavour. The vineyard area covers 1000 hectares and produces about 50,000 hectolitres annually.

Pacherenc-du-Vic-Bilh: The white *appellation* wines of Pacherenc-du-Vic-Bilh are only seen locally. They are made from the Arrufiat, the Gros and Petit Manseng, the Courbu, Sémillon and Sauvignon. It has no finesse, but is usually dry, with good acidity, and pleasant 'on the spot'. The Domaine du Crampilh is recommended.

The Coopérative Vinicole du Vic-Bilh-Madiran at Crouseilles produces a marvellous Madiran Rôt du Roy, which has complexity, backbone and generosity. This is their *tête de cuvée*; their straight Madiran is good, but does not last as well as the Rôt du Roy. They also have good *appellation* Béarn Rouge and Rosé, and a rare Pacherenc *moelleux*. The cooperative at Bellocq also specializes in Béarn wines.

Good domains are the Château de Peyros, Domaine Barréjat, Domaine Lalanne, Domaine Labranche-Laffont, and the Vignobles Laplace, which make more 'Bordeaux-style' wines, but good, and also Pacherenc of quality. Alain Brumont at Domaine Bouscassé and Château Montus makes traditional Madiran for ageing, while Gilbert Terradot at Château d'Arricau-Bordes is aiming for elegance. There is also the Union de Producteurs Plaimont at Riscle which has Madiran and the VDQS Côtes de St-Mont.

Jurançon: Jurançon is a white wine 'with a past', at least as far as Henri IV is concerned. There are about 500 hectares under vine, to the south of Pau. The wines are made dry or *moelleux*, from a battery of strange grapes – the Gros Manseng (generous yielding, and good for the *sec*), Petit Manseng, Courbu, Camaralet and Lauzet – the first three are the most important, with the Petit Manseng largely responsible for the special character of the classic Jurançon *moelleux* wines. It yields little and has a rich aromatic flavour. The climate is influenced by the Pyrenees and the ocean, and the harvest for these great *moelleux* wines begins about 15 October, when it is usually warm and sunny. However, the vintage may not end until end November – beginning December, after the first falls of snow on the Pyrenees and the first frosts. The combined effect of sun in the day and freezing at night leads to a concentration of the grape pulp which gives musts of a richness up to potential alcohol of 16–18 per cent. Thus, the grape is concentrated on the vine – described as *passerillage*. Pickers go through the vineyard several times, to ensure picking each bunch at the right moment. When the beginning of the winter is mild, with the south wind from Spain in the last days of the vintage towards the end of November, there is also *pourriture noble*, as well as the *passerillage*. Fermentations are at a cold temperature and they stop of their own accord when the alcohol reaches 13 per cent. It can be seen why total production of these wines is about 7,000 hectolitres annually, while Jurançon *sec* produces about 20,000 hectolitres. When climatic conditions are not favourable, only a small amount of the *moelleux* can be made from those small plots of Petit Manseng which undergo this process; the rest makes Jurançon *sec*, which is floral and full. The taste and aromas of these wines have been compared to acacia flowers, honey and grilled hazelnuts, apparently bestowed by the relationship of mineral and organic acids with the sugar. Although attractive when young, these wines age beautifully, becoming the colour of amber and taking on a bouquet of cinnamon, guavas and nutmeg, depending on the exact origin of the wine. Two excellent sources of Jurançon *moelleux* are M. Chigé at La Chapelle-de-Rousse, with his Cru Lamouroux, and M. Alfred Barrère at Lahourcade with his Clos Cancaillaü. The Clos Uroulat is also recommended. A good Jurançon *sec* is the Clos de la Vierge from the Cave Brana. The Coopérative Vinicole de Gan-Jurançon has a good range of wines, going up to the greatest.

14 *Savoie and Bugey*

The wines of the mountains of Savoie always seem delicious and tempting, perhaps because one is often drinking them after a hard day's skiing, which is hardly fair on other viticultural regions. But the wines do bear vinous exploration, even if in less-favoured years they illustrate the difficulties of growing vines in a mountain climate. 80 per cent of the wines of Savoie are white, with some light red and rosé, and sparkling and *pétillant* wine. Although the wines of Savoie have risen to *appellation* status, it is worth considering at the same time their VDQS neighbours, the wines of Bugey to the west nearer Lyon, because they are very similar and are certainly not inferior to their more elevated, in all senses of the word, cousins in the mountains. The *appellations* and grape varieties in Savoie and Bugey are extremely, and unnecessarily complicated. Overall, there is the *appellation* Vin de Savoie for red, white and rosé wines, which covers a mass of communes, fifteen of which can add their name to the title Vin de Savoie on the label. There are also three white wine *appellations*, Seyssel, Crépy and Roussette-de-Savoie.

The great danger in Savoie wines is acidity, as when the ripening conditions are not sufficient, the reds are thin and the whites horribly acid. The Jacquère white grape variety is the most commonly planted in Savoie, with acidity and not much alcohol, often bottled from the lees, giving it a *perlant* character – it should be drunk in the year after its birth. It is mostly grown between Aix-les-Bains and Montmélian. The Altesse, or the Roussette, is by far the best grape variety in this terrain, giving wines of character and great flavour. The Gringet is of the Savagnin or Traminer family, the Mondeuse, white and red, is very local, the Chasselas is well-known over the Swiss border where it makes Fendant, and the Roussanne is a high-class refugee from the northern Rhône. The Molette is a local variety used in sparkling wines, and the Cacaboué is reputed to come from St-Péray, but its presence is almost academic now. Among the red varieties, the character of the Gamay and the Pinot Noir is well-known, while the Persan is very rare and has a hint of Pinot Noir about it.

The best wines are considered to be Vins de Savoie from Abymes and Apremont, the rare Chignin-Bergeron made from the Roussanne, the Roussette-de-Savoie, with village name, made from the grape of the same name (the Altesse) and the Roussette-du-Bugey with village name, both medium dry – if it is just Roussette-du-Bugey *tout court*, it can be made purely of Chardonnay. Crépy, made between Thonon and Geneva, can have a touch of bubble about it and, if not too acid, be very refreshing. Seyssel from the Roussette, can aspire to complexity.

Good wines are produced by: the Domaine des Granges Longes at St André-les Marches, Montmélian (Abymes); Yves Ollivier at Chambéry (Abymes and Apremont); Jean Masson and M. Simiand at Apremont; the Coopérative Le Vigneron Savoyard at Apremont; and Jean Perrier at St-André-les-Marches (Apremont). Pierre Boniface, also at St-André-les-Marches, undoubtedly makes the finest Apremont at the moment, using the most modern methods and tasting with the greatest care when blending between his vats. The result is an ethereal mountain wine of floral character. The André Quénard family at Torméry, Montmélian, have excellent Chignin-Bergeron, and others, the Château-Monterminod at St-Alban-Leysse has Roussette and Mondeuse, while François Vial in the same village has Vin-de-Savoie Persan. Good Bugey producers are Eugène Monin at Vongnes, Camille Crussy at Flaxieu, and Jean Peillot also makes good Roussette-du-Bugey Montagnieu. Goy at Ballaison has good Crépy. The Château de Ripaille, overlooking Lake Geneva, makes good Vin de Savoie from the Chasselas. Wines that come from the *négociant* houses of Donati, Maison Mollex, or through M. Claude Marandon, a broker who specializes in the wines of Savoie, will be good. Mercier at Douvaine has Crépy, as well as Fichard at Chens-sur-Léman.

The sparkling wines of Savoie and Bugey are mostly drunk locally, as production cannot satisfy export demand. The famous Varichon & Clerc sparkling wine is now just Champagne-method Mousseux Blanc de Blancs, when it started as Seyssel. Seyssel-Mousseux must have their second fermentation in bottle, Champagne-method. Sparkling Cerdon from Bugey must be made by the Champagne-method or the *rurale* method to have the VDQS title. However, there is a great deal of artificially carbonated wine in the area, mostly drunk in Lyon.

15 *Jura*

This beautiful mountain region near the French/Swiss border was particularly devastated by the phylloxera, and reconstruction was hard work because of the slopes and the difficulty of attracting labour. Although one does not want all wines to taste alike, the original character of the local grape varieties, which are much used, does not attract everyone. The red Ploussard, or Poulsard, lightly tinted rosé, can give fruity, delicate light reds or rosés, but it can also be acid and thin. The red Trousseau has more colour and body, and both these are usually mixed with the Gros Noirien, which is the local name covering Pinot Noir or Pinot Gris. The white wines are dominated by the Savagnin (or Naturé, or Traminer of Alsace), mixed with the Melon d'Arbois (or Chardonnay) and the Pinot Blanc. About 600 hectares are under vine.

Côtes-du-Jura is the overall *appellation*, and covers the red, rosé or *gris*, white, yellow wines, as well as *vins de paille* and sparkling wines by the Champagne method. The *appellation* Arbois covers the same categories, while the *appellation* L'Etoile omits red and rosé, and the *appellation* Château-Chalon must be made from the Savagnin alone; this last is the archetypal *vin jaune*. The soil is basically chalky, the vineyards are high, and the climate very continental, with severe winters. The heart of the region is between Lons-le-Saunier and Arbois. As in Alsace, there is often little distinction between red and rosé; the name on the label is more the personal decision of the wine-maker than anything else. There are the wines from around Arlay-Voiteur, quite light and supple, but with more body when occasionally made with 100 per cent Pinot Noir, and those from Arbois made from the Ploussard which mix a certain fruity delicacy with tannin. But when the wines are just light, with drying tannin, they lack charm. The reds from the Trousseau can be almost Burgundian in character. Both reds and rosés can be acid if there is not enough sun. The whites can be made almost entirely of Chardonnay, when they taste nicer when young, or almost entirely of Savagnin, when they need ageing – the best of both can have a complex flavour.

Vin jaune is a very special category of wine, and the slightly maderized taste will appeal to Sherry lovers. It is made with the Savagnin grape grown on marly soil and picked very late, fermented slowly over several months, and then left in old oak casks for a minimum of six years. There is no topping up, and a film of *flor*, the yeast cells found in fino Sherries in Spain, protects the wine from the worst aspects of oxidation, while imparting its own special taste. *Vins jaunes* are bottled in the 65-centilitre *clavelins*. They can be kept for years, and have a curious taste which combines a honey-like flavour with dryness, and a *goût de terroir* common to all the white wines of the region, but exaggerated in *vins jaunes*. The finish can resemble walnuts. The esterization of these wines can be of real interest, although perhaps an acquired taste. *Vin de paille* obtains its name from the fact that the red and white grapes are dried on straw mats to increase the sugar content, but now also by hanging up the bunches in a dry, well-ventilated attic or room. This process must last a minimum of two months, before the grapes are vinified with extremely long fermentations, and three to four years in cask. These are dessert wines of complexity and class, with the special taste of the area. *Vins jaunes* and *vins de paille* are both, necessarily, expensive.

After Pasteur, Henri Maire is the best-known *fils d'Arbois*. This huge commercial enterprise also comprises important domain holdings in the Jura, and examples of all types of wine. The Rolet family at Montigny-les-Arsures also produce very good wines of all types, as do Roger Lornet, Lucien Aviet and Jacques Puffeney in the same village. Other good producers are the Château d'Arlay, Marius Perron at Voiteur (especially for Château-Chalon), the Château de la Muyre at Domblans for its Château-Chalon, as well as Jean Bourdy at Arlay. The Caveau des Byards at Voiteur is a good source of supply for most types of wine, as is the prettily named Fruitière Vinicole d'Arbois, while Joseph Vandelle at L'Etoile makes good Etoile Blanc and *vin jaune*. Luc Boilley at Chissey-sur-Loire, produces Côtes-du-Jura.

Index

Bellevue, Ch. de (Morgon), 147
Bellevue, Ch. de (Rochefort), 210
Bellevue-La-Forêt, Ch., 265
Bel-Orme-Tronquoy-de-Lalande, Ch., 42
Benais, 216, 217
Bergerac, 262
Bergerac, Côtes-de-, 262
Bergheim, 192
Bernarde, Domaine de la, 249
Bernardins, Domaine des, 239
Berrière, La, 205
Berthiers, Les, 223
Bertrands, Domaine des, 249
Béru, 159
Beugnons, 158
Beychevelle, Ch., 52-3
Beyer, Léon, 195
Bèze, Clos de, 120
Bizay, 212
Blagny, 136
Blanc, Clos, 126
Blanc Fumé (grape), *see* Sauvignon
Blanchot, 157
Blanquette-de-Limoux, 258
Blauburgunder (grape), 11
Blaye, 102-3
Bodet, Ch., 102
Bonnes-Mares (Chambolle-Musigny), 124
Bonnes-Mares (Morey-St-Denis), 123
Bonnet, Ch., 147
Bonnezeaux, 209, 210
Bordeaux, 30-108; classifications in 33-6; grape varieties, 36-9; map, 38; vintages, 103-8; when to drink wines, 39-40
Bordeaux, Premières Côtes de, 85
Borie, Jean-Eugène, 51, 54, 61, 63
Bosquet, Domaine de, 256
Bouchemaine, 212
Bouchet (grape), *see* Cabernet Franc
Bouchot, Le, 223
Boudots, Aux, 129
Boudriotte, La, 140
Bougros, 158
Bouilh, Ch. du, 103
Bouis, Ch. Le, 260
Bourboulenc (grape), 229
Bourg, 102-3
Bourgogne, *see* Burgundy
Bourgogne Hautes Côtes de Beaune, 141

Bourgogne Hautes-Côtes de Nuits, 130
Bourgogne Passetoutgrain, 142
Bourgueil, 216-8
Bouscaut, Ch., 75
Bousquet, Ch. du, 103
Bouzy, 185
Boyd-Cantenac, Ch., 48
Branaire-Ducru, Ch., 51-2
Brane Cantenac, Ch., 46
Bressandes, Les, 135
Breuil, Ch. Le, 42
Brézé, 212
Brilette, Ch, 66
Brissac, 211, 212, 214
Brouilly, 148
Brouilly, Côte de, 148, 149
Broustet, Ch., 83
Brûlées, Aux, 129
Brunet, Georges, 251
Bugey, 269-71
Burgundy, 109-155; classification in, 115-7; grape varieties, 113-5; map, 110; shippers, 150-1; vintages, 151-5; when to drink wines, 117-8
Buxy, Cave Coopérative de, 144
Buzet, Côtes-de-, 261

Cabernet Franc (grape), 11, 36, 207
Cabernet Sauvignon (grape), 36
Cadet-Piola, Ch., 93
Cahors, 264-5
Cailleret, Le, 140
Caillerets, Les, 137
Cailles, Les, 129
Caillou, Ch., 83
Caillou, Ch. Le, 263
Cairanne, 244, 245
Calisanne, Ch. de, 252
Calon-Ségur, Ch., 64
Camensac, Ch. de, 42
Campaux, Domaine des, 249
Cancaillaü, Clos, 268
Canon, Ch., 92
Canon (-Fronsac), Ch., 102
Canon-La-Gaffelière, Ch., 93
Cantegril, Ch., 84
Cantelaudette, Ch., 85
Cantemerle, Ch., 41-2
Cantenac-Brown, Ch., 46
Capbern, Ch., 65
Caramany, 258
Carbonnieux, Ch., 73-4
Cardaillan, Ch. de, 83

281

All Futura Books are available at your bookshop or newsagent, or can be ordered from the following address:
Futura Books, Cash Sales Department,
P.O. Box 11, Falmouth, Cornwall

Please send cheque or postal order (no currency), and allow 55p for postage and packing for the first book plus 22p for the second book and 14p for each additional book ordered up to a maximum charge of £1.75 in U.K.

Customers in Eire and B.F.P.O. please allow 55p for the first book, 22p for the second book plus 14p per copy for the next 7 books, thereafter 8p per book.

Overseas customers please allow £1.00 for postage and packing for the first book and 25p per copy for each additional book.